Judging the Past in Unified Germany

Over the past decade, no modern democracy has taken more aggressive steps to come to terms with a legacy of dictatorship than has the Federal Republic of Germany with the crimes and injustices of communist East Germany. In this book, A. James McAdams provides a comprehensive and engaging examination of the four most prominent instances of this policy: criminal trials for the killings at the Berlin Wall, the disqualification of administrative personnel for secret police ties, parliamentary truth-telling commissions, and the restitution of private property. On the basis of extensive research and interviews in Bonn and Berlin over the 1990s, McAdams gives new insight into the difficulties faced by German politicians, judges, bureaucrats, and public officials in their attempt to pass judgment on the affairs of another state. He argues provocatively that the success of their policies must be measured in terms of their ability to use East German history to justify their actions.

A. James McAdams is Professor and Chair of Government and International Studies at the University of Notre Dame. He is the author of *East Germany and Detente* and *Germany Divided: From the Wall to Reunification*, coauthor of *Rebirth: A Political History of Europe Since World War II*, and editor of *Transitional Justice and the Rule of Law in New Democracies*. In 1997, he was awarded the DAAD Prize for Distinguished Scholarship in German Studies.

Judging the Past in Unified Germany

A. JAMES McADAMS
University of Notre Dame

PUBLISHED BY THE PRESS SYNDICATE OF THE UNIVERSITY OF CAMBRIDGE
The Pitt Building, Trumpington Street, Cambridge, United Kingdom

CAMBRIDGE UNIVERSITY PRESS
The Edinburgh Building, Cambridge CB2 2RU, UK
40 West 20th Street, New York, NY 10011-4211, USA
10 Stamford Road, Oakleigh, VIC 3166, Australia
Ruiz de Alarcón 13, 28014 Madrid, Spain
Dock House, The Waterfront, Cape Town 8001, South Africa

http://www.cambridge.org

First published 2001

Printed in the United States of America

Typeface Janson Text 10.25/13 pt.   *System* LaTeX 2_ε [TB]

A catalog record for this book is available from the British Library.

Library of Congress Cataloging in Publication Data
McAdams, A. James.
    Judging the past in unified Germany / A. James McAdams.
        p.   cm.
    Includes bibliographical references.
    ISBN 0-521-80208-3 – ISBN 0-521-00139-0 (pbk.)
        1. Germany – History – Unification, 1990.   2. Justice, Administration of –
    Germany (East)   3. Germany (East) – Politics and government.   4. Restitution
    and indemnification claims (1933–) – Germany (East)   5. Justice and politics –
    Germany.   6. Justice and politics – Germany (East)   I. Title.
    DD290.29 .M49   2001
    943.08 – dc21   00-064185

ISBN 0 521 80208 3 hardback
ISBN 0 521 00139 0 paperback

For Jackie and Erin

Men make their own history, but they do not make it just as they please; they do not make it under circumstances chosen by themselves, but under circumstances directly encountered, given and transmitted from the past.

—Karl Marx, *The Eighteenth Brumaire of Louis Bonaparte*

Contents

Illustrations

Preface

The issue of retrospective justice has become one of the most compelling controversies of our time. In the 1980s and 1990s, dictatorial regimes throughout the world were suddenly replaced by an assortment of new democracies. Among many difficult choices before them, these governments were faced with one particularly nagging question: What steps should they take, if any, to come to terms with the crimes and abuses of their predecessors? These governments' responses to this challenge soon resulted in a proliferation of scholarly books and articles on the merits of seeking to redress these injustices. Some commentators argued persuasively that the new democratic regimes had an obligation to the victims of dictatorship to settle accounts with their oppressors and, to the extent possible, to repair their wrongs. Conversely, critics warned with equal passion and conviction that these policies would undermine democratic values and institutions. In their view, newly formed democracies would be better advised to steer away from their burdensome past and to concentrate instead on healing rifts and divisions among their citizens.

In contrast to these arguments, both of which I find plausible, I adopt a different approach in this book. Rather than weighing in on the morality of one or the other position, I take the pursuit of some form of retrospective justice as a given – a set of policies already instituted by a government – and seek to articulate a means of evaluating its success or failure. How should we know – for that matter, how should policymakers know – when governments are doing the right thing in acting on a record of dictatorship? As the reader will see, I provide an answer to these questions based upon the way political actors and administrative officials use history to justify their decisions.

As someone who has been interested in the politics of East and West Germany for some time, I did not need convincing that unified Germany's response to this challenge would be intriguing. But I also had two specific reasons for launching into the project. First, I had a hunch that the timing for this study would be propitious. Although many accounts have been written since 1990 of the FRG's reckoning with the legacy of East German communism, I believe we are now in a much better position to analyze the effectiveness of these policies. I never had any doubt that Germany's handling of the topic of retrospective justice would be ambitious and controversial. But now that the scope and impact of its policies have been fully exposed over the past decade, we can offer reasoned conjectures about which of its approaches worked best and which did not.

Second, in writing this book, I wanted to satisfy my curiosity. Throughout the 1980s, I traveled regularly to East Berlin to conduct archival research and interviews on relations between the two German states. In the process, I developed a wide array of professional contacts with East German government and party officials. Thus when the Wall fell in 1989, I found myself repeatedly asking what I should think of these individuals' behavior under the communist regime. By what standard should some, or perhaps all, of them be held to account for their government's abuses? Or was the East German experience so different from, or even incommensurable with, that of the liberal West that these offenses would be best passed over in silence?

The reader will readily detect from my sources that I have followed an eclectic approach in seeking answers to these questions. From the beginning, I wanted to piece together the policies that were actually implemented by the Federal Republic over the 1990s because these developments were not always clearly spelled out in the secondary literature on retrospective justice. To this end, I sought to read broadly in the legal commentaries, legislation, judicial decisions, administrative reports, parliamentary debates, and national and local news accounts that were relevant to the topic. Yet the whole story could not be revealed through published sources alone. When I wanted to understand major statutes better (some of which, such as the Property statute, are ferociously complicated), to reconstruct the motivations of decision makers or to gain insights into the hidden issues behind the public controversies, I relied heavily on interviews with both well-known policymakers in Bonn and Berlin and their equally well-informed administrative assistants and advisers behind the scenes. In all cases, I sought to cross-check my written and oral sources to ensure accuracy.

In the process of conducting this research, I have incurred many debts. For my chapter on criminal prosecutions, I am grateful to both the Justice Senator's office and the Public Prosecutor's office (II) in Berlin for providing me with many of the unpublished court decisions on the Wall trials. For my chapter on the uses of the Stasi files, I am indebted to the Federal Authority for the Records of the Stasi (BStU) in Berlin and to its director, Joachim Gauck, for many insights. Several of the BStU's current or former employees – David Gill, Klaus Richter, Gerd-Dieter Hirsch, Herbert Ziehm, Michael Zabel, and Siegfried Suckut – steered me through the thicket of the Stasi Records law and helped to clarify the process of administrative screening. For my chapter on the Bundestag's Enquete commission, I am grateful to the body's chair, Rainer Eppelmann, its chief of staff, Marlies Jansen, and many other staff members who answered innumerable questions about the ins and outs of the parliamentary inquiry. During my visits to Bonn, the German Society for Foreign Affairs kindly provided me with an office and made available its magnificent library, as it has done so many times in the past. Finally, back in Berlin, the Federal Office for the Settlement of Open Property Questions opened its doors widely to facilitate my research on the Property statute. Without the gracious assistance of its staff, especially Gabriela Körner and Birgit Schöneberg, I would never have been able to write the chapter on property restitution.

For this project, I have been fortunate to receive regular advice and encouragement from two eminent Germanists. My colleague Donald Kommers, a leading authority on the Federal Constitutional Court, has been an unfailing source of support, an intellectual light and inspiration. More recently, Peter Quint, who knows the constitutional aspects of German unification as well as anyone, has carefully critiqued all of my arguments and provided many invaluable insights.

Over the years this book was in gestation, I have benefited from the good counsel, expertise, and friendship of many scholars with interests in German affairs, human rights scholarship, and comparative politics. Many of them generously read all or parts of this book: Thomas Banchoff; Anthony Berardi; Jean and J. D. Bindenagel; Heinrich and Karin Bortfeldt; David Crawford; Gert-Joachim Glaeßner; Andrew Gould; Alexander Hahn; Helmut Hubel; Gerd and Ines Kaiser; Kevin

Krause; Henry Krisch; Gregg Kvistad; Hans-Heinrich Mahnke; Scott Mainwaring; Garth Meintjes; Juan Méndez; John Miller; Wilson Miscamble, C.S.C.; Dirk Moses; Norman Naimark; Mark Roche; Brad Roth; Kim Scheppele; Jürgen Schnappertz; Gunnar Schuster; Paul Schwartz; Timothy Scully, C.S.C.; Wolfgang Seibel; Uwe and Inge Stehr; John Torpey; Richard Ullman; Andrzej Walicki; Wolfgang Wiemer; and José Zalaquett.

Over the course of this project, I have had four excellent research assistants, each of whom played an important role in the preparation of this book: Michael Williams, Andreas Feldmann, John Wingerter, and Joseph Foy. Judy Bartlett aided me in overcoming the inevitable computer glitches. Above all, Kathee Kiesselbach, my administrative assistant in the Department of Government and International Studies, continually made it possible for me to perform my duties as department chair while keeping my scholarly pursuits alive.

Along the way, several institutions helped to facilitate this project. I am especially indebted to the John D. and Catherine T. MacArthur Foundation, which awarded me a timely Research and Writing Grant in International Security to start the book in the first place. At Notre Dame, I am thankful for the continuing support of the Helen Kellogg Institute for International Studies and the Institute for Scholarship in the Liberal Arts.

I owe a special word of thanks to my editor, Lewis Bateman, who convinced me to publish this book with Cambridge University Press and has been a superb and unflagging source of guidance and encouragement throughout the publication process. My thanks also go out to all of the other members of the Cambridge team, including Alan Young, who have devoted so much attention to this book, as well as to John Joswick and Eleanor Umali who provided excellent copyediting. Finally, I thank the editors of the *Review of Politics* for allowing me to republish sections of Chapter 2, which originally appeared in that journal (58, no. 1 [1996]: 53–80).

My greatest debt of gratitude is to my family. My wife, Nancy, has always been a vital part of everything I do, including my scholarship. She knows what this book means. Throughout this long project, my daughters, Jackie and Erin, never gave up on me despite my many trips abroad to conduct research or, most recently, many late hours at the computer screen. I dedicate this book, with much love, to both of them.

I could not have come this far without the guidance and support of the individuals and institutions mentioned above. Of course, any errors in this book are mine alone. I am also mindful that, in choosing to write about the subject of retrospective justice, I have put myself on contentious ground. Opinions on the topic are as diverse and as deeply felt as on any contemporary issue of public policy. I hope this study will add new fuel to the debate, both about the German experience in particular and about the relationship between justice, historical interpretation, and democratic prospects in general.

A. James McAdams
Notre Dame
September 7, 2000

Note

Anyone writing about German unification immediately encounters the problem of what terminology to use for the different Germanys and different German citizens before and after October 3, 1990. In this book, I have adopted the following conventions. I refer to the two German states before unification, the Federal Republic of Germany and the German Democratic Republic, as West Germany and East Germany. I refer to the people who lived in those states as West Germans and East Germans, respectively. However, after unification, I speak of eastern Germany and western Germany, and when contrasting the citizens of the two parts of the nation, I speak of western Germans (or westerners) and eastern Germans (or easterners).

Additionally, to make my account more readable, I frequently refer to the two German governments before 1990 as Bonn and East Berlin. Also, I refer to the government of unified Germany as Bonn, for most of the political decisions relevant to my account took place in that city. Of course, I am aware that the Bundestag voted to make Berlin the federal capital in June 1991, but it was not until 1999 that the city became the country's fully functioning capital. For the years after 1999, I refer to Berlin as the German capital.

Finally, this study contains legal and political terminology with which some readers may not be familiar. For this reason, I have provided a brief description of the German court system (see appendix). I have also included a glossary of frequently used terms and abbreviations (see p. 223).

1

Introduction

ON JUDGING THE EAST
GERMAN PAST

Looking back over the last two decades of the twentieth century, one would be hard pressed to find a state that took more varied steps to come to terms with a legacy of authoritarian rule than the Federal Republic of Germany (FRG) in the wake of national unification. This is no inconsequential statement. With the toppling of an unprecedented number of dictatorships over these years and a wave of audacious new experiments in democracy, the twin themes of truth telling and retrospective justice acquired worldwide prominence.[1] Moreover, by the 1990s, the United Nations and much of the international community had embraced aggressive measures (e.g., ad hoc tribunals on ex-Yugoslavia and Rwanda, an International Criminal Court) in the hope of creating a universal system of rights protection.

This claim about the FRG's distinctiveness is also not intended to diminish in any way the German people's efforts since 1945 to face up to their historical responsibility for the crimes of National Socialism and the Holocaust. At the beginning of the twenty-first century, this process of confrontation and atonement still seems unfulfilled. What distinguishes unified Germany's handling of the more modest human rights abuses and offenses of the former German Democratic Republic (GDR) is simply that the FRG's leaders launched into the task with a breadth of approaches and an almost religious devotion to thoroughness that was unmatched by any other country at the time.

Until the early 1990s, only a handful of new democracies had actually succeeded in bringing any of their former dictators or major rights violators to trial – most notably Greece in 1974–75, Argentina in 1985, and Bolivia in 1986–93. When given the choice, most transitional governments had opted to spare themselves the risks and controversies of criminal proceedings.[2] In contrast, these sanctions were to play a major part in the FRG's reckoning with the record of communist rule in East Germany. By the end of the decade, public prosecutors had reviewed over 62,000 possible cases of GDR-era injustice and issued more than 1,000 indictments for a wide variety of criminal offenses.[3] Provocatively, the courts were asked to consider for prosecution not only the most glaring crimes from the years the SED (Socialist Unity Party) was in power, such as the shooting of would-be escapees at the Berlin Wall and the kidnapping and murder of political opponents by the Ministry of State Security (MfS) or Stasi, but also a host of lesser offenses. These included crimes – judicial corruption, espionage, mail tampering, athletic doping, and electoral fraud – that would probably have received little or no attention in most other settings.[4]

In addition, German lawmakers were among a handful of democratic leaders in the early 1990s (the postcommunist government of Czechoslovakia was another prominent example) to use noncriminal sanctions to prevent persons who were directly implicated in the old regime's abuses from assuming positions of responsibility in the new political order. In accordance with this policy, the German Unification treaty of August 31, 1990, provided for the dismissal of any officials or administrators who had collaborated with the Stasi or could be linked to human rights violations in the GDR if their actions were sufficiently serious to make them "appear unsuitable," in the treaty's parsimonious language, for continued public service.[5] Also, though in a much looser fashion, German administrative law allowed for the review of hundreds of thousands of other civil servants – teachers, police officers, judges, and prosecutors – whose loyalty to the FRG's "basic democratic order" might have been compromised by their affiliation with the East German state.[6]

As in other transitional settings, commentators hastened to point to the inevitable limitations upon the uses of positive law in redressing wrongdoing and correcting past mistakes. Yet even these constraints do not appear to have presented serious obstacles to policymakers. Evidently, what some persons who had suffered under the former SED dictatorship wanted most from their new leaders was not retribution or even revenge. Rather, they desired a kind of moral affirmation that, they hoped, would come from knowing more about what had transpired under the communist regime and what lessons might still be learned from the experience.

In this case, the Federal Republic followed the example of many non-European democracies in the 1980s and 1990s – Chile, Argentina, El Salvador, and South Africa – by using an assortment of strategies for raising popular awareness about the petty crimes and personal betrayals, sordid incidents and misfortunes, misguided policies, and errors in judgment that had long been obscured behind the protective facade of the Wall. Notably, in spring 1992, the Bundestag formed a special investigative body, or Enquete commission, to meet these demands and charged it with the task of formulating a comprehensive judgment on the "history and consequences of the SED dictatorship in Germany." Concurrently, the parliament enacted innovative legislation to provide citizens in both parts of the country with access to the millions of files and personal dossiers that had been compiled on their lives by the East German secret police. Also, state and local authorities oversaw a panoply of initiatives throughout the decade (open forums on the Stasi, televised confrontations between perpetrators and victims, museum exhibits, scholarly conferences, memorials, and the like) that were meant to fill in the remaining gaps in public understanding about the GDR and to ease the region's transition to democracy.

Finally, in several noteworthy respects, the FRG was unequaled in the steps it was willing to take to repair the SED's injustices and, as daunting as the task may have seemed, to set aright the balance sheet of Germany's postwar history. Some of the FRG's policies were fairly uncontroversial. Beginning in spring 1990, East Germany's last transitional government, under Prime Minister Lothar de Maizière, and then its federal successor, under Chancellor Helmut Kohl, lost little time in overturning the convictions of hundreds of persons who had been wrongly convicted of political crimes under the old order. In 1992 and 1994, the Bundestag passed comprehensive legislation to rehabilitate the victims and provide them with monetary compensation for their losses.[7]

In other ways, however, the FRG's leaders took corrective measures that other governments would have barely considered imaginable in the early stages of democratization. In particular, this ambition was evidenced by their readiness to confront the thorny issue of property ownership in eastern Germany.[8] Well before October 3, 1990, the formal date of unification, a massive trust agency, the *Treuhandanstalt*, had begun the immense task of dividing up and privatizing thousands of industrial enterprises and businesses that had previously been centralized

3

under the commanding heights of the socialist state. Still, this under-taking paled in comparison with the Kohl government's meticulous efforts over the same period – at times, meticulous to a fault – to re-dress decades of unresolved claims to private property ownership in the East. In the ensuing years, German claims offices and administra-tive courts found themselves in the unenviable position of having to determine whether literally millions of homes and apartments, parcels of land, and country gardens should remain in the hands of people who had occupied them for years and even decades under the socialist system or should instead be returned to their original owners.

With the benefit of hindsight, one can see that much of Bonn's ag-gressiveness on all of these fronts is explainable in terms of the unusual circumstances that attended the fall of East German communism in 1989–90. Unlike the more fragile Latin American democracies, the equally precarious transition in South Africa, or most postcommunist experiments in eastern Europe, such as Poland and Hungary, it clearly mattered for the German search for justice that the GDR's demise had been both swift and complete. To say the least, there were no dis-gruntled military officers waiting in the wings of the federal chancery in Bonn for the first excuse to stage a coup d'état. Nor did the Kohl government ever have to worry that its police forces might conspire to subvert the Basic Law (*Grundgesetz*). Consequently, German policy-makers possessed an unusual – though not unlimited – degree of leeway in deciding whether one or another form of retrospective justice made sense in the context of a common national future.[9]

Adding to the FRG's comparatively greater zeal in addressing these questions, some lawmakers were motivated by uneasy memories about the handling of an only marginally more distant period in German history – National Socialism.[10] Had either of the two German states managed to deal with the crimes of the Nazi era in a convincing manner in the aftermath of World War II, it is possible that the comparisons that were to arise in the early 1990s between Hitler's despotism and the "second German dictatorship" (that of the SED) would have been more muted. As commentators were soon to observe, however, the deficit in both states' actions was sufficiently glaring that one could not have passed over the subject of East German injustice without simultane-ously bringing "another past, the Nazi past, into view once again."[11]

Certainly, many Germans in the West believed their first chancel-lor, Konrad Adenauer, had done less than needed to consolidate the country's break with Nazism. At a formative time in the Federal Republic's history, his government had been reluctant to embrace the example of the allied tribunals at Nuremberg. German courts were slow to prosecute Nazi war criminals, and for years thereafter – in the estimation of many critics – not nearly enough was done to bring the enormity of the Hitler regime's crimes to the forefront of public consciousness. Further aggravating the situation, even during the glory years of German democracy in the 1950s, some former National Socialist officials, including several of Adenauer's closest advisers, were allowed to retain high-level judicial, diplomatic, and administrative posts.[12] Two decades later, the Federal Republic would pay a heavy social price for these policies when a generation of young people rebelled against their parents' omissions.[13]

Notwithstanding the shortcomings in the West German *Vergangenheitsbewältigung* (policy of overcoming the Nazi past), observers could find even more evidence that the SED's leaders in East Berlin had been negligent on this issue to the point of irresponsibility. To be sure, in the first years after the war, the eastern zone's Soviet military occupiers tried and imprisoned proportionately more Nazi offenders than the West (even while they terrorized tens of thousands of other Germans who had fought against Hitler yet potentially threatened Moscow's control over the region). For a brief period, the newly founded GDR followed this example. In the so-called Waldheim trials of April–June 1950, its government handed down over 4,000 convictions for a variety of loosely defined offenses that varied from membership in the NSDAP (Nazi party) to service in the Wehrmacht.

However, this commitment to prosecutions was basically abandoned in subsequent years. By adopting the view that the German communists had already suffered the consequences of Hitler's tyranny in the 1930s, the SED proved willing to absolve its citizens, including many National Socialists and sympathizers, of any further need to wrestle with the implications of the Nazi period. In return for this largess, the East German people were only expected to align themselves with the party's putatively antifascist traditions. As a result, by the time German unity was restored, commentators could contend that few of the GDR's citizens had developed even the most rudimentary vocabulary for conceptualizing their nation's involvement in the atrocities of National Socialism.[14]

In this light, it makes sense to think that as long as the political will was present in Bonn and Berlin, conditions were ideal for Germany's leaders to take the kinds of sweeping measures that they exhibited with respect to the GDR. In fact, this impetus was provided on two major fronts from the first moment discussions were under way about the prospect of national unification.

On the eastern side of the inter-German border, the impetus was expressed passionately and vociferously by the handful of oppositionists and dissident intellectuals who played a key role in the GDR's waning days in setting the moral and political agendas for their part of Germany.[15] As participants in the improvised Roundtable discussions with the dying SED leadership from December 1989 onward and then as deputies to the first freely elected East German parliament, the Volkskammer, after March 1990, these activists perceived in the GDR's record a rare second chance for the German people. East Germany's citizens could make up for the limitations of the postwar era by finally examining their most deeply held convictions about the nation's role in the tragedies of the twentieth century. The activist writer Jürgen Fuchs captured this sentiment, cautioning an interviewer in 1992 that "if we do not solve this problem in a definite way, it will haunt us as Nazism did. We did not denazify ourselves, and this weighed on us for years."[16]

Correspondingly, on the western side of the national divide, leading politicians and opinion makers in the governing Christian Democratic–Free Democratic coalition and in the major opposition parties needed little convincing about the importance of weighing these voices into their plans for a united Germany. This was a matter of basic political credibility. If the GDR's citizens were ever to feel truly a part of the national project, they reasoned, it was vital that the FRG appear committed to accounting for the SED's actions and prepared to provide the victims with political and legal vehicles for redressing their grievances.[17]

Nevertheless, despite the energy and massive expenditure of resources the Federal Republic ultimately devoted to this challenge, it is telling that slightly more than a decade after the fall of the communist system, participants and observers alike remain sharply divided over the wisdom and efficacy of Bonn's reckoning with the GDR.[18] In fact, among the complex sentiments still haunting unified Germany, commentators on both sides of the controversy continue to feel – albeit for markedly different reasons – that the public officials who responded to this charge did more to pit easterners and westerners against each other than to reconcile them to a life together under a shared political roof.

On the one side, an array of observers, from constitutional theorists and politicians to former SED notables and professional pundits, have taken the federal government to task for ostensibly abandoning the moral and legal restraints of the *Rechtsstaat* (constitutional state) in seeking to come to terms with the GDR record. For the harshest of these critics, measures like criminal trials, civil service screening, and property restitution have seemed like nothing more than cynical manifestations of "victor's justice" in the capitalist West's long-standing battle with East Berlin.[19] However, these were by no means the only onlookers who failed to be persuaded by the FRG's policies. Even among those willing to give German decision makers credit for intending to do the right thing, many remain convinced that the net effect of these measures was to slow progress toward national unity by undermining public confidence in the fairness and impartiality of Germany's ruling institutions. One prominent legal theorist has made the point succinctly: "What has happened, has happened. Our previous mistakes in attempting to overcome the communist past can no longer be repaired. But they can be stopped."[20]

On the other side, an opposing group of critics composed of the former dissidents who numbered among the SED's few vocal opponents in the GDR's later years and outspoken western conservatives has faulted the FRG for exactly the opposite failing. Supposedly, Bonn was not doing enough to overcome the memory of dictatorship in the East. According to this view, the most convincing way for policymakers to have won the hearts and minds of the eastern population would have been to have made retrospective justice a priority in the region's incorporation into the Federal Republic. Yet, despite the measures taken, many could easily think of instances when the Kohl government had seemed more attentive to legal niceties, formal rules of procedure and due process, than to the substantive goal of redressing past ills. As a consequence, these participants were prone to conclude that their interests had been relegated to a second-place status on the national agenda. "We expected justice," activist Bärbel Bohley intoned, in perhaps the most often cited complaint about the rigidity of her new country's legal system, "but we got the *Rechtsstaat* instead."[21]

Because of the rancor and bad feelings separating these two groups, it cannot be surprising that in this situation – as in other difficult settings, such as Chile's transition to civilian rule or South Africa's break with apartheid – the issue of who is right or wrong in the debate over the merits of retrospective justice often seems like a toss-up between equally defensible moral platforms. The advocates of retribution, disqualification, and related forms of corrective action seem, quite properly, to speak out for the neglected rights of the victims and the wronged. Conversely, the opponents of these measures appear to be on equally strong footing in their determination to safeguard the rights of the accused from arbitrary punishment and to maintain the rudiments of political stability.

Still, as morally unassailable as both positions appear, it would be a mistake to imagine, as commentators sometimes do, that the two sides have shared no common ground at all or that they have been unable to reach reasoned compromises. To the contrary, when one looks closely at these disputes, it is rare for either side to view the challenge of coming to grips with past dictatorships in all-or-nothing terms.

For their part, even the most vociferous proponents of aggressive measures on the GDR's wrongs have generally not gone as far as to insist that their demands be effected at any price or under any circumstances. In calmer moments, most would probably agree that generating a healthy degree of respect for the neutrality of the rule of law in eastern Germany is a vital goal. In fact, however much they may align themselves with the sentiment that "justice be done," these critics would not want their new leaders to fall prey to the same sort of capricious behavior that previously brought them into conflict with the SED. The cost to German democracy would be too high.[22]

By the same token, those observers who have found the most to fault in Bonn's initiatives have rarely been so callous as to maintain that persons who suffered significant harm or indignities under the SED should receive no form of acknowledgment or compensation for the wrongs done to them. Most would readily concede that material and symbolic gestures can be useful vehicles for introducing the human casualties of dictatorship to democracy. Hence, they have been positively disposed toward activities (e.g., public forums on the SED's abuses, the payment of compensation to the victims) that appear to have the best chance of healing hurts and injuries and fostering a spirit of forgiveness and reconciliation among Germany's citizens.[23] From case to case, notably, most have also been inclined to support some kind of sanctions in instances of egregious wrongdoing. High-ranking former secret police officials, it seems, should not be allowed to fill top civil service positions, and true criminals should be punished for their offenses.[24]

Nonetheless, although the two sides may not be quite as polarized over the morality of these issues as is often assumed, they do seem frequently at loggerheads over one issue that has proved much more difficult for them to set aside. This has been the matter of the FRG's competence to sit in judgment on the GDR's affairs. All of its political and economic advantages aside, was a liberal–democratic polity like the Federal Republic really in the position to make responsible judgments about decisions that were reached or events that transpired under conditions far different from those in contemporary western Germany? Or, from the skeptics' perspective, was the gap between the two countries' experiences not so great that Bonn would have been better advised to have focused its attention on future tasks and to have passed over the GDR's offenses in silence?

At first blush, the interpretative challenge behind these questions may not appear to be such an integral part of a state's decision to redress injustice, but this challenge is implicitly at the heart of nearly every controversy over the FRG's attempt to come to grips with the record of a second dictatorship in German history. All along, the advocates and the critics of retrospective justice have been able to agree on one point. If policymakers were to apply their moral and legal categories in a credible fashion to the GDR, these standards would have to make sense in the light of the circumstances in which people had once lived and behaved under SED rule.

That this problem could be framed in empirical terms at all was potentially good news for anyone who wanted to evaluate whether the Federal Republic was doing the right thing in taking such steps. By engaging the East German record directly, Bonn would have the opportunity to defend its right to pass judgment. Yet even to get to this point one would need to confront some fundamental ambiguities about the kind of state the GDR had been and the extent to which anyone who lived through the communist experience could realistically have acted differently.

Interpreting the East German Past

Let us begin by putting the GDR into context. The communist states of the past century were not just any type of authoritarian government, but, more like their fascist contemporaries than their defenders would ever admit, they aimed to gain and maintain complete control over their subject populations.[25] In their most horrific guises, during Josef Stalin's "second revolution" of the 1930s and the internal party purges in East Europe of the late 1940s and early 1950s, the worst of these regimes accomplished their objectives by terrorizing their citizens into submission and crushing any signs of opposition to their authority. Even in the 1960s and 1970s, after most of the Soviet bloc had moved away from the excesses and extremes of high Stalinism, their leaders still held fast to the overriding goal of dominating the societies below them.

Writing about his native Czechoslovakia in 1978 in terms that could easily have been applied to the GDR, the dissident playwright Václav Havel called attention to the numbing impersonality of late communist rule and the degree to which "life in such a state [was] thoroughly permeated by a dense network of regulations, proclamations, directives, norms, orders and rules." Under these conditions, Havel argued, it was hard to speak about a realm of personal autonomy apart from the dictatorial state. In his estimation, most people in these countries had been "reduced to little more than tiny cogs in an enormous mechanism and their significance [had been] limited to their function in this mechanism."[26]

Assessments such as Havel's of the communist era would be of no more than academic interest were it not the case that these states' liberal–democratic successors have then been at a loss to know how or even whether they can bring conventional notions of responsibility to bear upon these regimes.[27] For example, a widely shared precept of liberal accountability holds that if a democratic polity is to avoid the trap of judging its members by an amorphous standard of collective guilt, its leaders must demonstrate that the crimes and abuses in question can be linked to the behavior of specific persons. That is, guilt must be individualizable. Yet under conditions of absolute despotism, skeptics wonder, who can say that persons suspected of participating in injustice have really been able to stand up to their superiors or to avoid being swept up, like so many people around them, in their government's campaigns to dominate society?

In a like vein, defenders of liberal democracy will insist that people's actions be judged according to knowable and publicly recognizable standards. In line with a well-established principle of western jurisprudence, they contend that no one should be held responsible for violating laws or other social mores that were not in effect at the time of the infractions (*nullum crimen, nulla poena sine lege*). But here, too, the communist record defies easy categorization and evaluation. When conventional legal and moral codes have been routinely manipulated and distorted to serve the state's baser political ends, it is at minimum debatable whether even well-intentioned persons will have had either the means or the ability to distinguish right from wrong.

Finally, it is commonly assumed that fair-minded policymakers will seek to verify whether persons suspected of wrongdoing can reasonably have abided by a high standard of ethical conduct under the previous order. No one, liberal theorists underscore, should be penalized merely for having failed to perform supererogatory or self-sacrificing acts while living under an oppressive regime. However, here as well, participants and observers like Havel have raised serious doubts about the opportunities for moral action that were available to average citizens in the communist world. Even if one were to show that certain people sometimes found the courage to act nobly and to resist all forms of wrongdoing, it seems inappropriate from this perspective to hold an entire population up to this standard. The dictatorship's reliance upon brute force and intimidation alone suggests that many citizens will have failed to do the right thing simply because they feared putting their livelihoods and personal well-being on the line.

Ironically, when a successor government is faced with these interpretative dilemmas, the most egregious instances of state-sponsored violence and injustice – "radical evil," as Hannah Arendt described them[28] – may, from one angle, be easier to judge because of the enormity of the crimes at issue. When the number of dead can be counted in the millions or when a state's representatives are implicated in genocidal policies and acts of military aggression against their neighbors, the proponents of punishment and other corrective measures will have the luxury of being able to look beyond the ambiguities of individual culpability to condemn the offenses outright. In these instances, they can turn to the kind of sweeping terms that Justice Robert Jackson famously employed in his opening remarks for the prosecution at the Nazi war crimes trials in Nuremberg. He described the wrongs in question as "so calculated, so malignant, and so devastating that civilization [could not] tolerate their being ignored, because it [could not] survive their being repeated."[29]

Of course, it says something about the difficulty of pursuing retrospective justice in any circumstance that successor states have registered, at best, a mixed record in following through on such charges. Even the Nuremberg justices could not find their way around the need to establish individual culpability in the case of defendants accused of planning aggressive war and other atrocities. Moreover, even in these instances, the resulting convictions remain awash with controversy.[30]

For our purposes, therefore, these extreme examples serve to amplify the importance of historical context in weighing a government's options in many transitional settings. Some new democracies, like Argentina in the late 1980s and Chile and South Africa in the 1990s, have been confronted with acts of shocking cruelty and savagery that verge on the inhumanity of National Socialism. Yet, arguably, a majority of the offenses with which the postcommunist regimes of East Europe have grappled over the past decade – physical and mental torture, kidnapping, corruption, property theft, and blackmail – would not be sufficiently severe or intolerable to qualify as crimes against humanity under customary understandings of international law. Thus, when these governments have sought to address their citizens' demands for justice, it has generally not been enough for them to characterize the offenses as immoral or reprehensible. They have also had to prove to the skeptics' satisfaction that the persons who committed the offenses should have recognized the gravity of their misdeeds and have been able to draw the necessary conclusions for their conduct.

Just such a challenge was presented in the early years of German unification to the various actors – politicians, political activists, jurists, and government officials – who sought to address East Germany's ills and offenses. They could not take for granted, nor would their critics have allowed them to do so, that the GDR's citizens had enjoyed the freedom to decide how to live their lives. Further, it was unclear how much average East Germans had been able to avoid becoming involved in their government's abuses. Hence, the natural starting point for redressing injustice was with the history of the GDR itself and the empirically verifiable conditions of communist rule. At first glance, these circumstances appear to have been quite inhospitable to autonomous moral action.

The German Democratic Republic was founded on October 7, 1949. Particularly in its early years, under SED chief Walter Ulbricht, the regime waged an uncompromising internal war against any sign of independent thinking or opposition within and outside the party apparatus. Ulbricht jailed many of his critics and forced hundreds of others into permanent exile while his government channeled its energies into constructing a disciplined form of state socialism that would be strong enough to withstand the country's exposed position to West Germany. State control over noncommunist parties and other political organizations was progressively tightened, the largest industries and privately held businesses were nationalized and the first agricultural cooperatives introduced, and the country's westernmost boundary with the FRG was fortified through the uprooting and expulsion of thousands of families from towns and villages along the inter-German border. When discontented workers took their grievances against Ulbricht's policies into the streets in a nationwide uprising on June 16–17, 1953, Soviet troops were called in to crush the revolt, and many of the protestors were later executed. Then, in its most infamous act, the regime built the Berlin Wall on August 13, 1961, effectively putting a clamp on its remaining 17.1 million citizens' freedom of maneuver.

Admittedly, in the years after the Wall's erection, first Ulbricht's government and then its successor, under the leadership of Erich Honecker, took deliberate steps to improve the public image of their experiment with Marxism–Leninism. According to the official mythology, the times of turbulence and uncertainty that had attended the initial construction of socialism in the 1950s were behind the East German people forever, and the country's leaders were now committed to establishing stable routines, fulfilling unmet expectations, and realizing all of the attributes of the good life under socialist auspices. Under Honecker's stewardship in the 1970s, the party faithful expressed the desire to show their citizens the benefits of socialism in the here and now by increasing the quality of durable consumer goods and the availability of luxury imports, constructing modern housing, and improving the wage structure of the East German work force.[31]

Just below the surface, however, these initiatives were grounded in an unspoken bargain with the population that narrowed its life options considerably. In a formulation that theologian Richard Schröder has aptly termed the "invidious social contract," the regime agreed to improve the material well-being of all of the GDR's citizens and even to refrain from intruding into certain aspects of their private affairs. But, this deal was complete only as long as they, in turn, displayed a minimal level of political conformity and exhibited at least grudging consent to major party directives.[32]

Throughout the 1970s and into the 1980s, Honecker gave voice to this tacit understanding through several widely publicized overtures to potential critics of his government. In December 1971, he signaled a partial reformation of SED cultural policy by announcing that there should be "no taboos" in the areas of art and literature, but in the same breath he stressed that this relaxation of state control would only be possible if the country's artists and intellectuals proceeded "from the firm basis of socialism." Similarly, in March 1978, Honecker hosted an unprecedented meeting with representatives of the GDR's Lutheran churches at which he let it be known that Christians could henceforth expect to be accorded the same rights and privileges as their fellow citizens. But again, he stipulated that they would have to operate within the limits of acceptable behavior provided to them by the state.[33]

These public gestures were magnified tens of thousands of times over in the form of countless, more subtle deals the regime – or, rather, its thousands of agents in the party apparatus, the state ministries, and the police – regularly struck with individual citizens to regulate daily life in the country.[34] Writers would suddenly obtain long-sought publishing outlets for their manuscripts if only they acceded to the Ministry of Culture and Science's "recommendations" (officially, the state did not admit to censorship) for enhancing the socialist content of their works. With the GDR's borders closed, Lutheran clergy were given visas to travel to religious synods in West Germany in return for tempering their criticisms of government policy in their sermons. Again and again, the regime proved cynically adept at trading access to scarce commodities, like telephone connections, the right to purchase a family car, and high-quality medicines and medical care, in return for simple obedience to its policies.

The consequences of failing to abide by the implicit rules behind these bargains are well known. The party–state showed that it could be a harsh and unforgiving taskmaster when pressed to defend its core values. In a widely publicized incident in fall 1976, the Honecker regime demonstrated the limits to the personal freedoms it was willing to allow when it banished the dissident songwriter Wolf Biermann to the West and subsequently coerced other artists into leaving the GDR permanently. For every prominent case in which the SED cracked down on its critics, there were hundreds of unpublicized instances in which ordinary citizens experienced the full force of the state's repressive policies. Children were taken away from their families and put up for adoption as a result of parents' failed escape attempts. Independent-minded teenagers were expelled from schools or dismissed from jobs for refusing to give in to the party's commands. And, still other citizens were sentenced to lengthy prison terms for demanding that their government abide by the human rights provisions of the Helsinki conference on European security and cooperation.[35]

Less obvious, but more insidious, was the subtle way the regime used its private bargains to envelop some citizens in multiple webs of complicity in these practices. For example, SED apparatchiks were hardly known to protest when the party allowed them, in blatant contravention of the written law, to take possession of residences, dachas, and plots of land that had been confiscated from fellow citizens seeking to emigrate to the West. Some high-profile artists and intellectuals were all too easily persuaded to act as casual informants for the Stasi in return for modest perquisites, such as access to western currency (especially deutsche marks), the right to purchase a new car, or simply the chance to amplify their own sense of self-importance. Even the management of an enterprise as grisly as the prevention of escape attempts at the Wall and along the inter-German border was transmogrified by the state into an exercise in studied co-optation. Guards who were involved in shootings were obliged to treat their actions as state secrets and then rewarded with cash bonuses and official commendations for carrying out their socialist duty.

This background brings us back to the problem of retrospective justice. Was this "daily system of soft terror" (to quote the eastern German Social Democrat Wolfgang Thierse), which "required the passive participation and quiet acceptance of many," really so pervasive as to make subsequent attempts to assign responsibility for wrongdoing impractical or even impossible?[36] Some oppositionists and intellectuals were immediately attracted to this view.[37] For them, there was an undeniable appeal to underscoring the special and all-embracing character of their country's encounter with communism. After all, if concepts like individual responsibility and moral accountability were deemed incommensurable with their past experiences, one could sidestep awkward questions about the application of liberal notions of legality and morality to a decidedly illiberal set of circumstances and turn one's attention completely to more mundane tasks. For a while, even well-known West German politicians, including Bonn's chief negotiator Wolfgang Schäuble, flirted with this position as well. They were at pains to demonstrate to their interlocutors that the FRG was not a neocolonial power bent upon imposing its standards on others.

Additionally, it did not escape the attention of policymakers that by taking an agnostic stand on the roots of the GDR's ills, they could avoid raising potentially embarrassing questions about another subject as the Germanys came together. This involved the seeming passivity of the East German population during the years of national division. Civic activist Jens Reich, no friend of the SED, raised exactly this cautionary note in 1992 just as Erich Honecker was coming to trial for his role in the killings at the Wall. "Every expectation of punishment is fruitless," Reich lamented about the case against the former party leader, "because we were all participants. We consented to everything. We looked away. We held our tongues. We rolled our eyes. We knew everything better. Many even took part. Only a miserable few sought to stop what was happening."[38]

Under these circumstances, one can understand why these attitudes would present stiff challenges to the thousands of judges and lawyers, civil servants, bureaucrats, and politicians who were actually called by their professions to be practitioners of retrospective justice in the FRG. Had they had their preference, most would undoubtedly have chosen to see themselves as nothing more than disinterested implementers of official policy; indeed, in line with German administrative traditions, many did precisely that. However, as will be observed again and again in this study, they could hardly succeed at this task without becoming interpreters of GDR history as well. Invariably, this meant opening up the black box that was the SED dictatorship and searching for ways of understanding the East German record that would make sense in the light of their liberal principles.

In contrast to the picture of collective complicity in East Berlin's offenses that Reich and others were painting, this approach had some noteworthy social and political payoffs. If one could demonstrate that there was at least some room for moral choice and individual discretion under the former regime, or perhaps even that some of its major wrongs could have been avoided, Bonn would have a ready tool for combating harmful stereotypes about the East. At worst, the pursuit of justice would show that the bulk of the GDR's citizens had committed no greater crime in their years of relative quiescence than to fail to become heroes. But when approached judiciously, this way of viewing the past could also lend support to a more hopeful proposition. Regardless of their failings, quite a few of the FRG's newest citizens had possessed the good sense to keep their distance from their government's abuses. Some had even had the guts to fight for their beliefs.[39]

Indeed, why should easterners not have warmed to this message? The final months of their country's existence had been a time of heady exuberance and excitement as they looked forward to the political freedoms and economic opportunities of their country's incorporation into the FRG. Nevertheless, only a year or two later, many had become frustrated and embittered about the costs of this process. Once the initial exhilaration had worn off, they felt with some justification that they had been turned into second-class citizens by their western compatriots.[40] They were also convinced that it would take years before they were accorded the full protections of the rule of law.[41]

In retrospect, we know that many western Germans would eventually have grounds for rethinking any feelings of moral superiority they may have harbored over the East during this period. For example, in late 1999 and early 2000, the Federal Republic was shaken by a series of stunning reports, soon to be confirmed in the secret archives of the Stasi, about financial improprieties, hidden bank accounts, and illegal kickbacks within the predominantly western leadership of the Christian Democratic Union (CDU). Not only were prominent personalities like Schäuble implicated in this affair, but, more shocking, the "chancellor of unity" himself, Kohl, turned out to be complicitous in his colleagues' activities.

Outspoken easterners were delighted to hold up the CDU's misadventures as evidence that the residents of the "old" *Länder* (states) were no more virtuous than those who had been forced to live under the SED. But of course, by the time these revelations were made public, nearly 10 years had elapsed since policymakers had first begun to shape and mold popular attitudes through, among other things, their strategies for coming to terms with the crimes of the communist era. With this in mind, we cannot help wondering how one should assess the wisdom and effectiveness of Bonn's policies over these formative years as well as their likely impact on the attitudes and sensibilities of the citizens of both Germanys. In this study, we will see that the FRG's success in this endeavor would depend in large measure on two closely related factors. The first was its leaders' inclination to bring historical context to bear in reaching their judgments rather than to impose blanket judgments on the East; the second was their ability to reconstruct the East German record in ways that suited their liberal principles.

Four Types of Retrospective Justice

Were the politicians, judges, and other officials who took on the challenge of retrospective justice in the 1990s appropriately attentive to conditions in the GDR when they sought to repair the harms and injuries of 40 years of SED rule and to redress the demands of its victims? Even if this was their intention, was the historical material they worked with sufficiently pliable and accessible to allow them to make sense of the circumstances under which wrongdoing occurred, to separate major rights offenders from mere hangers-on, and to identify those ills that could still be meaningfully rectified? Fortunately, in seeking answers to these questions, we can take advantage of a convenient fact about the road to national unity. By the end of the 1990s, Germany's leaders had brought nearly all of these measures to closure. Yet as an examination of four of the very different types of retrospective justice Bonn pursued over this period will show, the political and economic resources the FRG brought to this undertaking were rarely enough by themselves to guarantee success.

We will turn first to the FRG's use of criminal sanctions as tools of retribution by focusing on the high-profile trials that took place during the first half of the 1990s of SED officials and border guards who were implicated in the shooting deaths at the Berlin Wall. During the proceedings, most observers could agree that these killings were among the former regime's most objectionable acts. Nevertheless, even among those who favored prosecutions, there were notable disagreements about how to justify these trials.

Policymakers and legal scholars alike were initially divided about the first of the preceding questions, the one of whether appropriate attention was accorded historical circumstances in their judgments. For many, the culpability of the accused was a self-evident consequence of their participation in a fundamentally unjust political order or *Unrechtsstaat*. Thus, some officials assumed that punishment was called for practically by definition. Over time, it would become clear to a majority of the trials' advocates that this endorsement, in effect, of a principle of guilt by association was incompatible with some basic protections of the rule of law. But even when a consensus was patched together about the need to evaluate the defendants' behavior in the light of the conditions in which the border shootings occurred, it would still be challenging for the trials' advocates to respond to the second imperative, that is, the requirement that the East German record be compatible with the pursuit of retribution.

After considering the contending arguments for criminal trials, we will turn to the FRG's dismissal of thousands of eastern civil servants, police officers, teachers, and other officials from public employment after they were revealed to have been covert informants of the Ministry of State Security. This example of the use of noncriminal sanctions as a tool of retrospective justice – disqualifying justice – was no less controversial than the trials because of initial doubts that the Stasi's archives could be used as reliable historical records to identify collaborators or to draw meaningful distinctions among different degrees of involvement in the ministry's operations.

However, these apprehensions about reconstructing the past were largely misplaced. On balance, on the basis of information collected from the MfS files, the factual reality of Stasi complicity would turn out to be easier to assess than the elusive matter of criminal responsibility for the Wall killings. But a more serious cause for concern was the disposition of officials to use this information with due care in justifying dismissals. Because this competence was dispersed among several different types of state and federal agencies, there was an ever-present possibility in the early 1990s that persons would be disqualified from employment in one part of the country for activities that agencies in other locations would not have considered excessively burdensome. As a result, only a few years into the hunt for Stasi collaborators, opinions rightly varied about the efficacy of these measures and their impact upon the eastern German populace.

A third type of retrospective justice in our discussion, which will be called moral justice, is provided by the Bundestag's sponsorship of the special investigatory commission into a host of unresolved questions about the SED's legacy. This parliamentary body had one advantage over the deployment of criminal and noncriminal sanctions: it was not tied down by the need to assess individual guilt and responsibility. Also, because its focus was broader and its hearings were not confined to events in the GDR alone, the commission held out the possibility of providing important lessons about the general experience of dictatorship for all Germans.

Yet despite these hopeful foundations, by the time the Enquete commission completed its first round of investigations in the spring of 1994, serious questions could be raised about both the postwar image of German history that it adopted in its final report and the implications of its findings for the reputations of many of the institutions and social groups it surveyed. We will contend that this matter, too, was affected by the body's inclinations. The problem was not so much that the Bundestag's deputies-cum-historians were incapable of collecting useful information about the past and using the opportunity to provide a public forum for compelling testimony about events in and between the Germanys from 1949 to 1989. In these specific functions, the commission arguably excelled. Rather, the deeper cause for concern was with its members' disinclination to use history to guide their decisions, and not the other way around. From the first, the body's proceedings were hampered by persistent conflicts of interest, including the nagging resentments of its eastern deputies and the crass electoral calculations of their western counterparts. As a consequence, the commission's depiction of contentious issues in the two states' past, such as the survival strategies of the GDR's Lutheran churches and the management of the West German *Deutschlandpolitik*, bore only a partial resemblance to historical reality and, in conjunction with other policies, probably did more to impede inter-German understanding than to further it.

Finally, the fourth type of retrospective justice that will be considered – corrective justice – is exemplified by the even more complicated issue of property restitution. Under any circumstances, the attempt to rectify hundreds of thousands of property-related injustices by returning businesses, land holdings, houses, and apartments to their original owners was bound to be a tense and tumultuous enterprise, not least for those persons who would be asked to give up property they had possessed for decades. In fact, Bonn's willingness to confront this issue at all may have done more to set eastern and western Germans against each other in the early stages of unification than any other matter relating to its handling of the communist period.

On one level, we will contend that these difficulties do not appear to have been due to an inability or disinclination on the part of officials to convey an accurate picture of wrongdoing under the old regime. True, the process of identifying original owners and reconstructing the circumstances under which many contested properties had changed hands was often painstaking and agonizingly slow. But in this case, administrators had the advantage of working with fairly well-defined legal categories and verifiable instances of injustice.

This was not so, however, on another level, when claims officials discovered that German history was not always a convenient guide to a just property order. Had they only had to deal with one coherent legal system in the nation's past, the challenge of adjudicating multiple claims to ownership would have been fairly straightforward. But in 1990, policymakers on both sides of the national divide recognized that the issue of restitution could not be confined, either accurately or fairly, to the four decades of communist rule alone. Property-related injustice extended all the way back to the beginning of the National Socialist era. For this reason, precisely because they took history seriously, the architects of the property settlement would often resolve a dispute to the satisfaction of one group of claimants only to find that they had seemingly committed a fresh injustice in the eyes of another.

Given the difficulty of ensuring that public officials were appropriately disposed to address the issue of historical context and the uncertainty that these conditions would be amenable to liberal standards of judgment, the reader may wonder whether German decision makers ever had any alternatives. Would the FRG not have been better off had the country's leaders simply decided on the day of unification to forego the issue of retrospective justice entirely and to concentrate their energies instead on making less confrontational values, like forgiveness and forgetting, into the hallmarks of the new political order? Certainly, it is hard to imagine that they wanted to make as daunting an undertaking as unification more difficult than it had to be. Nonetheless, as will become evident in the four different cases in this book, the choices before them were rarely this easy.

One manifest constraint upon Bonn's freedom of maneuver was that a decision to do nothing would still have amounted to taking a stand on the disputes. For the victims, this stance would have suggested that no injustice was so grave as to merit the risks of corrective action. Indeed, to have taken no action at all on the GDR's offenses would have been tantamount to telling many easterners that the harms and misfortunes inflicted upon them over 40 years of communist rule were of negligible importance to the construction of the new German nation–state. In 1990, few politicians wanted to go quite this far.

But in addition, authorities were operating under another, less evident constraint. Many of their options had already been shaped and

JUDGING THE PAST IN UNIFIED GERMANY

bounded by decisions reached in the waning days of East German communism or even before then – as the property conflict would suggest – during the tumultuous decades preceding the GDR's founding. It is essential to appreciate this often understated fact. In comparison with the travails of many new democracies in the developing world, Bonn was clearly better situated to bring its institutions and ways of thinking to eastern Germany. But this is not to say that the East had no effect on the Federal Republic. It, too, was in the position to influence western policy, both because of the numerous and vocal social actors who demanded that the federal government recognize their interests and because of a variety of additional political and legal faits accomplis that grew out of the GDR's fall. In this sense, as will be seen repeatedly in this study, officials in the Kohl government may have had the upper hand in shaping the direction their policies would take, but as the epigraph from Karl Marx suggests at the beginning of this book, they rarely had the power to do exactly as they pleased.

To concede these points is not to say what specific choices German policymakers should have made over the decade, nor is it to cast a sweeping judgment on the utility of one or another form of retrospective justice. In some respects, the critics' apprehensions were well founded. Some of Bonn's attempts to act upon the East German record probably did have a less than desirable impact on the course of German unification – especially upon eastern attitudes about the meaning and practice of the rule of law. Nonetheless, other steps seem to have had much more salutary consequences for the public mood in the East and perhaps also for the quality of German democracy. As will be suggested in the conclusion to this study, these benefits may extend to the way many Germans will come to regard their nation's unique moral responsibility for the consequences of dictatorship over the twentieth century.

To appreciate these caveats fully, we turn to the central theme of this book, the relationship between historical interpretation and the pursuit of justice.

2

Criminal Justice

PROSECUTING GDR OFFICIALS

On March 14, 1966, two East German children, ages 10 and 13, were shot to death while playing in the vicinity of their country's border with the West Berlin district of Neukölln. We will never know what prompted them to stray so close to the border fence. Perhaps they were curious about the barrier that separated their tiny garden community from the homes of more prosperous Germans only a few hundred feet away. We do know, however, that two border guards used between 40 and 50 rounds of ammunition to prevent them from going any farther. The 13-year-old was killed instantly. His companion succumbed to his wounds several hours later in an East Berlin hospital reserved for the *Volkspolizei* (People's Police). Technically, the guards could have been punished for their actions because the use of weapons against children was expressly prohibited in the border code of the German Democratic Republic. But instead, they were given bonuses and commended for their initiative. Simultaneously, the vast machinery of the East German state was deployed to cover up the incident. The bodies of both victims were immediately cremated, and their parents were informed that their sons had died in an unspecified accident at another location.[1]

Were it not for the opening of the Berlin Wall on November 9, 1989, and the unification of the two German states 1 year later, this incident and countless other tragedies at the inter-German border might never have come to light. Yet, when they did become public in the early 1990s, as a result of the prosecutions of many of the persons linked to these killings, these atrocities instantly exposed all of the complexities and awkwardness of Bonn's attempt to sit in judgment on the actions of the SED regime.

To be sure, only the rare person would have rushed to defend every, or even most, aspects of the GDR's border policy. Few onlookers would have argued that it was a normal practice in the affairs of a modern state to use deadly force against unarmed citizens who had committed no greater offense than seeking to flee their country for the freedoms of another. Moreover, even the most hardened representatives of the communist system would have taken little satisfaction at the news that their government's policies had resulted in the deaths of two innocent children.

Nonetheless, it was far from self-evident to many observers how the Federal Republic was supposed to address these actions beyond expressing indignation and horror. Had the shootings taken place on the territory of the old West German state, the FRG's criminal code could have been used to prosecute the offenders, for there could have been no doubt about their knowing what they had done was wrong. In fact, on September 30, 1997, just such a trial was concluded in Berlin, resulting in the conviction of a western German right-wing radical for the attempted murder of two East German border guards in 1970.[2] But the GDR was not the Federal Republic. One could reasonably imagine that GDR officials had operated according to very different standards of personal comportment than their counterparts in the West.

Accordingly, a recurrent question for those who hoped to justify criminal trials in the Wall deaths was, Should this different context play any role at all when West German judicial officials sought to bring their own legal instruments to bear on the East German past? One almost instinctual response of some prosecutors was to deny the relevance of historical circumstances entirely on the grounds that the guards and other agents who were implicated in the border shootings were answerable to a higher law that superseded their obligation to uphold their country's laws and practices. On the face of it, this position would seem to have had at least two advantages. It allowed authorities to focus squarely on the immorality of the acts in question and made arguments by the accused that they were merely following the orders of their superiors more difficult. However, this stance had the potential drawback of invoking a fairly amorphous standard of retrospective justice at a sensitive juncture in the FRG's history. Because eastern Germans were suddenly being introduced to a legal system that was profoundly different from the one they had known in the past, many were understandably uneasy about how they would be judged by their compatriots in the West.

In contrast, there was another way of approaching the border killings that did not preclude appealing to the preceding standards. This was to reconstruct the historical conditions under which the guards and their superiors had acted and to hold them accountable for breaking laws that had actually been in effect in the GDR. The manifest appeal of this approach, which the courts were gradually brought around to adopting over the 1990s, was its reliance upon a more fair-minded understanding of individual responsibility under communist rule. Only those persons who could be directly tied to violations of the codified law would be made to pay for the GDR's worst excesses. Furthermore, by taking this approach, one could hope to avoid the problem of ex post facto lawmaking that was sure to bedevil the invocation of higher norms alone.

Nevertheless, as sensible as this avenue may have appeared to its proponents, it was far from enough to overcome all doubts about these processes. There was no guarantee that the historical record would automatically provide jurists with the evidence they required to support their charges in the Wall deaths. At times, the courts were able to substantiate their prosecutions by pointing to clear and undeniable cases of culpability within the East German decision-making hierarchy. But at other points, their credibility must have suffered when the thirst for justice led them to portray the GDR past in a manner that was inconsistent with the experience of those who lived through it. Thus, even when judicial authorities could make history work for them, the recurrent issue was whether they would be inclined to do so.

Competing Arguments for Justice

In ordinary times, reasonable people will always disagree about the uses to which the law should be put in redressing past wrongs. But of course the fall of the GDR after 40 years of antagonism and severely strained relations between East Germany and West Germany was far from a normal circumstance. Consequently, one had only to scratch the surface of the legal argumentation offered in support of criminal trials in the early 1990s to see that there were, in fact, radically different ways of interpreting the FRG's obligation to act on the offenses of its former adversary.

For many Germans – both the eastern victims of the SED's policies and the western politicians and policymakers who saw themselves as having occupied the moral high ground during the decades of national division – the demand for justice was part and parcel of their nation's continuing historical responsibility to act upon the legacy of German authoritarianism. According to this view, individuals like SED chief Honecker and his subordinates were not merely guilty of having committed specific criminal offenses during their time in office. As representative of the country's ruling regime, they were responsible for setting into motion and then maintaining a distinctively unjust political order, or *Unrechtsstaat*, that had already led the German people to ruin between 1933 and 1945. This was a state in which – to quote Karl Jaspers' well-known judgment about the Nazi dictatorship – the entire legal system had frequently served as a pretext "for pacifying the masses of its people and forcing them into submission."[3]

Admittedly, those who sought to justify prosecutions on these grounds did not always agree about how far one could go in likening the Honecker regime to the system of injustice propagated by Hitler. For some observers, such as Rudolf Wassermann, a former president of Germany's Federal Administrative Court and an outspoken proponent of a judicial reckoning with the past, there were "disturbing" similarities between the two systems. "The campaign of destruction against 'Marxists' and 'alien peoples,'" Wassermann explained a few years after the Wall trials had begun,

> had its parallels in the communist struggle against the bourgeoisie as a "class enemy." The one group disregarded human rights from the standpoint of race while the other did it from the class standpoint. The oppression in [East Germany] was even more tangible than under national socialism, because communist rule had no legitimacy at all and people had to be forced to go along, while almost to its end, the national socialist system was based upon the broad consent of much of its population.[4]

In contrast, other critics of the East German dictatorship used more cautious language in comparing the SED's rule with that of the NSDAP. When pressed, they were willing to concede the different origins of the two dictatorships and the much greater extent of the crimes committed under the Nazis.[5]

Yet both groups could agree on one point that was central to the characterization of the GDR as an *Unrechtsstaat*. Because of the distorted nature of East Germany's legal system, no one – from Honecker down to the lowliest border guards – could be allowed to excuse or to justify manifest violations of human rights by claiming that they had operated within the law of their land. To allow them to hide their crimes behind the elaborate web of legal fictions that had been created to give the GDR its veneer of legitimacy, these critics felt, would be to make a mockery of the idea of law as it was understood in the West. As legal theorist Eckhard Jesse has underscored, this step would have been equivalent to "factually affirming" the abuses of the old East German order.[6]

Within the body of German jurisprudence, there seemed to be an excellent precedent for dealing with the protests of innocence that could be expected from the GDR's representatives at their trials. In cases when former Nazi officials had sought to excuse their crimes by claiming fidelity to the law of the Third Reich, West German courts had often appealed to a natural law standard set by one of the Federal Republic's most eminent legal philosophers, Gustav Radbruch. In a formulation still associated with his name, Radbruch argued that the courts could not allow themselves to be bound by the strictures of positive law in reaching their judgments. When a conflict existed between the codified law and a higher conception of justice, and the contradiction between the two assumed, in Radbruch's carefully chosen words, an "intolerable dimension," it was not only appropriate but imperative that the law be declared "unjust [*unrichtiges Recht*]" and subordinated to the cause of morality.[7]

Nonetheless, as much as leading members of the new all-German government, such as Justice Minister Klaus Kinkel, Interior Minister Wolfgang Schäuble, and Chancellor Helmut Kohl, may have agreed with the moral ideal behind this sentiment, they could point to two manifest problems with relying *exclusively* upon suprapositive standards to justify the postunification trials. The first problem was the appearance that Germany's predominantly western leadership was bent upon imposing a kind of "justice of the victors (*Siegerjustiz*)" upon the defeated leadership of the GDR. This problem would have been great enough had the Federal Republic maintained no contacts with the communist regime before 1989 and hence been driven by the desire for revenge alone. Yet, whatever disputes and difficulties may have existed between East and West Germany over decades of separation, Bonn's relations with the GDR could not fruitfully be compared with those of a militant and expansionist dictatorship on the order of Nazi Germany. Despite years of rhetoric about keeping the national question open and promoting basic human rights in the East, Kohl's Christian Democratic–Free Democratic governing coalition had developed a relatively cordial working relationship with East Berlin by the end of the 1980s. This was borne out by the welcoming reception Honecker received during a semiofficial visit to the FRG in September 1987, a mere 2 years before the opening of the Wall.[8]

Who knows? Had Kohl and his colleagues been operating in a political vacuum, they might have been disposed to ease the transition to a united Germany by imposing sharp limitations on the number of prosecutions that eventually took place, but the stormy months surrounding the GDR's fall were anything but a vacuum. Policymakers were not only pressured to respond to demands for justice from both German populations but also had to take into account that, since October 1989, the East German regime had begun to establish precedents of its own for redressing these grievances.

The immediate occasion for East Berlin's measures was Honecker's ouster from the SED leadership on October 18, 1989, and his replacement as general secretary by Egon Krenz, long his heir apparent. In a desperate attempt to manufacture a semblance of legitimacy, the Krenz government had sought to exploit the GDR's legal system to demonstrate its commitment to thoroughgoing political reform. In late October, the regime took the first steps in this direction by setting up a special commission to investigate accusations of police brutality against civil rights demonstrators. Then, in early November, it turned its attention to Honecker himself. On November 8, the SED's tenth Central Committee plenum declared the country's long-time leader to be principally responsible for the GDR's troubles and expelled him from the party. Four days later, East German prosecutors began to investigate Honecker and other party *Prominenz* for abusing their power.[9] These initiatives set the stage for further proceedings and prosecutions during the GDR's next two short-lived governments under reform communist Hans Modrow until March 18, 1990, and under Christian Democrat Lothar de Maizière until October 3, 1990.

Against this backdrop, following unification the Kohl administration was understandably concerned to show that it took the issue of redressing GDR-era injustice seriously but would act only on the basis of western legal norms. Hence, the chancellor stressed that his government was "strictly against" the politicization of any conceivable proceedings against Honecker or anyone else associated with the SED regime. "We do not hold political trials," Kohl announced.[10] Other members of his cabinet emphasized that the FRG's credibility in these processes would only be ensured if it concentrated on the worst cases of actual guilt. It was crucial, Schäuble maintained, that Bonn be seen to be magnanimous in its actions and not self-righteous.[11]

In addition, as Germany's leaders deliberated over the prospect of undertaking such prosecutions, they were concerned about a second, even more delicate issue. This was the impact that the appeal to a higher – but, by itself, relatively loosely defined – conception of justice might have upon the FRG's ability to portray itself as a law-governed state, or *Rechtsstaat*. As citizens of the newly unified German nation, Honecker and everyone else in the GDR regime were entitled to all the protections afforded by the Basic Law.[12] They enjoyed the presumption of innocence. They could be punished only in proportion to the severity of their crimes. And, most important in this context, they had the advantages of the constitution's explicit prohibition on ex post facto lawmaking (Art. 103 [2]). The architects of national unity were so attentive to the principle of *nullum crimen, nulla poena sine lege* that they incorporated it directly into the Unification treaty of 1990. In a notable exception to the extension of West Germany's legal system to the East, the accord specifically stipulated that the FRG's criminal code could only be applied if instances of allegedly criminal behavior were already considered punishable "according to the law of the German Democratic Republic applicable at the time [such actions were committed]."[13]

We should recognize that this nod in the direction of preexisting East German statutes was not as radical as it may have appeared at first glance. In the years before national unification, but particularly after the signing of the inter-German Basic treaty of 1972, West German courts had generally recognized the normative character of GDR law for Germans residing in the East.[14] Furthermore, this reliance upon East German statutes did not mean that the FRG's courts were subsequently bound to exclude all suprapositive norms from their decisions. Quite the contrary, jurists could still look within the body of GDR law for evidence of moral categories commonly recognized in the West.[15]

Nonetheless, the presence of this simple protection against arbitrary lawmaking had the provocative consequence of forcing onlookers to view the GDR in a new light. Unavoidably, once decision makers conceded that East German officials could be held accountable for specific violations of their own laws, the next step of treating the GDR as a much more complex entity than the undifferentiated and essentially "lawless" *Unrechtsstaat* had to be taken.

In two key addresses in February 1992, Kinkel admitted as much when he warned against allowing anyone brought to trial the opportunity to dismiss or play down their crimes as merely "the independent activities of systems, apparatuses, and organized collectivities [*Großgruppen*]." "Even in a dictatorship," Kinkel emphasized, "an individual's room for maneuver is not as small as the perpetrators would like us to believe."[16] Apparently, the justice minister was fully aware of the implications of this statement for the way one assessed the historical reality of the GDR. If there was room for individual choice under the SED, there must also have been recognizable standards of behavior, legal and otherwise, that the party's representatives and other officials had simply decided to ignore. Again Kinkel: "Even the criminal code of the GDR treated manslaughter, bodily harm, [false] imprisonment, and violations of the peace as punishable offenses. In many ways, the GDR's rulers disregarded and infringed their laws, and thus they can be prosecuted today according to the criminal code of the GDR."[17] In this sense, the recognition that there had actually been a viable concept of law under the SED was the best, and perhaps the only, alternative to the imposition of retroactive standards of justice.

By late 1992, when the FRG's courts finally worked their way up to the most famous of the Wall trials, those of Honecker and his fellow members of East Germany's National Defense Council (NVR), a majority of judges had been brought around to Kinkel's more subtle characterization of the legal culture of the GDR. However, this way of thinking about the communist state was by no means automatic. Even before the best-known cases began, Kinkel and like-minded policymakers still needed to overcome the reservations of other judicial authorities who believed it was enough to judge the GDR according to a special standard of justice. This tension was nowhere more evident than in the first of several prosecutions that commenced in 1991 of the lowliest figures on the country's power hierarchy, the Berlin Wall border guards.

Seeking Justice within the Law

In retrospect, it may appear logical that the proceedings against the GDR's rulers were preceded by the trials of the persons who could be most directly tied to the killings at the Wall and along the inter-German border.[18] If one demonstrated that they had violated the GDR's laws, some prosecutors reasoned, would it not be easier to hold accountable the powerholders above them? In fact, we will have reason to suggest shortly that more convincing cases for prosecution, both historically and legally, could be made against the seniormost representatives of the East German regime. Yet even to get to this point, the courts would first need to arrive at a consensus about the general criteria to be used in adjudicating these cases.

The first border guard trial started on September 2, 1991, and eventually led to the conviction of two soldiers for killing 20-year-old Chris Gueffroy (the last victim of the Wall) on February 5, 1989. From the first day of the proceedings, however, the trial was marred by controversy. The credibility of the presiding judge, Theodor Seidel, was instantly impaired when word spread that he had once belonged to an organization that smuggled refugees out of East Germany and therefore might be biased in the case. For that matter, he made no effort to hide his political sentiments at the trial. Making matters more complicated, Seidel was never able to insulate his court from the frenzied attention of the media. But for our purposes, the most problematic aspect of the trial lay in how Seidel went about finding the defendants guilty of their crimes.

In their defense, as one could have anticipated, the former guards appealed to the doctrine of "obedience to superior orders" made famous by Nazi officials at the Nuremberg war crimes trials. In the face of substantial evidence against them, they admitted to using their weapons on persons who had sought to flee the GDR illegally, but they countered that they were only carrying out their duty as soldiers and acting well within the law of their country. On one level, these claims had some foundation. The East German penal code (§213) made it a criminal offense for anyone to leave the GDR without official permission. Furthermore, the country's border troops seem to have enjoyed some latitude in enforcing this statute. The Revised Border law of 1982 expressly stated that "the use of physical force [was] allowable when other means were not sufficient to prevent serious consequences for the security and order of the border territory" (Section 26.1). Also, the law permitted the use of firearms "to prevent the imminent commission of a crime" (Section 27.2).[19]

Given these provisions, one might have expected Seidel to begin by wrestling with this defense. Yet, to his way of thinking, the real issue was what kind of state the GDR had been. Explicitly citing the Radbruch formula, Seidel emphasized that one could not respect the laws of a regime whose leaders enjoyed "no form of legitimation (*durch nichts legitimiert waren*)." In his view, the legal standards of the GDR were unenforceable because they stood – again, he used Radbruch's terminology – in "crass contradiction to the generally recognized foundations of the rule of law."[20]

In taking this stand, Seidel conceded that he could be accused of drawing an implicit parallel with the Nazi regime whose crimes, he admitted, were much more extensive than those of the GDR. "Nonetheless," he added, "the court has no misgivings about following this legal approach in this case, for the protection of human life enjoys general validity and cannot be dependent upon a specific number of killings." In this light, the guards' claims that they had no choice in taking the lives of innocent human beings were not compelling. "Even in the former GDR," Seidel concluded, "justice and humanity were understood and treated as ideals." Hence, the soldiers must have recognized the immorality of their actions: "Shooting with the intent-to-kill those who merely wanted to leave the territory of the former GDR was an offense against basic norms of ethics and human association."[21]

From a strictly moral standpoint, Seidel's observations cannot be dismissed out of hand, and elements of his position would continue to find their way into subsequent individual decisions. As the judge rightly stressed in his ruling, drawing upon one of the two most prominent legal objections to the superior orders defense – the presence of a guilty or culpable state of mind[22] – the defendants themselves had shown in their testimony that they had known what they were doing was wrong. They admitted that they had routinely done everything they could to maintain the secrecy of shootings, such as Gueffroy's, after the fact. Also, demonstrating that they could have acted differently, they had refrained from using their weapons against would-be border crossers on occasions (e.g., official holidays, state visits) when such actions would have embarrassed their government.[23]

Yet was acting immorally the same thing as "breaking the law"? This question, which provided the basis for the other well-known objection to the superior orders argument, was decisive for the more famous trials to come.[24] On this count, many German scholars *and* several appeals courts parted ways with Seidel. There was widespread agreement about the guards' moral culpability, but these experts argued that

Seidel's exclusive reliance upon a higher law ran right up against the prohibitions in the Basic Law and the Unification treaty on ex post facto punishment.[25] This message was conveyed unmistakably at the second of the border guard trials, which began on December 18, 1991, and became a model for most subsequent proceedings. In this instance, two soldiers were charged in the 1984 shooting death of 20-year-old Michael-Horst Schmidt, who had attempted to escape over the Wall into West Berlin. Both defendants were found guilty, but this time, in contrast to Seidel's reasoning, the court was at pains to demonstrate that justice could be pursued within the bounds of East German statutes.

In her ruling of February 5, 1992, Judge Ingeborg Tepperwein explicitly took issue with the invocation of the Radbruch formula in this case (the guards' right to legal security, she insisted, took precedence over a higher moral code) and turned instead to the Border Law of 1982 to show that each of the defendants had exceeded his author ity in shooting to kill. Tepperwein conceded that the GDR's criminal law gave the soldiers the right to use coercive measures of some kind to prevent illegal border crossings. However, she noted that the East German code was similar to the law of the Federal Republic in one crucial respect: it required that the means employed to prevent a crime be proportionate to the crime being committed. In this instance, the judge argued, "the flight of a single, unarmed person from whom there was no apparent danger to other persons or things" could not be considered a violation serious enough to justify the use of deadly force. Moreover, Tepperwein added, GDR border law specified that the guards seek to "preserve human life if possible" (Section 27.5). Therefore, she concluded, one could reasonably have expected the soldiers to have chosen only the "mildest means" available – for example, "a single, deliberate shot at the legs" – to fulfill their obligations. They not only failed to act upon this option in shooting Schmidt, but they showed themselves to be culpable by failing to provide their victim with immediate medical attention. As the evidence before the court demonstrated, such care could have saved his life.[26]

It is easy to see why observers would consider Tepperwein's reliance upon East German law to be a step up from the more ambiguous foundations of the first border guard trial. At least her more historically minded approach had the advantage of placing the guards within a legal context in which they could have found guidance to act differently. As long as this small room for choice was available to them, they could not convincingly claim that they bore no responsibility at all for their actions. Indeed, no one had forced them to become border guards. They were part of an elite security force, 46,000 strong, that reported directly to the Minister of National Defense. Also, they could not have taken on this assignment without being constantly scrutinized for loyalty by, among other agencies, the Stasi.[27]

By the same token, one cannot help sympathizing with those critics who have also invoked GDR history to caution against holding the guards up to an idealized conception of East German law.[28] Even if the protection of human life was formally sanctified in the border code and reinforced by such legal documents as the GDR's constitution (for example, Article 30 (2) guaranteed the "personality and freedom" of every citizen), a commonly recognized part of the reality of the border regime was that no one would ever be punished for the use of deadly force. To the contrary, the possibility that shootings could result in the deaths of escapees was taken for granted by everyone involved. Border soldiers were routinely socialized to accept the proposition that there was no greater failing than to allow a successful escape. Thus, when they did have cause to use their weapons, as we have seen in the case of the 1966 killings of the two East German children, they were generally praised and rewarded for doing so.

To her credit, Tepperwein took these facts into account in deciding the issue of punishment. Despite finding both defendants guilty, the judge suspended the guards' sentences after reading her decision. Like Seidel, Tepperwein emphasized that obedience to superior orders could not be used to excuse or to justify their behavior. However, she acknowledged that the two soldiers were operating under conditions that militated against completely independent action on their part. "Not selfishness or criminal energy" had led to their crime, Tepperwein concluded, but "circumstances over which they had no influence, such as the political and military confrontation in divided Germany [and] the special conditions of the former GDR."[29] It was appropriate that their punishment be administered accordingly.

As sensible as this nuanced view of the East German past might have appeared at the time, it gave rise to a tantalizing question. If the border guards were not completely responsible for their actions – indeed, if Tepperwein was right and they could not be considered fully autonomous actors – would it be possible to bring those individuals to trial who had decided the border policy in the first place?

A "Trial of the Century"

It may be only a coincidence that Germany's high appeals court, the Federal Court of Justice, voted to uphold Tepperwein's verdict – at least in its essential aspects – in the second border guard trial on November 3, 1992.[30] The date of this ruling came a mere 9 days before the anxiously awaited trial of SED General Secretary Honecker was set to begin in Berlin.

Coincidence or not, the proximity of the two cases provided a fitting rejoinder to those dispirited eastern German rights activists who were regularly voicing concern that only the least of the offenders were being made to pay for the crimes of the communist past. Even under the GDR's last transitional governments, continual attempts were made through the summer of 1990 to bring Honecker to trial on charges as wide-ranging as the abuse of power, high treason, and murder.[31] But only on May 14, 1992, did the Berlin prosecutor general's office finally release a nearly 800-page indictment that formally charged Honecker and five other defendants with "indirect complicity [in manslaughter]."[32] The indictment maintained that, as members of the GDR's secretive National Defense Council (NVR), Honecker and former secret police chief Erich Mielke, Minister–President Willi Stoph, Defense Minister Heinz Keßler and his chief-of-staff Fritz Streletz, and Suhl district party secretary Hans Albrecht had enjoyed "unlimited influence" in determining how their state's border was fortified. They had been responsible for all of the decisions, from the selection of soldiers to the deployment of weapons and exploding mines, that ensured that the border regime ran "like clockwork." On this basis, the indictment held that they, and not the guards on the periphery of the chain of command, should be considered the "key figures in everything that happened."[33]

These charges were a far cry from the guilt by association that one might have tied to an *Unrechtsstaat*. But more to the point, they were much easier to substantiate than the claims made against the border soldiers. The indictment provided a detailed outline of the procedures of the NVR and painstaking descriptions of 68 of the hundreds of killings that had taken place on the inter-German border between 1961 and 1989. In addition, the document's authors acted like court historians in meticulously linking each of the defendants to the crimes he was alleged to have committed. The indictment demonstrated that on

August 12, 1961, Honecker himself, in the presence of Mielke and Stoph, had given the order that led to the construction of the Berlin Wall.[34] This decision had then led to numerous follow-up meetings – on September 20, 1961; November 29, 1961; April 6, 1962; June 13, 1963; October 23, 1969; July 14, 1972, and so forth, in abundant historical detail – at which all of the defendants had eventually taken part in "further steps to increase the security of the border." At one particularly notable meeting of the NVR, on May 3, 1974 – a time when the GDR was supposedly welcoming greater contacts between its citizenry and the capitalist West – Honecker had specifically endorsed the "unhampered use" of firearms to prevent escapes, and he had called upon his coleaders to "praise those comrades who used their weapons successfully."[35]

At no point can the prosecutor general's office have underestimated the political difficulties involved in seeking to prosecute the GDR's leaders for these offenses.[36] As commentators liked to point out, Honecker was, with the exception of Admiral Dönitz, the first German head of state to be put on trial in over 800 years. Indeed, during the first half of 1992, no one could even be sure whether the chief defendant would be present in the courtroom to hear the charges against him. In the wake of unification, Honecker had fled to Moscow, where he found refuge in the Embassy of the Republic of Chile; his return to Germany literally required the collapse of the Soviet regime and heavy diplomatic pressure on the part of the Kohl government. Nor was Honecker's presence in Berlin bound to make the proceedings any easier. Ironically, he was held in the same Moabit prison in which he had once been confined by the Nazis. As the "trial of the century" began, the worldwide media attention and high emotions that converged on the city guaranteed that Kohl's and Kinkel's hopes of avoiding a political spectacle would be tested.

From the standpoint of the defense, conditions were ideal for suggesting that a miscarriage of justice was at hand. In his one and only statement before the court, on December 3, 1992, Honecker gave one of the more spirited speeches of his career (amazing, in this writer's opinion, given his abysmal oratorical standards in the past) in which he portrayed himself and his colleagues as the victims of a cruel twist of fate. Feigning modesty, Honecker advised his listeners that the indictment gave him no choice, "without being an historian, [but] to recapitulate the history that had led to the [construction of the] Wall."

It was not, he insisted sarcastically, "'criminal' individuals, such as I and my comrades," who bore responsibility for the barrier in Berlin and the deaths at the border. Rather, the roots of this tragedy lay in the world-historical conflict that had begun with Hitler's rise to power in 1933 and culminated in the formation of two opposing German states after World War II and the hysteria of the Cold War. Now, the injustices of earlier eras were about to be repeated with his own conviction. "One would have to be blind or consciously close one's eyes to the events of the past," Honecker lectured his accusers, "to fail to recognize that this trial is a political trial of the victors over the defeated, [or] to fail to recognize that it amounts to a politically motivated misrepresentation of history."[37]

These would not prove to be insuperable objections for the courts. Honecker's characterization of his and his colleagues' room for maneuver was one-sided at best. But first, there was a more immediate complication for those seeking to prosecute the East German leadership – a fact that nobody could deny about the majority of the defendants: their advanced age. Within the Basic Law, there is arguably no more important guarantee than its opening promise (Article 1 [1]) to protect "human dignity."[38] Given the rapidly deteriorating health of many of the defendants, German prosecutors were aware that a long and exhausting trial would amount to a violation of this right. Thus, on November 13, only a day after the trial had begun in Berlin, the court temporarily suspended all proceedings against Willi Stoph because the former prime minister was experiencing heart trouble. Only a few days later, similar steps were taken in the trial of Erich Mielke on the grounds that the one-time secret police chief, also in failing health, was simultaneously being tried for the murders of two Weimar-era police officers.[39]

In both cases, it is noteworthy that there was little if any public opposition to the court's actions. However, when the attorneys for the defense requested that the same protections of the law be applied to Honecker, the reaction was quite different. Undoubtedly, a decisive element in the public outcry that ensued was that Honecker, more than any other figure, personally embodied the crimes of the GDR government. Yet Honecker's health problems were also more serious than those of the other defendants. Because most, although not all, medical experts gave the GDR's former leader less than a year to live as the result of a cancerous tumor that was spreading in his liver, it was clear that to postpone his case was to ensure that he would never be brought to justice.[40]

For weeks, the contending attorneys engaged in macabre debates about the condition of the defendant's liver. How *much* pain was he experiencing? How *big* was his tumor? How *fast* was it growing? When *would* it kill him? As these battles ensued, the presiding judge, an avowed anticommunist, Hansgeorg Bräutigam, seemed almost fixated upon bringing about Honecker's conviction, regardless of his health or mental state. Nevertheless, on January 12, 1993, Berlin's constitutional court intervened to stop the proceedings.

From the first, because Berlin's constitution as well gave priority to the protection of human dignity, the judges on the court had to ask themselves what the point of the trial would be were the defendant not around to face possible punishment. Their conclusion was a significant statement about the German conception of the rule of law. If the trial were allowed to become an "end in itself (*Selbstzweck*)," they reasoned, the FRG would be as guilty of violating the basic rights of its citizens as was the GDR. "The individual," as the judges put it, "[would] become a simple object of state measures," and a fundamental distinction between the two political orders would be obscured. As a result, the court dismissed all of the charges against Honecker on the grounds that continuing the case would violate the state constitution.[41]

For many politicians, the decision to free Honecker was an outrage. The minister–president of Mecklenburg–Vorpommern, Berndt Seite, proclaimed Honecker's subsequent departure for Chile a "slap in the face" of the victims of the Wall. Likewise, Saxony's outspoken environmental minister, Arnold Vaatz, claimed that the judgment reinforced earlier suspicions about the border guard trials: "One hangs the little guy, but lets the big shot get away."[42] Lending fuel to his critics' arguments, Honecker himself was quick to proclaim victory upon his arrival in Santiago.

But was this really a victory for Honecker? More to the point, did the Berlin court's decision confirm the cynical view that the *Rechtsstaat* was incapable of responding to its citizens' demands for judicial retribution? Despite the loss of the trial's most prominent participant, the trial court's subsequent behavior suggests that it was still determined to abide by the legal standards of the prosecutor general's indictment of May 1992. More important than the prosecution of Honecker himself, the proceedings against the three healthy members of the NVR continued after his departure. Finally, on September 16, 1993, Keßler, Streletz, and Albrecht were all found guilty of the charges against them, the first two for being "instigators" in the border deaths and the last for being an accessory.

These convictions present a provocative picture of the trial as it might have been had Honecker only been sufficiently healthy to endure the proceedings. Throughout the intervening 8 months following his departure and leading up to this verdict, the three defendants had sought to maintain, like Honecker before them, that they were not individually responsible for the shootings at the Wall. The Soviet Union, it seemed, had been the prime mover behind the construction of the barrier in August 1961. In their professional capacities, East Germany's leaders had done nothing more than to act upon their government's sovereign right, and its obligations to the Warsaw Treaty Organization, to safeguard their country's external security. If there had been deaths along the inter-German border, these incidents were the regrettable consequence of years of hostility between the eastern and western military blocs.[43]

Admittedly, these claims were not without historical foundation. Moscow had played a key role in the erection of the Wall, and the GDR had been at the center of some of the Cold War's greatest tensions. However, in coming to his judgments against Keßler, Streletz, and Albrecht, the presiding judge, Hans Boß, who replaced Bräutigam on January 7, 1993, refused to be persuaded that these arguments represented the whole story about the border killings.[44] Applying the same legal standards that Tepperwein had used in the second border guard trial, he contended that the NVR members had clearly played a key role in deciding how the inter-German border was secured. They knew, Boß asserted, that the killing of their citizens "was wrong [Unrecht]" because even GDR law recognized the primacy of protecting human life over serving state interests. But, he added, "[the defendants] chose to put up with this wrong out of political considerations."[45]

Boß conceded that the trial would have been easier had experts been able to locate the smoking gun they had hoped to find in the top secret protocols of the NVR, that is, an explicit order requiring the border guards to shoot *to kill* (*Schießbefehl*). In any case, the evidence showed that the members of the council assumed that such extreme measures would be used. They knew, Boß noted, that "their actions would lead to deaths on the border. They consciously accommodated themselves to the possibility of such deaths."[46] In this sense, there was an identifiable "causal link" between their actions and the soldiers' violations of the GDR criminal code: "Without their decisions and commands, the succeeding chain of command would never have been set into motion, and the actions of the border soldiers which led to the deaths of the victims would never have followed."[47]

In contrast to the turmoil of the trial's early stages when Honecker was in the courtroom, Boß's ruling was notable for the care with which he delivered it. In a telling reference to the ambivalent feelings of the Kohl administration, the judge acknowledged the awkwardness of his position as a westerner seeking to reach a satisfactory judgment on the East German past. "It would have been better," Boß advised his listeners in his oral statement on September 16, 1993, "if East Germany had tried its own leaders." Unfortunately, this was impossible: "German unification came far too quickly to allow for this."[48] Partly for this reason, Boß chose to take mitigating circumstances into account in sentencing Keßler, Streletz, and Albrecht to milder jail terms than those requested by the prosecution. Without excusing the officials' actions, he pointed out – quite generously, in this writer's opinion – that the defendants had themselves been "prisoners of German postwar history and prisoners of their own political convictions." In the absence of the Cold War, the judge reasoned, there would have been no division of Germany, and presumably none of these individuals would have committed the crimes for which they had been convicted.[49]

The trial might have come to an end at this point. However, given the high public visibility of the proceedings, Boß postponed the implementation of the three sentences until the Federal Court of Justice had the opportunity to review his decision. On July 26, 1994, the court delivered its verdict, not only upholding the decision on nearly all counts but also taking his conclusions one step further.[50] Whereas Boß held that Keßler, Streletz, and Albrecht had only participated indirectly in the killings at the inter-German border (the first two as "instigators" and the last as an "accessory"), the appeals court underscored their individual culpability by labeling them "indirect perpetrators" (*mittelbare Täter*). It would be an inadequate reflection of the three figures' roles as "behind-the-scenes actor[s] at the peak of a hierarchy," the judges contended, "were they only to be treated as participants" whereas the border guards were convicted for having "committed the [crimes]."[51] As members of the NVR, they had all taken part in the decisions relating to the use of deadly force at the border; they must have known these decisions would be carried out; and, despite their denials of complicity, they must have been regularly informed of the injuries and deaths sustained in escape attempts.

To be sure, in modifying the lower court's decision, the federal court altered only one of the defendants' sentences; Albrecht was sentenced to serve an additional 7 months. But the overarching meaning of the ruling was clear. Much more than the low-ranking soldiers who had acted on their behalf, the three remaining members of the NVR bore the main burden of guilt for the deaths at the Wall because they really could have acted differently.

Judicial Architects of German Unity

For those who had feared that nothing of consequence would come from the post-GDR trials, this judgment against Honecker's colleagues could not easily be ignored. As will be seen later when the German Bundestag's hearings on the SED dictatorship in Germany (Chapter 4) are considered, some participants, and particularly former dissidents, had desired an even more dramatic statement about the significance of the convictions. Had not a major part of German history also been on trial, they wondered, when Honecker and his associates sat in the docks? Did not the courts have a special responsibility to aid all Germans, and particularly all eastern Germans, in making sense of their nation's troubled past? The simple, and indisputably correct, response to these questions is that the courts' charge, as servants of the *Rechtsstaat*, was only to determine the guilt or innocence of the accused. Just the same, even though the judges may not have recognized it as such, their studied attention to the specificity of the crimes in question was an illuminating statement about the challenge of coming to terms with the GDR era.

We have already encountered some examples of what the courts thought about the record of East German communism. Adherence to the strictures of the Basic Law meant that judicial authorities were given a strong incentive – at least, from the second border guard trial onward – to approach the 40-year history of the GDR in more exacting terms than those allowed by the ambiguous concept of the *Unrechtsstaat*. As the Federal Court of Justice reasoned in its November 1992 ruling upholding the convictions in the border guard trial, representatives of the East German state apparatus could be tried precisely because the GDR was a far more complex entity than the increasingly lawless state that had existed under the Nazis. For all of its shortcomings and imperfections, the codified law had evidently meant *something* in East Germany even if it was irregularly applied. "[U]nlike under the national socialist dictatorship, there was no doctrine in the GDR according to which the simple whims of those who happened to be in power could become law." "Laws," the court insisted, paraphrasing a passage from the East German constitution, "were binding."[52]

In taking this stand, the court, it is important to note, did not choose sides in the age-old debate between positivistic and suprapositivistic interpretations of the law. Far from rejecting Radbruch's invocation of natural law, the judges simply said that the use of this standard to evaluate the abuses of the SED regime would "not be easy," for as they explained, "the killing of people at the inter-German border could not be equated with National Socialist mass murder." At the same time, however, the court declared that the prosecution of the GDR's offenses would still be "valid" when – here, the court drew upon Radbruch-like terms – "the state exceeded the utmost limits that by general conviction every country imposed upon it."[53] In this sense, when the judges appealed to preexisting GDR statutes in making the case for convictions, they were not justifying East German laws per se. They were trying to show how thinking persons could have recognized the difference between right and wrong in this society.

As an interpretation of the GDR's past, this perspective was enlightening. The court was saying that even in such a dictatorship, specific individuals had a choice in committing the crimes for which they were accused. They could have followed the law and the conventions of conscience clearly existing in their society, but they had consciously chosen to do wrong. To quote Berlin's justice senator (and later Federal Constitutional Court president) Jutta Limbach: "Only through the trials has it become clear that the governmental abuse of power is not a natural disaster. Rather, it is a mosaic of individual deeds committed by responsible persons."[54]

As valuable as this corrective may have been from a legal or even historical standpoint, we should recognize that the judges' stand was equally significant from a social and political perspective as well. After all, if some individuals had knowingly violated their country's standards of acceptable behavior, was it not reasonable to conclude that there were other easterners, even former soldiers, policemen, and politicians, who had just as deliberately chosen to do the right thing? If this premise was assumed to be true, could the Wall trials not have something important to say about the terms according to which the eastern German population was being integrated into the FRG?

Forty years ago, Otto Kirchheimer anticipated the courts' social function in a classic work, *Political Justice*. "Successor justice," he wrote, "is both retrospective and prospective. In laying bare the roots of iniquity in the previous regime's conduct, it simultaneously seizes the opportunity to convert the trial into a cornerstone of the new order."[55] At the time he was writing, Kirchheimer was primarily concerned about the abusive ends to which legal procedures could be put by successor regimes, and he warned against allowing judicial bodies to become compliant tools in the replacement of one dictatorship with another. This danger was not a problem with West Germany's more robust and well-established legal system. Nevertheless, Kirchheimer's insight about the courts' prospective function rings true when one views the Honecker trial and others like it as possible cornerstones in the construction of a united Germany.[56]

Let us imagine that, instead of focusing on the connection between the codified law and instances of wrongdoing in the GDR, Germany's courts had followed the looser model of retributive justice enunciated by Seidel at the first border guard trial. In this case, arguably, the impression might have been created that Honecker and his colleagues were being prosecuted not so much because of their deeds but rather by virtue of their participation in an immoral and unjust state apparatus.

Naturally, for those who were calling for the FRG to impose swift justice, such a procedure appeared to have many advantages. In applying only an abstract conception of injustice to the shootings at the Wall, the courts would seemingly cut right to the heart of East Germany's status as an *Unrechtsstaat*. Also in this view, many of the cumbersome and tedious aspects of the German legal process – the "pedantry and juristic nit-picking," to quote one such critic of the trials, Neal Ascherson[57] – would be eliminated.

However, if one takes the courts' social and political functions seriously, there was an undeniable drawback to this approach. This lay in the implications of the concept of the *Unrechtsstaat* for anyone who had ever been associated with the East German state. In this case, in a world in which guilt was not unambiguously identified with the violation of specific laws, there was very little to prevent many eastern Germans from becoming citizens of the Federal Republic with a nebulous cloud of collective responsibility hanging over them. If one added to the SED's over 2.3 million members all of the officials in the country's state bureaucracy, its armed forces, and its police, not to mention the tens of thousands of people who had secretly acted as "unofficial collaborators" of the Ministry of State Security, the list of the guilty could easily include a third of the East German population. This was the sort of blanket indictment that dissident Jens Reich feared (see Chapter 1), when he worried that proceedings like the Honecker trial would have disastrous consequences for the reputation of the GDR citizenry.

In contrast, as long as they avoided the politicized climate of the early stages of the Honecker trial, the courts involved in the Wall proceedings were offering a potentially more upbeat message about the German future. In insisting upon a stricter definition of criminal culpability, they were making a distinctive claim – not everyone was guilty. This may not seem like an unusual or provocative pronouncement. But if one takes into account the intense social and economic turbulence at the time of the courts' rulings and the questions many of the GDR's former citizens were asking of each other about personal responsibility for the regime's crimes, there is every reason to think the presumption of innocence had a special relevance in eastern Germany. In this instance at least, the rulings of judges like Tepperwein and Boß held out the promise that equal standards would be applied to all.

Additionally, in setting this example, the courts may have conveyed a salutary message about the purposes of the German *Rechtsstaat*. Even for those who were convicted of their crimes (or those sympathetic to their plight), the way the judges reached their verdicts bespoke a legal culture that was very different from that which had been dominant in the GDR.

To see the point, one has only to consider the treatment accorded Honecker. Had his health been better, the East German leader would in all probability have been found guilty of the same offenses as Keßler, Streletz, and Albrecht. Boß intimated as much in his ruling, noting that the role "of the general secretary of the central committee in particular" had to be taken into account in assessing the National Defense Council's responsibility for the border killings.[58] However, precisely because the former SED chief could not have survived his trial, Honecker – the man, and not the former politician – was accorded the constitutional protections of human dignity. Whereas state interests had frequently defined the administration of justice in the GDR, the mercy and compassion the courts showed in this instance demonstrated that a different standard prevailed in the Federal Republic. The value of human life outweighed the public clamor for retribution.

Then, too, hopeful lessons could be derived from the courts' readiness to take extenuating circumstances into account in handing down their sentences. It is notable, for example, that out of the scores of border guard trials conducted in the first half-decade after unification (1991–96), only two soldiers were actually forced to serve jail time for their crimes, one in Berlin and the other in Brandenburg; in both instances, this was only because their offenses were unusually heinous. Even the guard most directly responsible for the 1989 killing of Gueffroy would eventually have his sentence suspended on appeal by the Federal Court of Justice in March 1994.[59] As we have seen, similarly lenient standards, although sentences nonetheless, were applied in the convictions of Keßler, Streletz, and Albrecht. For these reasons, one could cautiously side with that body of legal opinion that held – in the observation of one ex-president of the Federal Constitutional Court, Ernst Benda, during the proceedings against Honecker – that the post-GDR trials had the potential to become a positive "learning process" for the FRG's new citizens.[60]

The Risks of Going Too Far

It would be misleading to conclude this chapter without calling attention to the still significant risks for the reputation of the German *Rechtsstaat* that were bound to accompany every additional trial that was conducted in the name of retrospective justice. In one judgment, the civil libertarian critics of the proceedings were surely correct. Only a fine and tenuous line separated responsible efforts to pursue justice from the baser desire for vengeance. If the trials really were to become a meaningful learning experience, the 16 million remaining residents of eastern Germany would need to be convinced that judicial authorities were meting out no more justice than was absolutely required by the nature of the offenses in question and in the light of the historical conditions at work when the crimes were originally committed.

In fact, as novel as Germany's proceedings may have seemed to their advocates in the first few years after national unification, it is worth recalling that the Federal Republic was not the only democracy to have wrestled with the issue of settling accounts with former dictators. One useful example is provided by the trials that took place in Argentina's transition to civilian rule in the mid-1980s.

In the Argentine case, the officials who prosecuted nine members of the military junta who had levied a reign of terror on the country during the so-called dirty war of the late 1970s were presented with a seemingly ideal circumstance, not unlike that faced by unified Germany. Had they desired, these authorities could simply have imposed sweeping judgments upon the members of a dictatorial regime who were by all accounts, and particularly according to international legal norms, guilty of manifold human rights violations. However, also like the Germans, Argentine officials chose instead to take the risks of retroactive lawmaking to heart and to prosecute the accused junta leaders for acts that could be shown to be subject to domestic law at the time they were performed. In roughly the same manner as in the German case, prosecutors collected abundant evidence to this effect, detailing the exact violations of the law and the personal involvement of each defendant in their commission. On these bases, on December 8, 1985, five of the nine military commanders were found guilty of a variety of crimes. The outcome was not predetermined, however, for the other four were acquitted.[61]

In addition to carefully following the manner in which these trials were conducted, those in charge of the Argentine proceedings were attuned to a related problem that should have been apparent to German prosecutors as well. It was one thing to hold those at the pinnacle of the chain of command accountable for their actions but quite another to undertake prosecutions at every other level of the old governing structure, where proof of criminal behavior was harder to obtain and complicity more difficult to measure.[62]

As has already been suggested, it stretched credulity somewhat to maintain that the Berlin Wall guards were fully responsible for all of the deaths that occurred along the inter-German border. Strictly speaking, one could find evidence to support the view that they had violated East German laws in using their weapons against would-be escapees. But if one were completely candid about the historical record, it would be necessary to factor into this equation the substantial constraints under which these individuals operated, their socialization and pressure from their peers, as well as the limitations on their ability to act otherwise.

Likewise, Germany's courts were facing no small challenge in making the case that a seamless vein of guilt existed at every other point of the decision-making hierarchy.

In some instances, these efforts seem to have been more credible than in others and even defensible in view of the broader message the courts' were conveying to German society, whether this was their conscious intention or not. For example, on September 10, 1996, six former generals of the National People's Army (NVA) were found guilty by a Berlin court for their part in 19 instances of manslaughter or attempted manslaughter at the Wall (including the death of Gueffroy) and subsequently sentenced to prison terms of between $3\frac{1}{3}$ and $6\frac{1}{2}$ years. On a purely abstract level, it made sense to think that midway between the NVR and the border guards, there was bound to be an identifiable group of persons responsible for expediting the deadly chain of command at the border. The court's achievement was to reconstruct the circumstances to show that this had, in fact, been the case.[63]

In an impassioned statement, the presiding judge, Friedrich-Karl Föhrig, contended that all six officers, with former deputy defense minister and border troop commander Klaus-Dieter Baumgarten at their head, had played an instrumental role in defining the security regime that led common soldiers to take the lives of others. The NVA generals routinely updated the order to apprehend or, if necessary, "destroy" (*vernichten*) fleeing refugees; they oversaw the laying of mines and installation of automatic shooting devices; and they supervised the perverse practice of rewarding border guards for successfully using their weapons. Anyone "who issued these commands," Föhrig emphasized, "or who worked in a position responsible for their implementation, was, legally speaking, a *causa* for the death of a 'border violator.'" Indeed, in their everyday behavior, these midlevel representatives demonstrated responsibility for the consequences of their actions by showing that they could turn this killing machine on and off as it suited their government's purposes: "When it was politically opportune, the soldiers did not have to shoot. Whenever the international reputation of the GDR was at issue, those in power were no longer solely concerned with the heavy use of munitions but [suddenly] remembered human rights."[64]

In other cases, however, there is good reason to conclude that the courts were on shakier historical ground in arguing for prosecutions. To see the point, let us consider the legal gymnastics in the decision by the Berlin prosecutor general's office to continue what it had begun with Honecker by bringing an additional seven of his colleagues to trial. At first glance, this follow-up trial, which began on January 15, 1996, appeared no different than its celebrated predecessor. Once again, well-known names from the GDR were being held to account for crimes committed under the old order. However, this interpretation would be to miss the ways in which the prosecutor's office not only expanded the scope of its investigations to facilitate these indictments but also went beyond a reasonable standard of individual accountability in the process.

As we have seen, the first trial of the GDR leadership was based exclusively upon membership in the NVR, the agency specifically responsible for border security. But in the new trial, it is telling that only three of the seven persons included in the initial indictment of November 30, 1994, belonged to this body. This time around, the prosecution chose instead to use the much broader criterion of membership in the SED politburo as the measure of complicity.

Just as significant, this second indictment seems to have been based upon a fundamentally different understanding of culpability than the one that had been used to prosecute Honecker. Only two of the persons named in the document, Erich Mückenberger and Kurt Hager, were charged with "active involvement" (*aktives Tun*) in decisions affecting the border regime;[65] moreover, prosecutors seemed unconcerned that both men had been responsible for areas (economic policy and cultural affairs) that were far afield from security questions. In contrast, the other five members of the politburo (Krenz, Günter Schabowski, Horst Dohlus, Günther Kleiber, and Harry Tisch) were charged not so much for what they did, but, remarkably, for what they *failed* to do. As members of the SED's highest body, the indictment held, they must have known they had the power in their hands to do more to secure the rights "to life and freedom" of the GDR's citizens. However, the prosecutors charged, they consciously failed to take advantage of this possibility "to work to achieve a humanization of the border regime and thereby prevent the killing and wounding of escapees."[66]

From a moral standpoint, this accusation was undoubtedly well deserved. Typically, six of the defendants indignantly denied this charge, though one of them, Schabowski, broke ranks with his colleagues. In his statement before the court on February 26, 1996, he acknowledged that the deaths at the Wall were the logical consequence of his and others' stubborn faith in Marxism–Leninism and of their, in his words, "misguided attempt to free humanity from its troubles." In this sense, Schabowski mused, everyone who had been a part of the SED regime shared a degree of moral responsibility for the crimes and injustices of the old regime. "As a former follower and protagonist of this world-view," he admitted, "I feel guilt and pain at the thought of those killed at the Wall. I ask for the forgiveness of the victims' relatives, and I must also [be prepared] to accept when they refuse me. Indeed, were I unable to adopt this view, it would be impossible for me to continue living."[67]

Nonetheless, one can readily imagine the problems with using the argument for moral responsibility to justify criminal trials. As Schabowski stressed in his defense, his personal failure was not at all the same thing as criminal liability. In any case, he insisted, under the conditions existing at that time in the GDR he could not have realistically done anything to alter the prevailing policy at the Wall: "Any effort to move in this direction under the then-existing conditions would have immediately been perceived as an attempt to call into question the general line [of the party] and the personal authority of the general secretary. This would not have had the slightest chance of working, in the politburo or in any other body."[68]

Of equal cause for concern, it is hard to see how the attempt to bind law and morality together in this fashion could have contributed to the healthy respect for the rule of law that we have said was conceivable in the later stages of the Honecker trial. Quite the contrary, the expansion of charges to include individuals who were less directly responsible for the border casualties can only have suggested that broader segments of the eastern German citizenry were still threatened with the burden of collective guilt. No doubt, this possibility was reinforced by the impression, deserved or not, that prosecutors had thrown out a cardinal principle of accountability from the earlier proceedings. Now, individuals could be tried for what they had *not* done, for their moral failings. Later on, the courts would revise this charge. But for the time being, this definition of culpability was both a dubious standard for any liberal polity and an oddly ahistorical reading of the East German past.

Why were German prosecutors willing to risk sending such a potentially unsettling message about the rule of law to the GDR's former citizens? To listen to many of the politburo members on trial (although not so much Schabowski), one would think that Germany's leaders were merely continuing a cynical campaign of victor's justice against their former adversaries in the GDR.[69] However, we can offer an alternate explanation for the prosecutors' behavior that is both more charitable *and* more revealing of their motivations. This is to say that they were trying to carry to completion an undertaking they had begun with the initial trials of the border guards. In the familiar words of one prosecutor, Heinrich Kintzi, it would have been a "skewed picture" of the GDR's legacy of injustice had German courts only convicted the least important figures and failed to pursue "those who had more responsibility and, correspondingly, also bore much more guilt."[70]

In this sense, the decision to expand the list of those indicted from the SED leadership must have seemed to German officials like the commonsensical next step in the process of using the courts to come to terms with the past. In seeking to follow this logic, however, these officials seem to have lost sight of the elementary truth that had earlier been an implicit part of the decisions of judges like Boß. This was the notion that the pursuit of justice had to be combined with a realistic appreciation of the options that had, or had not, been available to decision makers.

An Ambiguous Message about Culpability

Against this background, the Federal Constitutional Court must have missed out on an important opportunity to clarify the reach of the law when it delivered a long-awaited ruling on the constitutionality of the judgment in the Honecker trial on October 24, 1996.[71] The occasion for the court's decision was an appeal by NVR members Albrecht, Keßler, and Streletz (and one former border guard). The claimants argued that their rights under Article 103 (2) of the Basic Law were violated because the Berlin state court and the Federal Court of Justice had supposedly ignored preexisting statutes that legitimated the shootings at the inter-German border and had chosen to base their rulings on legal standards that were foreign to the GDR. In rejecting these arguments, the second senate essentially upheld all of the lower courts' decisions. Yet it was how the justices came to this conclusion that suggested a rather ambiguous understanding of how much the GDR's former citizens were protected from unfair or arbitrary ex post facto judgments.

Much like the earlier decisions, the constitutional court could have dismissed these claims by identifying competing East German statutes that showed that the GDR's leaders had willingly and knowingly violated their country's laws in encouraging border soldiers to use any means necessary to prevent border escapes. In its description of the earlier cases, the high court referred to several statutes that could have been employed to make this case, and, at scattered points in its judgment, it intimated that the lower courts had done the right thing in using such a standard.

Nonetheless, rather than taking this path themselves, the justices appealed to a legal rationale that was curiously reminiscent of Seidel's judgment in the first border guard trial. In principle, the judges argued, the citizens of a *Rechtsstaat* could rest assured that they would only be held accountable to legal standards in effect at the time of their actions. But, the justices added, this constitutional guarantee was grounded in the expectation that such standards had been devised by a democratic government that would have taken basic human rights into account in crafting its laws. The same guarantee could not be extended to cases in which a nondemocratic government had perverted the law to justify "the worst criminal injustice." In these instances, the court declared, explicitly invoking the Radbruch formula, the contradiction between the positive law and justice was so great that the Basic Law's promise of legal security had to be subordinated to the higher norms of humanity.[72]

In coming to this judgment, the FCC could not be faulted for wanting to keep the Basic Law's prohibition on ex post facto lawmaking from being misused to justify particularly crass forms of injustice. As the justices explained, one could not allow the members of the NVR to defend their actions simply by falling back on laws they had once enacted to give their system its veneer of legitimacy. Nevertheless, what one missed in the high court's decision – failing a few passing references to GDR statutes – was a clear indication of why the accused should have known in their specific circumstances that they were committing criminal behavior.[73] Indeed, in their primary reliance upon Radbruch, the justices seemed to recommend a standard of personal responsibility that was open to abuse. Taken to an extreme, all that a particularly vengeful court would have needed to do to establish guilt was to show that a given individual had been involved in the commission of an act that, in the court's estimation, had violated basic principles of morality.

To its credit, the court indicated that this appeal to a higher law could only be resorted to in "extreme, exceptional cases." Yet here, the judges left their listeners guessing about why the GDR represented so grave an exception that the normal guarantees against retroactive judgment should be suspended in the Wall killings. Muddying the waters all the more, the court's one small foray in the direction of greater specificity was to acknowledge that German courts had once wrestled with "similar" circumstances in their postwar prosecutions of Nazi injustice.[74] As the justices must have known, even to invoke the National Socialist period as a point of comparison with the crimes of the GDR era was to engage in a precarious undertaking in view of the manifest differences between the two regimes. In any case, the court had little to say beyond this point to clarify its wishes.

For those observers who worried that the FRG's representatives were giving short shrift to basic principles of fair treatment in their handling of the Wall deaths, there was probably some solace to be found in the more concrete and focused nature of subsequent decisions by lower courts. Hence, judges would typically combine an invocation of the Constitutional Court's appeal to higher principles with a pointed examination of the circumstances under which wrongdoing had occurred and an assessment of why the accused should have been aware of the illegality of their actions at the time of their transgressions. All the while, however, doubts were bound to arise about the motivations of prosecutors in bringing such cases to trial. Did they intend merely to identify the individuals most closely associated with the border killings? Or were they driven instead by the more ambitious desire to establish a perfect chain of guilt all the way to the top of the East German regime, regardless of whether their claims were supported by the historical evidence?

This issue was nowhere more apparent than in the outcome of the so-called politburo trial, which resulted in the conviction of SED leaders Krenz, Kleiber, and Schabowski on August 25, 1997; all proceedings against the other four original defendants (Mückenberger, Hager, Tisch, and Dohlus) were suspended for reasons of ill health or death.[75] As we have suggested earlier, this particular prosecution was grounded on the dubious proposition that the accused were guilty not for what they had done but for what they had failed to do: to humanize the GDR border regime. Apparently, some jurists shared this uneasiness. When the case finally came to trial before the Berlin regional court in August 1995, the presiding judge – once again, Bräutigam – summarily revised the original indictment to charge all of the defendants with "active involvement" in the border deaths.[76]

In retrospect, this may have been the more appropriate charge all along, had it been made at the right juncture and with appropriate attention to the nature of the claims against the defendants. But, the timing of the decision was sure to raise questions about the court's determination to judge each of the accused according to the same equal and fair standards.

Certainly, there could be little doubt about Krenz's complicity in the shaping of the border regime. As a member of the NVR and as the central committee secretary specifically charged with security questions, he had directly participated in decisions, as the court outlined in its 1997 decision, that led to two identifiable deaths at the inter-German border. In contrast, the degree of Kleiber's and Schabowski's responsibility for these crimes was debatable because neither had been associated with the defense council. Nevertheless, no one would have contested the court's reasoning in its opening decision that both figures had been involved in "steering" the East German state at its highest level. The GDR's security and military organs were directly subordinated to the politburo.[77] Also, by virtue of their high positions, both had been routinely informed about the casualties at the Wall. But when it came to demonstrating the specific role each defendant had played in the border killings, the court was largely reduced to deducing culpability from the general activities of the politburo.[78] And, notably, it had nothing to say about the mitigating considerations that had been such a central feature in Judge Boß's September 1993 ruling against Keßler, Streletz, and Albrecht.

No doubt, the finding that the two defendants were as guilty as Krenz (of "limited intent to commit murder") was a useful way of justifying the legal processes that had been set in motion with the first border guard trial of 1991. "It would not have been consistent with the gravity of the deeds in question," the court insisted, "to fail to treat the behind-the-scenes decision makers as perpetrators." This perspective was especially important, it added, "since the degree of responsibility often increases rather than decreases with the distance from the point of the [crime]."[79]

Still, to the extent that outsiders could regard the court's judgment as a foregone conclusion, based more on the necessity of obtaining convictions than on the weight of the evidence, the reputation of the rule of law in eastern Germany would have been impaired. As we have found, it was possible, though with certain limitations, to delve into the circumstances behind specific border shootings. Plus, one could identify concrete reasons for why those implicated in killings would have been aware of the potential consequences of their actions. Yet, as the FCC decision and the judgments against Schabowski and Kleiber suggested, the authorities' determination to act on these bases could not always be taken for granted.

FIGURE 1. West German negotiator Wolfgang Schäuble (left) and his East German counterpart Günther Krause (right) sign the German Unification Treaty on August 31, 1990. GDR Prime Minister Lothar de Maizière stands in the middle. (Courtesy of Bundesbildstelle.)

FIGURE 2. Former SED chief Erich Honecker (with clenched fist) leaves the Chilean Embassy in Moscow on July 29, 1992, after agreement is reached to return him to Germany to face charges for the killings at the Berlin Wall. (Courtesy of AP/Wide World Photos.)

FIGURE 3. In a visit to the Stasi archives on February 3, 1992, Commissioner Joachim Gauck (right) shows German President Richard von *Weizsäcker* (left) some of the millions of secret files the East German Ministry of State Security collected on its citizenry. (Courtesy of Bundesbildstelle.)

FIGURE 4. German citizens take part in a public tour of the Stasi's former headquarters in Berlin-Lichtenberg. They are looking at some of the thousands of bags of shredded documents left behind by the secret police after the "storming of the Normannenstraße" on January 15, 1990. (Courtesy of Bundesbildstelle.)

FIGURE 5. In a hearing of the Bundestag's Enquete commission on the SED dicta-torship on November 4, 1993, the eastern German pastor Rainer Eppelmann (second from left) chairs a panel with three prominent participants: Chancellor Helmut Kohl (far left), former SPD chairperson Hans-Jochen Vogel (second from right), and former Foreign Minister Hans-Dietrich Genscher (far right). (Courtesy of Bundesbildstelle.)

FIGURE 6. The English-style Guggenheim villa in Potsdam, which was taken from its original owners under the Nazi "aryanization" laws of the 1930s, was just one of hundreds of thousands of eastern properties subject to rival ownership claims after the GDR's demise. (Courtesy of AP/Wide World Photos.)

FIGURE 7. Dignitaries arrive in Berlin, on November 9, 1999, for celebrations marking the 10th anniversary of the fall of the Berlin Wall. From left to right, former Soviet party chief Mikhail Gorbachev, Stasi-files Commissioner Joachim Gauck, former U.S. President George Bush, German Bundestag President Wolfgang Thierse, Chancellor Gerhard Schröder, and former Chancellor Helmut Kohl. (Courtesy Bundesbildstelle.)

FIGURE 8. Although only invited at the last moment to address the ceremonies com-
memorating the Wall's fall, Joachim Gauck spoke for many easterners when he proclaimed that the GDR's citizens had brought the German nation the "historical gift"
of a revolution made in the name of freedom. (Courtesy Bundesbildstelle.)

3

Disqualifying Justice

THE SEARCH FOR STASI
COLLABORATORS

On March 14, 1990, Wolfgang Schnur, a well-known East German lawyer who had once defended draft resisters, was abruptly forced to resign from his post as chairperson of the citizens' party Democratic Awakening when evidence surfaced that he had routinely delivered reports on his clients to the Ministry of State Security (MfS) for nearly 20 years. The event was significant because Schnur's resignation came a mere 4 days before the GDR's citizens went to the polls to vote for their country's first freely elected parliament, the Volkskammer. As the leader of one of the three parties in the conservative "Alliance for Germany" coalition, which won the Volkskammer election on March 18 and enjoyed the vocal backing of Helmut Kohl's Christian Democratic Union, Schnur could have become prime minister in the new government had his inglorious past not been exposed. Thus, as revelations mounted that other well-known politicians had conspired with the secret police as well – Martin Kirchner, general secretary of the eastern CDU; Ibrahim Böhme, chairperson of the newly refounded Social Democratic Party – it was not surprising that calls were raised in the East to review all candidates for major political and administrative posts for MfS ties and to exclude the worst offenders from office.

At least superficially, the case for undertaking these measures was even more straightforward to its advocates than that which had been used to undergird the Wall trials. After all, the disqualification of Stasi agents and informants like Schnur from administrative positions in the new Germany was a milder form of retrospective justice than the application of criminal sanctions. In view of the MfS's activities, these disqualifications also seemed to present a much lower threshold of culpability. One only had to ask whether an individual's behavior and attitudes were compatible with the Basic Law's commitment to a "free-democratic basic order" (Article 18).

In the case of many MfS agents, there was serious room for doubt about this issue because of what the Stasi was. Over the years, the Stasi had managed to destroy entire families by deliberately sowing mistrust between husbands and wives, parents and children. Under pressure from the MfS, teachers and school administrators had been persuaded to inform on their students in exchange for petty privileges and cash bonuses. University professors had been spied upon by their colleagues. And, tips from collaborators had regularly resulted in harassment by the police, beatings, and even long prison sentences for persons suspected of "negative enemy" tendencies. Dissident Gerd Poppe spoke for many victims, observing: "The Stasi systematically sought to destroy our personal and professional lives. It was criminal. Worse than that, it was evil."[1] Thus, it was far from excessive for him and others to maintain that persons associated with the organization should be carefully scrutinized before they were allowed to remain in government service.

Making the identification of the worst offenders seem all the more compelling was that, in a manner befitting the traditions of German officialdom, the MfS had kept voluminous and detailed records on all of its operations. Presumably, these files included the names of every agent and every informant. Accordingly, the proponents of screening demanded that the East German government and, later, the Kohl administration, capitalize on the information in the Stasi's holdings to determine which of their compatriots had sold their honor to the secret police and to assess the complicity of each in its misdeeds.

Indeed, even if West German officials had reservations about this endeavor, as many did at first, they could not have ignored the momentum gathering in the East. By summer 1990, the Volkskammer had already taken steps to routinize these procedures. In a draft law on the management of the archives, the parliament stipulated that the Stasi files be utilized "in the course of lawful security checks" and for other "politically relevant" reasons.[2] As a result, even before the Germanys came together, Bonn was launched down a path that most of the neighboring East European democracies, with the notable exception of Czechoslovakia, were reluctant to consider.

Certainly, the benefits of screening potentially millions of citizens were not evident to all Germans. For one thing, even some of the secret police's victims had serious doubts about using the records of an organization like the MfS to construct a reliable picture of the East German past. Much as critics had inquired about the sifting of evidence in the Wall prosecutions, they wondered whether the ministry's archives would convey the complex constellation of circumstances under which ordinary people had been brought into the Stasi's fold. No doubt, some had committed major harm. But other citizens' associations had been more fleeting and inconsequential. Some had merely driven cabs or trucks for the Stasi. Others had been clerks, typists, and low-level administrators. Clearly, a responsible accounting of this chapter in the GDR's history would require one to make careful distinctions among these activities.[3]

Then, too, even if officials succeeded in drawing an appropriately balanced picture of the MfS, the skeptics stressed that there was no assurance that the image of the country's populace that emerged from the vetting of thousands of politicians, bureaucrats, and other public servants would be welcome news. Unlike the Wall trials, which affected a relatively small and self-contained group of perpetrators and crimes, the Stasi's corrupting influence had been suffused throughout the social landscape of East Germany, from the hierarchy of the Lutheran churches to state bureaucracies and schools, from trial courts to the ranks of the local police. One could not be confident that a population that had only recently entered into the process of unification would benefit from the turmoil of a sustained hunt for collaborators.[4]

Some of the latter fears would turn out to be exaggerated. As a matter of record, fewer eastern Germans were directly caught up in the Stasi's machinations than initially feared, and of those, it is fair to say that not all were guilty of genuinely disqualifying offenses. The more experience German administrators and judicial authorities gained in handling these cases, the more they were able to find the right kind of historical evidence to draw such distinctions. Nevertheless, because the immense task of deciding whom to disqualify from their jobs was split up among different federal and state agencies in the East, we are wise to wonder whether these agents were consistently inclined to act on this basis. In fact, the available evidence suggests that this was not the case across the board. As a consequence, there were moments in the search for Stasi collaborators in the 1990s when one could easily have been misled into thinking that far more of the GDR's citizens were guilty of major violations of public and private trust than was actually true.

Contending Views on the Stasi's Reach

Most scholars will agree about the event that touched off the Stasi controversy in the first place. On the evening of January 15, 1990, hundreds of demonstrators streamed through the gates of the central headquarters of the Ministry of State Security in Berlin–Lichtenberg's Normannenstraße and took control of the last, and most secretive, of the commanding heights of the SED regime. This was not the first time that citizen activists had occupied Stasi offices; similar protests had been staged one month earlier in Erfurt, Dresden, Leipzig, and several other locations. Also, the "storming of the Normannenstraße" was not quite the romantic act of popular insurrection that its participants perceived it to be at the time. Eyewitnesses would later recount that officers of the secret police had a hand in allowing the would-be liberationists to enter the complex of buildings that comprised the Stasi *Zentrale* (central offices) – apparently so they could destroy incriminating documents.[5] Still, the event promised something quite unimaginable only a few months before. The East German people could finally take possession of the millions of personal dossiers and records that the ministry's agents had compiled over four decades of dictatorship. Yet, a difficult question arose, What, if anything, should they do with these holdings?

For many oppositionists, the simple answer to this dilemma was captured by the words an exuberant protestor had spray painted on a building within the MfS headquarters: "I want my file." Because the hallmark of the former dictatorship had been its ability to conceal its activities behind a wall of secrecy and deception, these activists insisted that Germany's new leaders immediately open to public inspection the more than 100 miles of documents, tapes, and microfilm that constituted the Stasi's records, both in Berlin and in other cities. As the activists saw it, the old regime's victims were entitled to know exactly what had been done to them, and by whom, during the years the secret police had ruled their lives. The exposure of these misdeeds and, even more important, of the perpetrators behind them would provide a much needed foundation for the kinds of trusting relationships required in the new society to come. Joachim Gauck, the Rostock pastor who would soon be named federal commissioner of the archives, epitomized this view. "If after more than 55 years of Nazi and communist dictatorship," he later explained, "citizens were going to trust elected officials under the new democratic system, it was important that those officials be trustworthy." Gauck added, "The intention was . . . to respond to the East German people's minimal demand that persons who had conspired with the regime, unbeknown to their fellow citizens, should be deemed unsuitable for public positions of trust."[6]

For an opposing group of participants, however, the files were a dubious resource for any democracy. In the immediate aftermath of the Normannenstraße occupation, concerns about their accuracy were legion. Many protesters feared that Stasi officials had intentionally left behind falsified documents to discredit their enemies and divide German policymakers. Furthermore, it was commonly supposed that agents of the ministry had managed to destroy their most incriminating records before they could be recovered. Ironically, the activists who occupied the *Zentrale* initially had a hand in this process, for they feared that some records would be misused by foreign intelligence agencies. The same reasoning apparently also played a role in the Modrow and de Maizière governments' curious decision to allow the Stasi's espionage department, the *Hauptverwaltung Aufklärung* (main headquarters for foreign intelligence), to administer a "self-dissolution" through late spring 1990.[7]

Nevertheless, even if one assumed that the bulk of the MfS's holdings had not been tampered with, the critics considered it absurd to utilize such materials to identify wrongdoing or to rebuild a divided society. How, they inquired, could their government seriously hope to rectify the injustices of a bygone dictatorship when it insisted upon basing its judgments on the records of an organization that had violated most standards of human decency to collect them? Would not the nation's political climate be gravely impaired if federal authorities bowed to eastern pressures to open the files?

In the eyes of the West German decision makers who entered into this debate in spring 1990, the conflict suggested a classic confrontation between two opposing, yet equally justifiable, conceptions of privacy. On the one hand stood the citizen's right to "informational self-determination" that the FCC had affirmed in a landmark decision almost a decade earlier.[8] Hansjörg Geiger, a strong western proponent of opening the files, explained the principle this way: "Only he who is in the position to know what information has been collected about him will be able to express his human dignity and develop his personality in the manner guaranteed by the Basic Law."[9] On the other hand, there was the countervailing right to privacy of future Schnurs, Kirchners, and Böhmes who might be named as perpetrators or informants in the files. According to the advocates of this position, illegally obtained information, whatever its apparent value, could never be used to impugn the reputation or integrity of anyone.[10]

In the conventions of German jurisprudence, the standard solution to a conflict of this type is to seek a "practical concordance" between the two parties such that each has a chance of realizing its right to the fullest extent. In fact, if we look down the road a bit, this was the Bundestag's intention when it enacted the so-called Stasi Records law (*Stasi-Unterlagen-Gesetz*, or StUG) on December 20, 1991. This statute finally regularized the issue of citizen access to the MfS holdings. To satisfy the one side, the new law granted the secret police's victims the opportunity to consult their personal files. But, to placate the other, it established strict controls over who could see this information and over the uses to which it could be put. For example, the interests of innocent parties were to be protected from unwanted disclosures, and in a concession to eastern rights activists, restrictions were placed on the ability of western intelligence agencies to use information gathered from the archives.[11]

Nonetheless, to get to this point, one had first to contend with the skeptics' assumption that the eastern German population would be thrown into turmoil by the revelations of dishonesty and personal betrayal which, they felt, were sure to follow the opening of the files. Had the Stasi been just any institution, it is possible that these apprehensions would not have been so pronounced. However, the Stasi was no ordinary institution. In large part thanks to its success over the years in convincing the populace that it was "a perfect surveillance organ" whose army of full-time operatives (*hauptamtliche Mitarbeiter*, or HMs) and unofficial collaborators (*inoffizielle Mitarbeiter*, or IMs) could reach into every corner of the GDR, few East Germans had any idea who among their compatriots had made the fateful choice to cooperate with the secret police. Hence, to live with the Stasi was to live with daily anxiety. Many feared that it had managed to infect nearly every human relationship.

It says something for the organization's mystique that at the time of the Volkskammer vote news agencies gave widely divergent and, we now know, exaggerated reports about the extent of Stasi penetration of East German society. Although cautious observers put the number of actual collaborators in the hundreds of thousands, others ranged from one to two million informants, and higher.[12] Also, few of these commentators were careful to specify whether they were speaking about current figures for 1989 or the much greater number of informants over the history of the GDR. As a result, it was hard to distinguish between the real Stasi and the mythical organization, an omniscient *Staat im Staat* (state within the state), from which no deviant thought or action had been secure.

Under these circumstances, we can appreciate why members of the new GDR government elected on March 18 were openly hesitant about embroiling their country in a search for the ministry's agents. Some, such as controversial Interior Minister Peter-Michael Diestel, publicly broached the idea of destroying the MfS's holdings before they could inflict serious harm. The files could never be used to draw meaningful distinctions between guilt and innocence, Diestel argued, because the GDR's population had been completely corrupted by the experience of dictatorship. "If you ask me about guilt," he explained in April 1990, "then I would have to say that there were really only two [types of individuals] who were truly innocent in this system, the newborn child and the alcoholic, who was tanked up every day." In this light, one had to treat the Stasi's records – "these products of evil," as he called them, "products of the devil" – with the utmost care. Diestel acknowledged that these remnants of the old order might have a limited value in rehabilitating victims of political persecution. But the files could not be allowed to become "a problem for the construction of our democratic order." Indeed, because eastern Germany was desperately short of competent administrative personnel, Diestel expressed his readiness to look to the MfS's ranks in recruiting for his ministry.[13]

For a time, aspects of Diestel's position were echoed among long-standing opponents of the SED regime. In one of his first interviews as minister of defense and disarmament in the new government, the dissident pastor Rainer Eppelmann warned of the pitfalls of allowing eastern Germany's recently won democratic freedoms to be defined in terms of "denunciations, revelations, and acts of revenge." In his estimation, easily a third of the GDR population had worked "more or less intensively" with the Stasi. Thus, any attempt to exclude these individuals from public life would be tantamount to depriving the region of a meaningful political and societal voice in the unified German state.

Also like Diestel, Eppelmann contended that the issue of culpability could not be so easily reduced to a matter of who had, or had not, gone along with the secret police's entreaties. In fact, because the sway of communist ideology had been such a pervasive force in the lives of the GDR's citizens, Eppelmann sounded a bit like Václav Havel in warning about the difficulty of distinguishing among degrees of complicity: "each of us, at one or another point in our own lives, bears guilt for the fact that this system could exist as long as it did." He would not even exclude himself from this generalization. "I certainly wouldn't say about myself," Eppelmann mused, "that I was always courageous enough, persistent enough, uncompromising enough, and honest enough. I'd like to know what GDR citizen could make such a claim."[14]

Provocatively, even Interior Minister Schäuble expressed misgivings about allowing the region's first tentative steps toward democracy to be handicapped by the MfS's shadow.[15] By Schäuble's count, an astounding four million persons had maintained one or another form of contact with the Stasi over the years even if this involvement had been limited to such activities as writing reports about official trips to the West. For this reason, he could not see how eastern Germany would, in his words, "really have a chance to win a better future" if it allowed itself to become mired in controversy over the Stasi. To be sure, Schäuble admitted that there might be some merit in taking limited steps to come to terms with this dimension of the country's authoritarian legacy. Yet he could not help but sense that "a considerable part of the energy now being devoted to this task would be [better spent] by winning the future."[16]

Against this background, it should be clear why the opposing case for opening the files and searching for collaborators would have been difficult to sustain if one had tried to make it on historical grounds alone. As long as the MfS records themselves had not been examined, it was impossible to say whether they contained either a positive or negative message about the extent of popular involvement in the ministry's activities. Consequently, those activists who wanted to expose the Stasi's misdeeds to public scrutiny were initially reduced to justifying their positions by appealing to moral arguments.

For example, Joachim Gauck contended that eastern Germany would never be restored to good health unless its residents were forced to confront the hidden truths behind the walls of the Normannenstraße fortress. "After all of the great words of revolution," he argued, in response to demands that the files be destroyed sight unseen, "this is a matter of searching out those smaller, dirty words of betrayal that were the usual thing among our people. [This means] not denying the signatures [when we come across them], calling betrayal betrayal, and cowardice cowardice." By owning up to these ills directly, the East German citizenry would presumably embrace democracy with the right attitudes, "awake, informed, and driven by a will to achieve more justice and truth."[17]

For many of the same reasons, the poet Lutz Rathenow urged his compatriots to consider the heavy price of failing to take advantage of the opportunity to examine the inner workings of the MfS. If easterners did not immediately contend with the unpleasant realities in the files, he warned, they might never be able to overcome the suspicions of many western Germans that they, as a people, had been totally compromised by the Stasi. "One of the methods of the secret police," he reminded, "lay precisely in its ability to mystify its work. Its success was based on the aura that it was capable of attaining absolutely any objective, for example that every man and every women would collaborate with it, if only it wanted that to happen." For all of these reasons, the unavoidable first step to depriving the "zombie state security" of its power over the popular imagination lay in demonstrating that it had not been as successful as it claimed. "There is really no way of getting around this remaining mountain," Rathenow averred. "We just have to read right through it."[18]

As reasonable or as self-evident as these arguments may now appear in retrospect, one must admit that if they had been made in ordinary times, decision makers would have faced an uphill battle in deciding to use the misbegotten records of a police state as instruments of social justice. The threat to personal privacy was too great. Yet, even though Gauck and Rathenow had scanty evidence to back up their claims, two prominent features about the political climate during the GDR's last days seem to have shifted the weight of necessity to their side. Each of these developments originated in the East.

First, in the disorder and confusion surrounding the occupation of various MfS offices throughout the country, it was widely suspected that many of the personal dossiers the Stasi had compiled on the East German citizenry had found their way into the wrong hands. Accordingly, if the GDR's new government did not want to relegate the assessment of the ministry's operations by default to ambitious journalists, rumormongers, and would-be blackmailers, it made sense to think that it should immediately devise an institutional mechanism for governing the uses of these holdings as well as for weighing their reliability.

Second, as evidence continued to mount of politicians who had spied for the MfS (most notably, word circulated after the March 18 election that the Stasi's reach had extended even to prime minister de Maizière), the prospect of screening public servants became politically unavoidable. In the wake of the election, the parties in the East German parliament were persuaded, with varying degrees of enthusiasm, to take up this challenge within their own ranks, as much to protect the reputations of members who were being falsely accused as to identify possible collaborators. However, it did not take long for similar demands to be raised for the vetting of other occupations, from high-profile posts in government ministries down to grass roots positions in the schools, town councils, the courts, and the police.[19] "We have a right to know what happened to us," the dissident physicist Sebastian Pflugbeil proclaimed before a huge anti-Stasi demonstration in Berlin in late March 1990, "and we don't want to have any teachers, pastors, or judges who would have been willing to send us to [internment] camps only one-half year ago."[20]

East and West German negotiators took their initial, halting steps toward accomplishing the first of these tasks in August and September 1990 when they hammered together a compromise agreement that led to the formation of a provisional administrative body in Berlin to manage the MfS holdings until an all-German parliament had resolved all outstanding questions of access to the records.[21] This goal was finally realized with the passage of the StUG in late 1991. Following unification, Gauck was named the first commissioner of this agency, the Federal Authority for the Records of the State Security Service of the Former GDR (BStU), which soon became known colloquially as the "Gauck agency."

Simultaneously, although with notably less publicity in view of the controversies to come, Schäuble and his East German counterpart, Günther Krause, agreed upon language in two sections in the Unification treaty that addressed the question of what to do with public officials who had contributed to the apparatus of oppression in the GDR. One section of the treaty provided for the dismissal of anyone responsible for human rights violations under the SED dictatorship. Another spoke directly to the problem of Stasi collaboration, stipulating that evidence of secret police "activity" could constitute an "important ground" for disqualification. In both cases, the accord implied that it was up to the appropriate authorities to determine whether someone's continuing employment, in the treaty's carefully phrased language, was "unsuitable (*unzumutbar*)" under the circumstances.[22]

Even at this early stage, it would have been evident to anyone reading the treaty that these grounds for disqualification were elastic enough to provide substantial room for interpretation once administrators began to work with the MfS records. These provisions could even be used to safeguard the rights of individuals who were suspected of collaboration. For example, public agencies still had to decide what it meant to be *active* for the Stasi. And even then, the accord did not require the dismissal of everyone found to have associated with the ministry. As a further sign of its authors' desire to maximize the room for discretion, the treaty did not even specify a hard-and-fast standard for assessing employees' "suitability" for continued employment.

After the two German states were formally united in October 1990, the readiness of public officials to take advantage of this flexibility was in large part dictated by who was doing the judging and whether they were inclined to make sensible distinctions about the degree to which citizens had colluded with the Stasi. At two levels, one involving the Gauck agency's processing of requests for information from the MfS files and the other the review procedures of the German court system, the message these unofficial historians had to convey about the past was often positive and forward looking. The evidence showed that some persons had indeed mortgaged their honor to work with the secret police, although, the files' interpreters added, this behavior was not the norm in the GDR. However, at the intermediate level where the disqualification of collaborators took place, it was harder to be confident about this process. The official understanding of complicity was sometimes so broad and so loosely defined that one could not help wondering whether the critics' fears about the files' adverse impact on the East were justified.

Level One: Distilling Truth from the Files

From its first days of administering the MfS records, the BStU was the principal proponent of the view that the aggressive pursuit of GDR-era injustice need not result in a blanket condemnation of the East

German populace. In fact, had one only listened to the agency's chief, the potential pitfalls of taking up the Stasi issue would not have been apparent. Gauck summarized this perspective in an illuminating interview with the news weekly *Der Spiegel* in 1993, emphasizing that the citizenry of the former GDR was not at all a "people of traitors." It was a population with as complex an historical profile of good and bad motives, good and bad deeds, as any country. "The Stasi files do not demean the East German people," he declared. "Rather, in conjunction with other historical sources, they show us as we are, with our strengths and our weaknesses, which are very similar to the strengths and weaknesses of our West German compatriots."[23]

To make the point credible, however, Gauck and his coworkers essentially had to convince doubters to engage in two leaps of faith about the BStU's mission. The first point was that the holdings of the secret police were a reliable means for getting at the truth about the GDR past; the second, that collaboration had been such a conscious and deliberate activity that it could safely be linked to a relatively narrow segment of the eastern German populace.

With regard to the first point, it was probably unavoidable that the Gauck agency would come under fire for even suggesting that these records could serve the cause of truth telling. In GDR times, few of the Stasi's thousands of employees had ever been allowed comprehensive insight into the organization of its archives. According to the principle of "internal conspiracy," each employee knew only enough to fulfill his or her task, whereas the number of those entitled to a more comprehensive perspective on the records was deliberately restricted. Thus, a given individual might have access to a card catalog listing the names of persons of interest to the MfS but have no way of distinguishing informants from targets. Simultaneously, another employee might see the "cover names" of collaborators but be unable to connect this information with real names.[24]

Then, too, administrators were faced with an added problem. The collapse of central authority in the GDR and the occupation of Stasi offices by citizens' groups had left the secret police holdings in utter disarray. In the Berlin *Zentrale* alone, MfS operatives and overzealous activists had together managed to remove or to destroy many of the instruments that would have facilitated a quick identification of former collaborators. These included the central computing system that governed the archives' nearly 100 different card catalogs as well as large sections of the "F16" directory, which recorded the names of six million persons of varied interest to the MfS, informants and victims alike.

Nonetheless, these largely technical challenges do not appear to have been insurmountable problems for the BStU. With time, and the assistance of a handful of well-positioned (and sympathetic) MfS employees, the agency was able to retrieve much of the information that had initially appeared lost or inaccessible in the wake of the GDR's fall. At times in their search for IMs (unofficial collaborators), BStU employees were called to utilize the empirical skills of a careful historian. If a particular case file no longer existed, they could reconstruct many of its original components by comparing and cross-referencing data from other, still-existing files. Where had the individual in question been on a particular date? To what information had he or she been given access? Could this information have been made available in any other way? In this manner, the parts of a larger story would slowly come into focus.

This seems to have been the case with incriminating evidence the BStU collected against de Maizière in early 1991 after a former Stasi officer alleged that the GDR's last prime minister had covertly supplied him with information on his clients for over a decade. At first, a direct link between de Maizière and the unofficial collaborator known in some records as "Czerni" was difficult to establish. Both the latter's personnel card in the F16 file and five folders of operational reports on his activities had vanished from the ministry's central archives in the turmoil surrounding the occupation of the Normannenstraße headquarters. Yet by drawing upon scattered information in four other catalogs, the BStU was able to piece together a credible case that "Czerni" and de Maizière were the same person. "Czerni" must have been a highly placed member of the synod of the Lutheran churches (someone who, in the eyes of his handlers, could influence "the meetings of the synod in the sense of a positive picture of the relationship between state and church"). By profession, he must have been a lawyer. Finally, he must have lived at a certain Berlin address (Am Treptower Park 32). How much of a coincidence can it have been that de Maizière was the only person in the city to fit all three categories?[25]

Above and beyond the challenge of retrieving lost data from the archives, a more serious objection to the use of the MfS files to reconstruct the past was that they were factually unreliable.[26] On prima facie grounds, it is easy to see why this was a plausible concern. It was certainly conceivable that Stasi operatives had occasionally dressed up their reports to impress their superiors or otherwise promote their careers. Further, even if their motives were purer, it was also possible that agents could have been careless or sloppy in describing their activities. If a control officer failed to pay close attention to the crucial distinction between informants who had actually engaged in conspiratorial activity for the MfS (so-called *IM-Vorgänge*) and the much larger, broader category of eastern Germans who were merely considered prospects for collaboration (*IM-Vorläufe*), the consequences for personal reputations could prove disastrous.

For these reasons, Gauck and his colleagues would not have been very persuasive had they tried to maintain that such distortions of the truth never entered the MfS's record keeping. The possibility of human error was too great, and even the fabled Stasi was not run by superhuman beings.[27] Instead, Gauck and his colleagues took an approach to the problem that seems, to this writer at least, to have been much more convincing. This was to invite the skeptics to imagine what attitude the ministry would have had about its records when it compiled them. In the BStU's reasoning, the answer one provided to this question was directly related to one's conception of the Stasi's place in East German society. Had the MfS had a reputation for having little regard for the success of its operations, a common enough trait among various sectors of the economy, its officers might well have been unconcerned about who their informants were or about the accuracy of their reports. Yet, the BStU contended, precisely because the ministry took its mystique seriously as an organ that was supposed to "know everything and report everything worth knowing,"[28] it was logical to think its officers would have done everything in their power to know their agents' biographies and personal foibles in order to maximize their chances of receiving useful information from the field.

On the first score, officials argued that the Stasi files themselves provided the most convincing evidence to this effect. Generally, the first part of the personal dossier of an IM would include a detailed record of the efforts made to recruit him or her and would invariably conclude with documents showing that he or she had knowingly and – this was important – willingly offered services to the MfS: a handwritten statement of readiness to engage in intelligence-gathering activities (*Verpflichtungserklärung*), a formal promise to refrain from revealing these activities to family members and other persons (*Schweigepflicht*), and the selection of a cover name (*Deckname*). Similarly, the second and third parts of the same files would often include other evidence of complicity such as progress reports penned in the IM's hand, taped interviews between control officers and the informant, and signed receipts for expenses incurred in the course of an assignment. On the basis of such evidence, the BStU maintained that the majority of IMs had "neither been coerced nor blackmailed into collaborating with the MfS but had declared their willingness to do so out of 'personal conviction.'"[29]

In addition, agency officials could show that the supervision of these and other records was a routine, deliberate, and disciplined part of the Stasi's daily operations. For example, an entire department, the *Zentrale Auswertungs- und Informationsgruppe* (ZAIG), was occupied with the task of assessing the conscientiousness of informants and analyzing their reports. For every report that came back from the field, a corresponding control officer would ask basic questions about the quality of the information delivered. How knowledgeable was the IM, and how honest? How direct and how dependable were his or her sources of information? What were his or her biases, and how might these sentiments have interfered with an objective assessment of the assignment?[30] One high-ranking Stasi officer has described the process so well that it is worth quoting him at length:

> It was a basic precondition, as everyone who worked with the information knows, that [the files] had to be reliable. It wouldn't have been valuable at all to recruit someone who was a blowhard. The things we needed had to hold water; they had to be interesting. It was the rule for us to compare and contrast different sources of information. In scholarship, the truth content of every piece of information has to be chewed over; you are only a capable scholar if you use proven information to come to the right conclusions. This was the way we conducted our work [in the MfS] as well.[31]

Naturally, this interpretation of the MfS's operations was unlikely to satisfy all of the BStU's critics. In view of Gauck's readiness to defend the ministry's records, one prominent commentator even accused the commissioner of having become a "leading apologist" for the Stasi.[32] Nevertheless, even when critics succeeded in showing that the files contained inaccuracies here or there, Gauck and others could still defend them as legitimate sources of information about the East German past. They were not foolproof, department head Herbert Ziehm maintained, but they were "just as credible, or not credible, as the records of any other public agency [in the GDR]."[33] Indeed, one could have added that precisely this reasoning had made it possible for an earlier generation of administrators and historians to utilize the records of the Nazi regime to good effect, especially those of the Gestapo.[34] With all due caution, why should the Stasi's files not be used for these purposes as well?

At the same time, the BStU invited Diestel and other skeptics to engage in a second leap of faith about the hunt for Stasi collaborators. It was not the agency's purpose, Gauck contended on several occasions, to interfere with the lives of the vast majority of easterners who had committed no greater offense in their lives than to make their peace with the political realities of the communist system. Rather, the BStU's sole mission was to use the files to identify the much smaller group of persons who, of their own volition, had taken that extra and, in Gauck's view, indefensible step of selling their services to the MfS. Gauck expressed the distinction this way: "Accommodation [with the old regime] was normal, but overaccommodation, including working for the secret police, was not!"[35]

In part, this second leap was supported by the statistics the BStU successfully compiled in the early 1990s on the Stasi's penetration of East German society. According to these findings, the ministry had employed no more than 180,000 full-time officers since its founding on February 8, 1950. Of these, approximately 91,000 were still active when the Berlin Wall was opened in November 1989. Over the same 39-year period, the ministry could count between 500,000 and 600,000 total IMs in its service. Of these persons, however, only about 174,200 were active in various capacities in 1989.

These were big numbers in comparison with the secret police apparatuses of other authoritarian regimes, including the Nazi dictatorship. In 1936, the Gestapo had employed no more than 3,000 regular officers and perhaps 10,000 total informants.[36] Yet these were not the overwhelming statistics that onlookers had fearfully expected in the early days of unification.[37] Furthermore, if one combined the number of full-time officers with those the BStU was able to identify as active IMs at the time of the GDR's collapse, the result would be a relatively small segment of the country's adult working population (at most, about 2.5 percent, or 265,200 persons out of 10,520,000 citizens between the ages of 18 and 65).[38]

Just the same, it would be a mistake to think that the BStU's case for using the Stasi files could simply be boiled down to counting the heads of MfS informants or rejoicing because many East Germans had failed to follow suit. For Gauck and his associates, the real test of utility was the extent to which the archives allowed one to go beyond merely formal and legalistic understandings of complicity to focus on cases of real guilt and real culpability in the communist period.[39]

In an oblique way, Gauck addressed this issue in a 1991 book on the work before the agency. He admitted that even in the handling of the Stasi's regular operatives, the HMs (full-time employees), one could not reduce the final determination of "guilt, complicity, and innocence" to the MfS's narrow definition of collaboration. Although the ministry had nearly 100,000 full-time employees at its disposal in 1989, this did not mean that all of them should be lumped together in the special category of "perpetrators." In fact, Gauck suggested, using reasoning akin to that of the criminal courts in the later stages of the Wall trials, one needed to begin any investigation into the Stasi's activities by separating the agency's low-ranking employees – the cooks and soldiers, truck drivers and bank tellers – from the higher officers who had been responsible for its most oppressive acts. Only the last had committed offenses that made them unfit for future public service.[40]

By the same token, Gauck stressed that one had to be equally careful when categorizing the former IMs. In deference to the victims, he expressed sympathy with those who found "collaboration as an [IM] to be even more reprehensible than regular employment [by the ministry]" because, as he phrased the point, "these people could not be easily recognized by their victims, and they were committing a fundamental breach of trust." But again, he emphasized that a balanced assessment of someone's involvement with the secret police would have to take into account the specific circumstances that had given rise to this activity. Sometimes, Gauck noted, personal crises had led out-and-out opponents of the SED to ignore their better judgment and consent to deliver reports to the MfS. On other occasions, the psychological pressures to accede to the Stasi's demands were so intense that it was difficult to separate willing collaborators from hapless victims. Hence, if justice were to be done, one could only arrive at a single, self-evident truth after reviewing the files: "a great deal of differentiation was necessary."[41]

The implications of Gauck's argument should have been clear to everyone. It was not only feasible to draw upon the mountain of records to present a reliable picture of wrongdoing in the GDR, but, if one approached the task with the right amount of sensitivity to the difficult situations people had faced under the old regime, the verdict about popular entanglement in the ministry's operations was likely to be reassuring. Only a small minority of the GDR's citizens had made themselves unworthy of public trust by virtue of their associations with the MfS.

Strictly speaking, Gauck and his coworkers were at pains to emphasize that the BStU itself was not in the business of making such judgments. As an administrative organ, the agency was restricted by statute to providing other bodies, such as *Länder* governments and private corporations, with the tools they needed to make sense of the MfS's operations.[42] Once this task was accomplished, it was up to these bodies alone to determine whether evidence of their employees' dealings with the secret police constituted sufficient grounds for disqualification. In this light, the remaining issue – a big one – was whether these organs would heed Gauck's words of caution in deciding the fate of the former HMs and IMs.

Level Two: Screening for Stasi Activity

When we consider the waves of accusations and counteraccusations that accompanied the handling of the Stasi issue in the first few years of the GDR's incorporation into the Federal Republic, it becomes readily apparent that there was a significant gulf between the ideal image of screening that Gauck and others championed as the end result of their labors and the concrete demands of scrutinizing the past associations of more than one million eastern German workers. Even the Stasi files chief himself was forced to concede this point.[43] It was not simply that the various agencies that acted upon the BStU's findings – from civil service offices to parliamentary committees, labor associations to private corporations – applied arbitrary standards to their employees. Some did, whereas others were apparently more discriminating. Rather, the deeper problem was with the process itself. The leeway provided by the Unification treaty for evaluating "suitability" could just as easily be turned against employees as it could be made to work for them. As long as there was little consensus among policymakers about the meaning of culpability and, additionally, as political and economic considerations entered into these decisions, the memory of the Stasi would loom over the region.

We will probably never know exactly how many people lost their jobs in the course of the "destasification" of eastern Germany. The topic has been the subject of continuing speculation among journalists and other observers largely because no single German agency was assigned the task of monitoring these dismissals and because employers were not required to report their decisions to any central authority. At least one analyst has put the total number of disqualifications for MfS ties during the period between January 1991 and spring 1992 at over one-half million persons.[44] Yet this figure seems to conflate Stasi-related firings with the much greater number of state employees who were laid off as a result of the restructuring and modernization of the eastern German civil service.

In fact, as of February 28, 1997, the BStU estimated the total number of Stasi dismissals from civil service positions at 42,046. This figure was based on two assumptions: (1) that, on average, 6.3 percent of the 1,420,000 persons investigated for complicity were found to be either HMs or IMs, and (2) that 47 percent of the latter category (or less than 3 percent of the total number) were eventually dismissed. Of the remaining 435,000 persons investigated outside the ranks of the civil service, the same calculations would yield 12,880 dismissals (a generous figure because private industry was less inclined to dismiss employees for MfS activity). Thus, as of 1997, the total number of Stasi dismissals cannot have been higher than 54,926 and was probably lower.[45]

Even though the actual number of dismissals over the 1990s was lower than many analysts anticipated, one should not overlook the more serious cause for concern. This was that different standards of guilt and innocence were evidently applied from one case to the next.

For example, even at the earliest stages of the screening process, that is, before the BStU was asked to investigate employees for possible links to the Stasi, this problem was borne out in the different types of questionnaires public officials were required to complete to be certified by state review commissions. Some of the eastern *Länder* were inclined to use a narrow definition of complicity, presumably along the lines that Gauck himself would have considered appropriate for disqualification. Thus, candidates for judicial posts in Berlin and Brandenburg were asked only whether they had been *actively* involved with the MfS or any of its related agencies. In contrast, in other states, the official definition of culpability was much broader, sometimes to the point of including even the most casual connections with the Stasi. Hence, in Saxony and Saxony–Anhalt, would-be judicial appointees were questioned about *all* types of contact they may have had with the secret police, including, but not limited to, explicit collaboration. In Thuringia, state authorities were zealous even to the point of courting guilt by association and asked judicial candidates not only about their own activities but also about whether their families or loved-ones had ever had ties with the Stasi. "Have you," one questionnaire asked, "or has anyone else living in your home (your spouse, children – stepchildren and foster children – half- or stepsiblings – or their spouses, in-laws, or siblings, including half- and stepsiblings, or fiancés) ever been spoken to or written to about conducting any kind of intelligence-related or anticonstitutional activity against the Federal Republic or its allies?"[46] Given the decades of hostility between the GDR and the FRG, it is likely that a sizable segment of the eastern German population was complicitous under this loose standard.

As we can deduce from the literally thousands of dismissals that were later appealed before German administrative and labor courts over the first half of the 1990s, the same disparities apparently came into play when public agencies acted upon the Gauck agency's findings. A typical BStU research report on an employee's past might include all of the factual information one needed to determine whether he or she had ever had contacts with the secret police (e.g., an IM category, cover name, department, control officer, receipts, etc.). But in line with the agency's statute, the report's authors were conspicuously silent on the one question that interested state and local officials the most: Were these contacts, in fact, sufficiently burdensome to constitute legitimate grounds for dismissal? Lacking firm guidelines of their own, some state employers evidently chose to simplify their task by disqualifying anyone the BStU found to be "Stasi positive" regardless of mitigating circumstances or special considerations.

Lacking a centralized agency to collect the statistics, we are reduced to speaking impressionistically about this problem. But the stories of uncertain policies and apparent injustices abound. In Cottbus, in 1992, the conversion of hundreds of former GDR passport inspectors into federal border patrol officials was delayed for months after local authorities discovered that their previous employer had formally been subordinated to the MfS. In Leipzig, public officials were dismissed from their positions without the benefit of a hearing even though the Stasi records showed that they had been both informants *and* objects of surveillance. In Dresden, scores of university professors and assistants were fired in the wake of accusations that their contacts with the secret police had implicated them in unspecified crimes against humanity. And, in Berlin as well, suspected IMs were dismissed from their jobs merely for having made their residences available for "conspiratorial meetings" between agents in the MfS's employ.[47]

In some cases, we may attribute these heavy-handed measures to ambiguities in both the Unification treaty and the Stasi Records law about the exact meaning of Stasi "activity" (*Tätigkeit*). For example, commentators on the StUG have pointed to a lack of clarity in the statute about whether individuals are to be judged solely in terms of what they have done or instead in the potentially more encompassing terms of a professed intent to work for the MfS. In one section of the law, collaboration seems to be defined in the more restrictive sense, requiring active involvement with the ministry (StUG, §20 [6–7]).[48] But in another passage, notably under the heading "definition of terms," collaborators are simply understood as "persons who have declared a readiness to supply information" to the secret police (StUG, §6 [4] 2).

Even without such legal ambiguities, however, there can be little doubt that the emotionally charged climate that attended the opening of the Stasi files was far from conducive to the kinds of careful distinctions between "accommodation" and "overaccommodation" that activists like Gauck had preferred. In some cases, the principal determinant of how a given employee was treated appears to have been the politics of the federal state in which he or she happened to reside. In politically conservative Saxony, a CDU-governed *Land* whose policies were heavily influenced by key figures from the 1989 revolution (e.g., justice minister Steffen Heitmann, environmental minister Vaatz), any evidence of involvement with the MfS seems to have constituted sufficient grounds for disqualification from government service, and a restrictive civil service code was applied to this effect. Under these conditions, even Stasi drivers, cooks, and janitors were all subject to dismissal from their jobs, regardless of the nature or intensity of their previous commitments.[49]

In comparison with Saxony's handling of the MfS issue, Brandenburg was a picture of moderation and restraint. In part because the state was governed by a Social Democratic premier, Manfred Stolpe, who was himself accused of being an IM, the Brandenburg assembly was never able to agree on a commissioner to represent its interests to the BStU in Berlin. But the debates that took place over Stolpe's culpability in the early 1990s may also have led to a more differentiated handling of suspected collaborators. The state's civil service law was not only less intrusive into past activities than those of the more conservative eastern *Länder*, but the disqualification rate for some categories of state employees was noticeably lower as well. It is also noteworthy that, by mid-decade, Brandenburg officials, such as Minister of Justice Hans-Otto Bräutigam, were among the first voices to call for a winding down of any further vetting for MfS ties.[50]

Curiously, the one domain in which Stasi collaborators seemed to enjoy a decent chance of retaining their jobs, regardless of politics or location, was in private industry. Although the Unification treaty did not specifically address the disqualification of private sector employees, there can be little doubt that the scores of new companies and businesses that sprang up throughout the former GDR in the first half of the 1990s had the wherewithal to undertake a sweeping review of their ranks to match the most aggressive campaigns of the *Länder*. Also, the extent of MfS involvement among this segment of the eastern work force appears to have been nearly as great as that in the public domain.[51] However, as long as skilled labor was in short supply in the East, private employers were apparently more inclined to value the technical abilities and training of those who worked for them than to concern themselves with ancient history. As a consequence, as late as mid-1994, private firms had submitted only about 10,000 requests for background checks to the BStU in marked contrast to the well over 1.2 million inquiries filed by public agencies over the same period.[52]

When economic interests favored screening, however, it is telling that the case for moderation and restraint was more difficult to sustain. In the public sphere in particular, Stasi-related dismissals appear to have been directly influenced by the forces of supply and demand in the labor market. Accordingly, professions that could readily be replenished with qualified personnel from the West seem to have been especially hard hit by the screening process.[53] In others, however, where fewer persons with adequate training were available, state authorities were inclined to be, almost too conveniently, much more forgiving in their assessment of the Stasi records. Again, Brandenburg is a case in point.

As one would expect of a state that suffered from a shortage of qualified policemen and policewomen, over 95 percent of those individuals
who were investigated for Stasi ties were ultimately allowed to retain
their jobs even though it was widely known that police officials had
frequently worked hand-in-hand with the MfS in GDR times. But in
neighboring Berlin, a healthier labor market apparently lent itself to
a more tough-minded standard of culpability. With an ample supply
of qualified personnel in the city's western sectors, the Berlin government recommended the dismissal of an extraordinary 40 percent of
officials in the upper ranks of the police force who were vetted for
Stasi complicity.[54]

To the extent that policymakers were concerned about the implications of the decisions of both public and private agencies for the
reputation of the rule of law in Germany, they may have found a
small measure of comfort by comparing their experiences with the
other prominent example of screening in postcommunist East Europe,
Czechoslovakia's lustration law of October 4, 1991. Somewhat like its
German counterpart, this law provided for the disqualification of employees in high-ranking government posts for a period of 5 years if they
were found to have been agents or informants of the secret police (StB).
Yet in this case, unlike in Germany, both the original lawmakers and
the implementors of *lustrace* showed little concern for distinguishing
among different degrees of StB complicity. Nor did they even seem to
be open to bringing additional information to bear on their decisions.
Hence, the existence alone of an StB file would generally constitute
sufficient grounds for dismissal. At least in the German model, by way
of contrast, there was room for flexibility. The theoretical possibility of
treating such records in a differentiated fashion was vouchsafed by the
Unification treaty, the StUG, and the fundamental guarantees of the
Basic Law even if the principle was not always followed in practice.[55]
But of course, for those idealists who had hoped for the application
of even greater care to the Stasi review process, the results we have
described had to have been discouraging.

Level Three: Appealing Dismissals before the Courts

In view of these inconsistencies and the pall the search for Stasi collaborators cast over much of eastern Germany, it is revealing that the Gauck
agency's ardent defenders and its arch–civil-libertarian critics could

agree on one point. They were all inclined to bemoan the absence of more unitary guidelines and institutional safeguards to protect the rights of citizens who were subjected to these procedures.[56] Helmut Simon, a former FCC justice, spoke for many observers when he called attention to the ambiguous ground on which the screening process rested: "We simply cannot afford to throw the proven foundations of our Rechtsstaat overboard. It still comes down to this: 'giving the accused the benefit of doubt' and 'audiatur et altera pars' ('the other side should be heard as well')."[57]

This was easy to say. Yet the related challenge for commentators was to identify the instruments that were actually available to German policymakers for carrying out this task. In an ideal world, the BStU itself would have taken on the charge by assuring to each person whom it found to have colluded with the Stasi the right to a hearing to review the evidence against him or her. However, despite having more than 3,000 employees at its disposal by mid-decade, the agency was ill-equipped for the task. Its researchers were too preoccupied with organizing and processing the MfS's holdings to have taken on the added burden of hearing the complaints of tens of thousands of persons with varied ties to the secret police. More important, had the BStU taken this step, it would have jeopardized its own self-understanding as a neutral administrative body above the fray of ordinary politics. This was no small matter. As long as the agency was regarded primarily as a *processor* of documents and not as an interpreter of past behavior, let alone a court of final judgment, its representatives could comfortably see themselves as engaged in an activity that was no more controversial than the fulfillment of their statute.[58]

But there was also another often overlooked impediment to the introduction of more finely tuned screening procedures. As a federal state, the FRG relegated the right to review the qualifications of many of its public officials – from teachers and police officers to attorneys, notaries, and state parliamentarians – to the *Länder*. As a result, the new eastern German states and their respective subsidiary bodies (e.g., police commissions, school boards) were inclined to regard any outside interest in these questions as interference in their internal affairs.[59] The Interior Ministry made this discovery to its chagrin in 1991 when it unsuccessfully sought to carve out for itself a more active role in the screening of suspected collaborators. As one BStU state commissioner wryly observed about the resistance the ministry immediately provoked among the *Länder*, this was "the price [one] had to pay" for living in a democratic system that could not be "centrally directed" (the commissioner actually used the historically loaded term *gleichgeschaltet* reminiscent of Nazi times) like the GDR.[60]

Under these circumstances, the next best thing to a uniform standard of evaluation was provided by the review procedures of the German court system. If any institution was suited to offer a needed corrective to the politically motivated or incautious use of the Stasi's records, it was the courts by virtue of the law's emphasis on due process. Yet observers may have been surprised by the extent of the courts' engagement. Provocatively, the more they became involved in reviewing the cases of persons who had been dismissed from their jobs or otherwise penalized as a result of information from the files, the more they took it upon themselves to define the sphere of Stasi-related injustice in an even more narrowly focused fashion than Gauck and the BStU.

At the heart of the courts' stand, first of all, was a noticeably greater degree of skepticism about the utility of the Stasi's records for identifying wrongdoing, which echoed some of the cautionary perspectives that had first been expressed in early 1990. The criminal chamber of Germany's appeals court, the Federal Court of Justice, gave voice to this sentiment in a prominent judgment on May 5, 1992, when it dismissed an arrest warrant against an alleged terrorist that was based in part on scattered MfS reports. Significantly, the court did not dispute the possibility that the files could be used in some cases to provide evidence of criminal activity. But at least implicitly, the court took issue with the confident reasoning that had led BStU officials to assert that these documents were "just as credible" as the records of any other public agency. Noting that the Stasi's operations had never been procedurally consistent with the high legal standards of the *Rechtsstaat*, the court advised that all of the information in the MfS archives had to be subjected to "severe and especially critical scrutiny."[61] Only in this way, the judges emphasized, could one guarantee that the rights of the accused would be protected.

This issue came to the fore in early 1991 when the BStU claimed to have unearthed evidence that the popular rector of Berlin's Humboldt University, Heinrich Fink, had been a paid informant of the Stasi since the late 1960s. Among the materials the agency provided to the Berlin Senate was a registration card listing Fink under the cover name "IM Heiner," which supposedly tied him to a series of covert reports to the

Stasi on the activities of the GDR's Lutheran churches. Interestingly, Fink chose not to contest the existence of these documents when he was dismissed from the university. But in appealing the decision before a Berlin labor court, he contended that the BStU had failed to prove the most important charge of all, that he had knowingly worked for the Stasi as "IM Heiner." Notably, the local court agreed with Fink's defense, ruling on April 1, 1992, that it was not enough for the BStU to have asserted the likelihood of the rector's involvement with the secret police: "a simple probability cannot suffice." Instead, the court reasoned that the BStU was required to demonstrate that the accused had "consciously and willingly" worked for the ministry, for only evidence of a concrete connection could overcome the benefit of doubt to which Fink was entitled.[62]

Though the ruling came a month before the federal court's May 5 judgment on the criminal case, it affirmed the special care that was required in any recourse to the MfS archives. Still, in accord with the BStU's claims about the files' overall reliability, the judgment did not invalidate the evidentiary value of these holdings either. This point was spelled out when Fink launched an appeal to the state labor court to compel the Berlin Senate to restore him to his former position. In seeking reinstatement, Fink had good reasons for feeling confident about his chances. Two high-ranking Stasi officers (albeit those thought to be his former handlers) testified to his innocence, and he had the moral backing of hundreds of Humboldt University students and faculty who considered him to be the archetypical victim of western "victor's justice." However, this time around, the BStU was able to assemble more compelling evidence of Fink's complicity. Researchers proved that he had personally received an MfS-authorized service medal ("in gold") from the National People's Army in 1984 even though he had never been a military officer. Additionally, they produced telephone records to show that Fink had twice called a secret MfS telephone number in 1987, apparently to report on internal church discussions in Berlin–Brandenburg.[63]

For the state court, significantly, these findings were sufficiently substantial to reject Fink's request for reinstatement. Just the same, although the court found that the BStU had proved that Fink "had direct conspiratorial contacts with the MfS and [knowingly] supplied it with information," it took the opportunity to reemphasize the higher evidentiary hurdle now required for establishing Stasi complicity. As the presiding judge, Bernd Preis, explained, there was nothing wrong with the labor court's earlier decision in Fink's favor. The lower court had properly found that the BStU's initial evidence against Fink was incomplete and, the judge added, "in no way compelling." The case simply demonstrated that registration as an IM was not, by itself, evidence of conscious collaboration with the Stasi.[64]

In the spirit of this decision, a series of lower and appeals court rulings after 1992 reaffirmed the principle that meaningful collaboration should be treated as a deliberate and identifiable activity. For example, in a widely cited decision in July 1994, the eastern citizens' group, Neues Forum, was prohibited from publicizing a list of 4,500 ostensible IMs in the city of Halle on the grounds that the distribution of the names on the list without a formal hearing would amount to an unlawful infringement of each person's right to personal security. In this instance as well, judicial officials chose not to challenge the validity of the sources from which Neues Forum's list had been compiled. But very much in tune with the handling of Fink's case, they argued that the appearance of one's name in a Stasi dossier was not enough to establish knowing complicity.[65]

For similar reasons, throughout the mid-1990s various courts ruled that even the existence of a signed agreement to work for the Stasi was insufficient proof of collaboration. In at least one instance, a Berlin labor court found that an individual accused of being an "unofficial collaborator" may not have been the author of his purported agreement.[66] However, even though the authenticity of the MfS documents could not be called into question in the majority of these cases, the courts continued to espouse a relatively restrictive position on the question of disqualification. Dismissals from employment could only be justified on the basis of evidence of "conscious and final activity for the MfS."[67]

A second respect in which the courts offered a more refined perspective on the issue of GDR wrongdoing had to do with the elusive matter of "suitability" for public office. The Unification treaty established no absolute guidelines for terminating former MfS operatives, thereby leaving it up to the states and other authorities to weigh the facts to determine whether continued employment was justifiable. But here, too, a wide variety of labor and administrative courts intervened to narrow the standards for disqualification.[68]

In a January 1993 decision, the Federal Labor Court found that a cook could not be denied employment in a vacation resort merely because he had once written reports for the Stasi. It was still incumbent upon the state, the judges argued, to show that his previous position with the MfS had been important enough and his personal involvement extensive enough that he could no longer be considered suitable for public sector employment.[69]

Additionally, in several related cases, the courts ruled that the type of job being sought should be taken into consideration in assessing an employee's qualifications. As a higher administrative court found in November 1995, it was appropriate for a prospective fire captain who had once worked as an IM to be judged by somewhat less stringent standards than a police officer in a comparable position. In the latter case, public confidence in an essential element of the rule of law demanded that the state adhere to high standards in the selection of its official representatives. But in the case of firefighters, who occupy a much less prominent position in the public mind, the judges concluded that dismissals would require a "considerable degree of involvement [in the MfS]."[70]

In keeping with these rulings, in successive decisions in late December 1995 and early 1996, the screening chambers of the Federal Constitutional Court came out strongly in favor of further narrowing the grounds for disqualification for Stasi collaboration for certain categories of employees. In the first instance, involving a review of the law governing the licensing of former GDR attorneys, the judges affirmed that lawyers could indeed be dismissed from their jobs for having betrayed confidences about their clients to the secret police. But, the judges underscored, this step could only be justified if that information had led to, or could have led to, serious violations of human rights. The chamber added in a telling nod to the importance of preexisting standards that there was nothing unusual about taking this stand, for such behavior would "even have been contrary to the written and lived law of the GDR."[71]

In the second decision on February 15, 1996, involving the fate of a notary who had briefly collaborated with the MfS, the chamber found even more restrictive language to define the grounds that would constitute a loss of confidence in someone's capacity for public service. The judges contended that fairness to the accused entailed taking explicitly into account "whether, by way of example, the transmission of information of a denunciatory character had the intention or the expectation that it would [promote] inhumane consequences or circumstances incompatible with the rule of law." In this case, evidently, it did not. Because there was no evidence that the individual in question had inflicted any harm on the family on whom he had written reports ("no one was hurt [by his activities]," they noted), the court overturned the ruling that had led to the notary's original dismissal.[72]

Finally, a variety of courts were increasingly inclined to test the outer boundaries of Gauck's early appeal for differentiation by taking certain mitigating factors into consideration in reaching their decisions. In this vein, the Federal Labor Court ruled in September 1995 that a former civil service employee should be reinstated in his job despite his failure to acknowledge past ties with the Stasi on his application for the position. The judges agreed that the state had been justified in inquiring about his contacts with the MfS. But, they argued, the extent of his association with the secret police was open to interpretation, whereas there was every reason to think that he would still become a loyal and dedicated servant of German democracy. Since 1968 (presumably following the Warsaw Pact's invasion of Czechoslovakia), he had repeatedly given voice to his aversion to the GDR's system of government, even at the risk of jeopardizing his career. He had also been an enthusiastic participant in the events leading to the communist regime's collapse in 1989. He had only cast doubt on his character by failing to tell the truth on his application. Even here, however, the judges found his behavior understandable, for he had reasonably concluded, like many other job seekers in the first years of unification, that he would not be given a fair hearing.[73]

In rendering its decision, the court sided with several lower courts in taking another mitigating factor into consideration. It found that the employee's connection with the secret police was so far removed from the present that it no longer made sense to hold him accountable for his past errors.[74] By late 1996, this reasoning had become such a routine feature of judicial rulings on the issue of MfS disqualification that the Bundestag was persuaded to revise the Stasi Records law to limit the requests for information that could be made to the BStU. Provided that one had not engaged in serious criminal behavior or committed grave violations of human rights, the new law prohibited the Gauck agency from releasing data on one-time IMs if their formal contacts with the secret police had ended before December 31, 1975.[75]

The Competing Messages of Screening

By the end of the 1990s, in short, both the proponents and the opponents of using the Stasi files could have found ample evidence to support their positions, depending upon which level of the screening process they emphasized. On the one side, those who chose to concentrate on the court decisions could second the hopeful views that Gauck and others had articulated at the beginning of the decade. It was possible to identify the sources of Stasi-related injustice in the GDR and to make careful distinctions about degrees of wrongdoing without implicating the entire eastern German population in such offenses. This approach was implied by the courts' studied emphasis on due process and proportionality.

In fact, as the optimists turned their attention increasingly toward the more egregious cases of "conscious and deliberate" rights violations in the GDR and as the total number of dismissals for collaboration declined accordingly by the middle to late 1990s,[76] they could have added a corollary to this judgment. Although some eastern Germans had unquestionably violated the trust that others had placed in them by choosing to do business with the secret police, the evidence suggested, provided one interpreted it properly, that most had resisted these pressures. Indeed, officials at the BStU were happy to cite cases from the archives of individuals who had foregone the chance for personal advancement or financial gain and resisted the ministry's threats and entreaties.[77] Bundestag president Rita Süssmuth made precisely this point in an address on the fifth anniversary of the restoration of German unity. "It has become clear from the Stasi files," she declared on October 3, 1995, echoing Gauck 2 years earlier, "that the GDR was not at all a people of informants. Only a minority of around 2 percent of the population actually collaborated with the MfS. In fact, our access to the documents proves that there were many acts of civic courage and opposition among the [country's] citizens."[78]

On the other side, had one been looking for a bleaker message in the files, this could have been found in the process of assessing the democratic commitments of hundreds of thousands of eastern Germans over the first half of the decade. If the screening of public employees had been conducted in a disciplined and uniform manner in the first place and been confined strictly to the most serious offenders, it is conceivable that much of the confusion about the Stasi's role in East German society would have been avoided. But this was not the norm, nor could it have been easily implemented. From state to state, different standards of judgment were applied in determining which persons with clouded pasts would be allowed to retain their jobs or, conversely, which would be forced to relinquish their positions. In many instances, the way officials reacted to the brand "Stasi positive" apparently had more to do with location or economic utility than with an objective assessment of deeds.

It is true that these standards would be tightened with the passage of time and with increased experience on the part of the administrators charged with managing the MfS records. As a result, some persons who were initially penalized for their past activities would eventually be vindicated by the courts. For example, of 368 cases of disqualification brought before Berlin's courts by the end of 1996, at least 33 resulted in the reinstatement of the affected parties in their original jobs.[79] Still, it strains credulity to imagine that the casual onlooker would have taken the time and trouble to separate appearance from reality before forming an opinion about these processes. Hence, even though the courts' rulings testified to a much smaller degree of Stasi complicity than commentators had feared at the beginning of the 1990s, it seems likely that negative impressions of eastern Germany, once formed, would have been hard to change.

Then, too, it cannot have helped the collective image of the GDR citizenry that the search for Stasi collaborators rarely extended far beyond the new states in the East. Because the screening of public employees was left almost entirely to the individual *Länder*, few of Germany's western states (with the partial exceptions of Bavaria and Baden–Württemberg) ever instituted regular procedures for reviewing the backgrounds of their eastern emigrés. This had an ironic consequence. Had someone spent his or her entire life in East Germany, but then, amidst the turmoil of 1989 and 1990, made a calculated decision to move to the West before the official date of unification, he or she would have stood very little chance of ever being investigated for Stasi ties. For that matter, western German citizens were generally excluded from the vetting process anyway despite evidence to show that thousands had been active informants for the MfS before the opening of the Wall.[80]

Against this background, it can be no mystery why, well before the end of the decade, many western opinion leaders came out against using the Stasi's records to seek further revelations about wrongdoing in the GDR. In a moment of pique, even Chancellor Kohl hinted that, had he had his preference, he would have chosen not to allow "the completely evil stink [of the files]" to poison the atmosphere of unification.[81] Simultaneously, notable personalities like former federal president Richard von Weizsäcker, *Die Zeit* editor Marion Gräfin Dönhoff, and *Ostpolitik* architect Egon Bahr campaigned for a general amnesty for all Stasi informants.[82]

Nonetheless, it says something about the extent to which the issue of collaboration continued to sting in the skin of many eastern Germans that a vocal minority not only defended the policy but actually faulted Bonn for not going far enough with their efforts. For example, several of the BStU's state commissioners routinely criticized federal authorities for placing the emphasis in the examination of civil service employees "too one-sidedly on collaboration with the MfS" and for, in their description, "giving the MfS a special position which it never had in the apparatus of dictatorship."[83] In contrast, they claimed that a more historically informed approach would have been to include the entire SED nomenklatura in these investigations. In their view, the party had been the leading force behind the MfS and its crimes.

One way of responding to these demands was to point to the serious problems with putting such a strategy into effect. If it had been hard to show that proven Stasi operatives were guilty of disqualifying behavior, it was bound to be even more difficult to collect the same evidence against the party apparatchiks to whom these operatives were technically answerable. Furthermore, as critics of these proposals emphasized, one could not overlook a basic difference between MfS complicity and SED membership in everyday life in East Germany. Whereas people in the former category had made themselves potentially problematic civil servants because of the egregious betrayal of public and private trust implied by colluding with the secret police, party membership, if not internal party activities, had always been an open fact in the GDR. In this light, if SED members were singled out as well for punishment, one would need to demonstrate, as the FCC underscored in an important 1995 ruling, that some additional aspect of their behavior had made them unfit for public employment.[84]

There was another way of viewing these demands. This was to say that, much like those jurists who had previously sought to establish a seamless web of complicity around the Wall killings, the proponents of additional sanctions were simply looking in the wrong direction. Their mistake was in seeking to use the legal tools of the *Rechtsstaat* to provide the East with a deeper and more satisfying understanding of culpability. In the aftermath of World War II, Karl Jaspers called attention to this point by distinguishing among several different types of guilt which, in his opinion, had been incurred by the German people under the Nazi dictatorship. Among these, he included both criminal and moral guilt. The former category, he noted, in terms that were roughly comparable to the sort of disqualifying guilt used for Stasi operatives, was subject to the jurisdiction of a court of law and could be routinized accordingly. But the latter was subject to another court, the jurisdiction of individual conscience.[85]

In many respects, the first type of guilt was easier to pin down so long as one was inclined to look carefully. But the recognition of moral guilt, although more ephemeral, had the potential advantage of meeting the activists' desires for a more complete accounting of the diverse failings that helped to sustain multiple decades of authoritarian rule in East Germany. The challenge before them, as will be seen in Chapter 4, was to devise a suitable instrument for undertaking this broader assessment of the past and for inducing the citizenry to confront the demands of individual conscience. To this end, they turned to the Bundestag and to the closest thing to a German "truth commission," a parliamentary Enquete commission.

4

Moral Justice

ASSESSING THE COMPLETE
RECORD OF DICTATORSHIP

Less than a year into the process of national unification, many of the original dissidents who had mustered the courage to stand up to the SED regime had substantial grounds for worry. They feared that other eastern Germans had not really internalized the central moral lessons that, in their view, were to be drawn from four decades of communist dictatorship. The first months of the drive to national unity had been a time of tremendous exhilaration in the East as expectations soared that the GDR citizenry would immediately benefit from the fruits of West German capitalism. However, as rents and prices climbed and unemployment exploded in the wake of German currency union and the collapse of the region's basic industries, many easterners seemed, in the activists' eyes, to forget the deeper sources of their misfortune and to seek deceptively easy solutions to their problems.

Some younger eastern Germans vented their anger with the new system by associating with skinhead groups and neo-Nazi organizations and participating in scattered acts of violence against foreigners as epitomized by the bloody assault on a home for asylum seekers in the Saxon town of Hoyerswerda in September 1991. But just as disturbing for the former oppositionists, greater numbers of the citizens of the new *Länder* showed that they could still be swayed by nostalgic depictions of their former lives in the GDR. Demonstrating that popular memories about the shortcomings of state socialism were short-lived, many easterners who had not previously supported the SED did the unthinkable. They registered their discontent with the costs of unification by supporting the communist successor party, the Party of Democratic Socialism (PDS), in local and regional elections.[1]

There can be no doubt that a sizable measure of self-interest played into the activists' calculations in voicing concern over these developments. Despite the pivotal role they had played in the upheaval of 1989–90 and their many contributions to the peaceful transition out of communism, most had become politically marginal in a very short time. Surprisingly, self-styled citizens' parties, such as Alliance '90 and the East German Greens, won less than 5 percent of the eastern vote during the Volkskammer elections of March 1990. Furthermore, those self-described activists who successfully made the leap into the unified German Bundestag after October 3, 1990 (among them, Stephan Hilsberg, Angelika Barbe, Wolfgang Ullmann, Markus Meckel, Gerd Poppe, and Rainer Eppelmann), were rarely appointed to leading governmental or party posts. Moreover, they generally found their interest in wrestling with unresolved questions about the GDR past overshadowed by more mundane policymaking issues.

Yet aside from merely feeling neglected, the activists had genuine grounds for believing that the region's recent problems were at least partly attributable to the Federal Republic's inability to come to terms with the broader moral failings that had helped to sustain the East German dictatorship. Up to a point, most could agree that measures like criminal trials and the vetting of civil service employees were useful ways of beginning the process of bringing home the GDR's record of injustice. But because of their reliance on relatively narrow, legalistic definitions of guilt and innocence, these mechanisms tended to limit the public's understanding of the underlying forces at the root of the abuses and their contributions to the longevity of the communist regime. In the activists' view, far more ambitious steps were required to get the complete message about the East German experience across to its citizenry.

One proposal that was bandied about for months in late fall 1991 and early 1992 was for the German government to sponsor a series of public tribunals in the East that would enable the victims of the SED's policies to confront their oppressors in open settings and facilitate a candid discussion about the "difficult heritage of the 40 years of [GDR] history."[2] In the eyes of proponents like the Lutheran pastor Friedrich Schorlemmer, the Social Democratic politician Wolfgang Thierse, and Gauck, the advantage of such forums was that they could highlight the needs of people who had not been able to redress their grievances through the cumbersome and slow-moving procedures of the *Rechtsstaat*; moreover, the forums could bring victims and perpetrators together in a way that would never be possible through such devices as criminal trials.

However, even as the tribunal concept was being developed, it immediately ran into opposition in both parts of Germany because of apprehensions that it would transgress accepted notions of due process and legal security. Were East Germany's former officials, critics wondered, to be held up to public ignominy without being offered a reasonable chance to defend themselves? By what right did the tribunals' advocates assume they were entitled to sit in judgment on their eastern compatriots?[3]

Instead, the Bundestag took what its leaders thought to be the safer path, announcing in the early spring of 1992 that it would form a special parliamentary Enquete commission on the "history and consequences of the SED dictatorship."[4] On several occasions since the parliamentary reforms of 1969, policymakers had turned to such commissions of inquiry when they wished to solicit independent expert opinion on pending government legislation (e.g., the practice of psychiatric medicine, drug policy reform). In this case, an Enquete commission seemed to its advocates like the most sensible way of ensuring that a balanced perspective on the GDR would be presented to the German people. Because its members would be drawn from both parts of the nation and all of its major parties, one could expect them to approach their charge with a maximum of objectivity and fair-mindedness.

Nonetheless, there is reason to wonder whether this, supposedly the most historically self-conscious of the FRG's attempts at retrospective justice, actually realized its goals. Certainly, few observers would dispute the sincerity of the commission organizers to use the East German experience as a guide (to quote commission chairperson Rainer Eppelmann) "to change our laws, issue new decrees, and possibly correct our behavior so that we will not again find ourselves in the position of the ignorant child who, for a third time, touches the hot oven door and burns its fingers anew."[5] The history of the GDR would also prove eminently analyzable. However, the verdict one gives to the commission's work depends in great measure on the definition of success.

From a purely scholarly perspective, it seems indisputable that the over 15,000 pages of testimony and expertise the commission accumulated during its investigations represent a significant and lasting addition to the corpus of publicly accessible information about the GDR.[6] In many ways, these contributions complemented the huge stores of information made available at roughly the same time by the opening of the Stasi archives. Over a 25-month period, from May 1992 to May 1994, the body's 16 voting members (32 Bundestag deputies overall), 11 academic advisors, and substantial staff conducted a marathon-like 44 public hearings, met in 40 additional closed sessions, and held 150 related subcommittee hearings. As Eppelmann would later proclaim, "No university could have brought so many experts together so quickly."[7]

In the process, the commission considered some of the most hotly debated topics in the history of divided Germany. What motives did the GDR's leaders have in supporting a separate German state in 1949? Did the Socialist Unity Party ever enjoy meaningful autonomy in its relations with Moscow? To what extent did the GDR's Lutheran churches help or hinder their parishioners' efforts to call attention to the SED's human rights violations? Should West Germany's major parties have been better prepared to respond to the historical opportunity presented to them by the Wall's opening in November 1989?

Undoubtedly, the commission added an important element of personal catharsis to the task of redressing injustice by giving the floor to over 327 witnesses from both parts of Germany. To be sure, these hearings lacked much of the gut-wrenching immediacy of the confrontations between victims and perpetrators that would soon take place in the public sessions of the Truth and Reconciliation Commission in South Africa. Also missing was the systematic attention to individual cases and atrocities of Chile's National Commission on Truth and Reconciliation, its famous predecessor, which had wrapped up its hearings only a year earlier.

But of course, the value of personal witness cannot be discounted. Those testifying before the Enquete commission included not only high-profile figures in the FRG's relations with East Berlin, such as Chancellor Kohl, his Social Democratic predecessor Helmut Schmidt, and former Foreign Minister Hans-Dietrich Genscher, but also many of the unsung victims of SED rule. It can safely be said that these individuals would otherwise never have had the chance to tell their stories of everyday hardship and abuse. There was the woman who was harassed and finally arrested by the Stasi merely for requesting permission to visit her infant son in West Berlin, the industrial worker who was discriminated against when he refused to carry a weapon in his Kombinat's paramilitary training exercises, a school director who was forced out of his job because his religious beliefs prevented him from joining the SED, and two grieving parents who were kept from meeting with their daughter while she lay on her deathbed in West Germany.[8]

However, despite these virtues, the Bundestag initiative came up short on one crucial measure of success. Once again, the issue was how much the body's members were really committed to taking history seriously in accounting for the GDR's ills. As will be found by examining the commission's treatment of three sensitive topics in its final report to parliament of June 1994[9] (the relationship between the SED government and country's churches, the practice of the West German *Deutschlandpolitik*, and the seeming passivity of the East German population over decades of dictatorial rule), its members were driven as much by their own narrow political agendas as by the desire to uncover the truth about the moral choices that had been available in the GDR. Consequently, there were notable respects in which the commission failed to present the East German record in such a way that one could identify mistakes and missed opportunities while helping to bring the two German populations together again.

Finding Fault with the Churches

Among the many issues covered by the Enquete commission, it would be hard to imagine a more sensitive topic for the eastern activists on the body than the complex relationship between the GDR's Lutheran churches and the SED leadership in the years before national unification. On the one hand, if they were fully honest with themselves, many of those who had once congregated in opposition circles had East Germany's religious institutions to thank for providing them with a safe haven from a predatory state in times when the only other way of expressing their dissatisfaction with the ruling regime was to apply for permission to emigrate to the West. But on the other hand, to these same dissidents who were worried about learning the right lessons from the past and countering such tendencies as the rise of the PDS, the churches epitomized all of the moral folly that was associated with any attempt to do business with dictators. By the middle to late 1980s, in fact, the churches and the dissidents were practically at loggerheads over the issue, for each had arrived at fundamentally different ideas about what steps were necessary for effecting meaningful social and political change in East Germany. Although church leaders, like the outspoken managing director of the consistory of Berlin–Brandenburg, Manfred Stolpe, were convinced that the only realistic opportunities for improving the quality of life in the GDR were to be found in continued negotiations with the communist government, many oppositionists wanted to bypass the state entirely and bring the case for a new political order directly to the East German citizenry.

With the benefit of hindsight, it should be clear why the activists on the Enquete commission would later assume that the march of historical events was squarely on their side in reviewing this record. By the end of the decade, the church establishment seems to have greatly overestimated the progress that could still be made through contacts with the SED. Was this not the lesson to be gained, critics asked, from the undeniable intransigence of the Honecker government on key issues in its waning years and the regime's swift and total collapse in fall 1989 at the first expression of concerted opposition to its policies? However, to acknowledge this viewpoint alone would be to ignore the much more complicated circumstances that had led church leaders to establish contacts with the communist regime in the first place.

Over the first decade of the GDR's existence, there were few grounds for expecting that anything beneficial would come from the strained relationship between church and state. Despite an initial period of postwar euphoria when the Soviet occupation authorities were eager to incorporate religious institutions into a broad antifascist front, church–state relations had progressively deteriorated with the GDR's founding, especially after Walter Ulbricht announced the country's transition to socialism in 1952. As propagators of an alien belief system who maintained direct ties to West Germany through the all-German Evangelical Church in Germany (EKD), the Lutheran churches, in the SED's eyes, were among the most dangerous outposts of bourgeois thought in the GDR. Under these circumstances, although the government's policy on organized religion was arguably never as repressive as that of other East European communist states, one cannot discount the difficulties faced by church authorities. In flagrant violation of the GDR's 1949 constitution, religious instruction was prohibited in the schools, pastors were routinely subjected to police harassment and intimidation, and the SED relentlessly sought to wean churchgoers away from their faith through the propagation of scientific atheism. At the party's fifth congress in 1958, Ulbricht even went so far as to proclaim 10 commandments of socialist morality.

For their part, Lutheran authorities were no more inclined to modify their behavior to meet the demands of a hostile state. In the mid-1950s, for example, many came into repeated conflict with the regime over its efforts to popularize an alternative confirmation ceremony, the *Jugendweihe*. At the time, even otherwise compliant pastors and bishops took the view that there was no room in their flocks for young people who made the mistake of taking part in this Marxist passage to adulthood and accepting dialectical materialism as their faith.[10]

In fairness, the churches' uncompromising stand on relations with the GDR government probably made good sense as long as the border between East Berlin and West Berlin remained open. For the time being, they could count on receiving an uninterrupted flow of financial assistance and moral support from their counterparts in the West and even dream of the day the two Germanys would be reunited. But with the Wall's construction and the loss of this last opening to the FRG in August 1961, Lutheran leaders were grudgingly forced to concede, as Bishop Werner Krusche would tell the Enquete commission in December 1993, that a separate East German state was "no interim event or intermezzo."[11] Under these conditions, their only hope for restoring contacts with the Federal Republic was with the consent and cooperation of the party regime. Likewise, only the East German government could facilitate such mundane tasks as the construction and renovation of church buildings, let alone provide for an environment that was not totally inimical to religious observance. As a result, church officials slowly but deliberately searched for ways of expressing their institutional identity in an era of closed borders, of becoming a "church within socialism," as the slogan went, rather than merely alongside it or against it.[12]

One key step in this direction was provided by the churches' incorporation, in June 1969, into a united eastern German federation, or *Kirchenbund*, that was no longer formally tied to the EKD in West Germany. Another was signified by the church leadership's cautious but deliberate decision to seek a modus vivendi with the SED. This strategy seemed to pay off following Erich Honecker's ascension to the party leadership in 1971. For its own reasons, the East German government had come to believe that it had more to gain by cooperating with its religious institutions than by further efforts to isolate them. This meeting of the minds set the stage for a momentous summit meeting between Honecker and the executive board of the *Kirchenbund* on March 6, 1978. On this occasion, the SED general secretary announced that as long as the churches were willing to work with his government and contribute to a spirit of reciprocal trust and understanding, there was no reason why East German Christians should not enjoy the same rights and privileges as any other GDR citizens.[13]

Naturally, Lutheran leaders recognized all along that the regime's more accommodating posture was designed as much to channel their energies and co-opt them into supporting the status quo as to reward them for good behavior. In return for their implicit cooperation, state authorities showed that they were willing to accept the churches' legitimate position in East German society and even to engage the churches in dialogue on several subjects of mutual concern such as world poverty, the proliferation of nuclear weapons, and environmental protection. But at the same time, the churches were expected to toe a strict line on acceptable criticism of official policy, and their leaders were encouraged to exercise a restraining influence on pastors and parishioners who failed to adhere to this standard.

From the vantage point of the 1990s, the instances when the churches actually lived up to this conservatizing function may seem to stand out. This was the case, for example, in January 1982 when the dissident scientist Robert Havemann and a young East Berlin pastor named Rainer Eppelmann circulated a petition among the city's intellectual community that called for the removal of all "occupation forces" from East Germany and West Germany and for the neutralization of both German states. Although the so-called Berlin appeal soon garnered over two thousand signatures, it was revealing that the Berlin–Brandenburg church hierarchy (to which Eppelmann was subordinated) moved just as fast to distance itself from the document's provocative language. In its view, the appeal represented a "distorted view" of current realities in central Europe, and it was "unsupportable in the discipleship of Christ."[14]

Nonetheless, it must also be said that, over this same period, the churches contributed in significant ways to the germination of the oppositional culture that would eventually result in the revolutionary events of 1989–90. First, far from always kowtowing to official policy, Lutheran officials repeatedly demonstrated that, on decisive questions

of faith and conscience, there were unmistakable limits to their willingness to compromise with the state. For example, over the late 1970s
and early 1980s, many pastors put their careers and livelihoods on the
line by openly opposing the government's efforts to make paramilitary
training a mandatory feature of all secondary education in the GDR.
Then, too, the more the churches succeeded in defining an appropriate
niche for themselves in which they could accomplish their objectives,
the more they became, in the process, a natural sanctuary for countless
East Germans – conscientious objectors, ecological activists, would-be
émigrés, and other nonconformists – who no longer fit into the plans
of the governing regime.

Ironically, many of these same grass-roots activists would later fault
the church establishment for, in their view, failing to support them
when they most needed its help by taking a more overtly critical stand
on the SED's policies. But this dissatisfaction should not be allowed
to obscure an equally indisputable fact about the churches. Without
such a semiautonomous sphere in which to test their ideas and debate
contending strategies, the oppositionists would most likely not have
been prepared to capitalize on the regime's weaknesses as the decade
drew to a close.[15]

For all of these reasons, it would have been difficult for the former dissidents who sat on the Bundestag's Enquete commission to
deny that there were some positive moments in the churches' delicate
balancing act with the East German regime. Thus, when Eppelmann
opened the body's hearings on "the behavior of the Lutheran churches
toward the SED-state in divided Germany" in a public session in the
Thuringian city of Erfurt on December 14, 1993, it is telling that he
began his remarks by assuming an outwardly generous pose toward his
fellow clergymen. He underscored the commission's respect for those
churches which, in his careful depiction, "had searched for and found
an independent path in an environment that was defined by ideological and political antagonism." In the same spirit, he also extended the
commission's gratitude for "all of the help the churches of the GDR
made available to so many people in their differing times of need."[16]

Still, what Eppelmann went on to say showed that he and many
other eastern parliamentarians on the body could not easily forget, or
forgive, the compromises that these religious bodies had struck with
the party–state in the years when some Germans (himself included?)
had supposedly chosen a path of greater suffering for their beliefs.

According to the author of the Berlin appeal, the Lutheran churches, "to which many of us were and remain bound in a very personal and direct manner," were by no means free of "mistaken judgments, failures, and guilt." Why was it the case, Eppelmann probed, somewhat hyperbolically, that their leaders had been much slower to condemn religious persecution than their counterparts elsewhere in East Europe? Why had they not consistently come to the aid of militant pastors who were resisting the oppressive hand of the SED? For that matter, what was amiss with the churches as Christian institutions that had made them, along the way, the subject of such profound disappointment for so many East Germans?[17]

These complaints would have been completely understandable had the Enquete commission subsequently sought to maintain a balance between finding fault with the churches for their shortcomings and crediting them for their accomplishments. On the latter point, in fact, the body's members heard a great deal of positive testimony about the churches' achievements under difficult circumstances. Of the commission's 18 volumes of testimony and expertise, two entire volumes (or more than 1,600 pages) are devoted to the activities of the churches. Within these, one does not have to look hard to find examples of the salutary influence that religious institutions exercised on East German society. Indeed, one might even say the preponderance of evidence supports this conclusion. In hard times, the churches contributed to a greater sense of openness and hope among the East German people by offering alternatives to the government's official conceptions of truth and justice and by providing the first vital links among the disparate groups that would constitute the GDR's dissident culture.[18]

Yet, notably, when we turn to the Enquete commission's shorter and more important 305-page final report to the Bundestag of May 1994, it is revealing that many of the document's parliamentarian authors were almost instinctively inclined to side with testimony to the opposite effect.[19] Significantly, there is little in the Christian Democratic–Free Democratic majority opinion in the report to indicate that East Germany's religious leaders ever had defensible reasons for eschewing a policy of open confrontation with the East German government, let alone that this strategy would have allowed them to make progress in improving the general lot of Christians in the GDR.[20] In the final document, the *Kirchenbund*'s formation in 1969 is portrayed mainly as an "important partial goal of the SED's church policy" that was only adopted over the misgivings of most leading members of the EKD in both parts of divided Germany (p. 167). In like fashion, the notion of a "church within socialism" is described as a concept with "no lasting theological effect," which, the report adds, "hardly found acceptance in local congregations and was largely ignored" (p. 168). Finally, the *Kirchenbund*'s 1978 meeting with Honecker is characterized almost exclusively in terms of the controversy it provoked. "Many church critics," the final report advises, viewed the event as a "betrayal of the church" that bespoke an "increasing affinity of the churches to the socialist state." Moreover, subsequent encounters with SED officials were received with "incomprehension" by parishioners, many of whom, it notes, were fearful of the consequences of a "'truce' or even a 'kissing-up course'" between church and state (p. 169).

In fact, with only these pages as a guide, the uninformed reader could easily be misled into thinking that, in the last decade before the GDR's fall, the Lutheran establishment was interested in nothing more than solidifying amicable relations with the communist regime and was opposed on all accounts to allowing groups within its fold to jeopardize this understanding. For example, we are informed that with the rise of critical voices within their parishes and local communities, church leaders "saw themselves constantly challenged to abandon their own self-imposed taboos" (p. 171). Yet far from grasping the implications of these steadily more vociferous attacks on the SED's authority, the report would have us believe that those in command in the Lutheran hierarchy remained unflinchingly wedded to an accommodationist course. "Aside from differences of views in individual cases," the document's authors declare, "the church leadership of the GDR was inclined either to wait out this development or to reject it entirely" (p. 169). A more damning allegation is that, when the dissenting groups' protests started to take on a life of their own in the late 1980s, Lutheran authorities were largely opposed to this development: "Church leaders responded to these discussions, which on the one hand were closely tied to the realization of the Christian message but on the other hand often brought external influences with them into the churches' realm, by trying to limit them as much as possible" (p. 171).

In this light, to the extent the final report has anything positive to say about religious activity in the 1980s, it will come as no surprise that it is almost exclusively to praise those individual Christians and dissident pastors – among whose numbers several of the eastern German members of the Enquete commission could count themselves – who were bold enough to speak out against further negotiations with the communist regime (p. 168). "Within the churches," we are informed, "there was a growing number of people who regarded the refusal to accede to the real-socialist demands of the SED dictatorship as a 'commendable activity'" (p. 169). Although these individuals generally worked within the protected environment of the churches to express their views, their aims went far beyond the limited aspirations of the Lutheran hierarchy. "Here," one finds,

> critical questions were debated without a care for whether limits were being exceeded or taboos violated. Here, meaningful social change was realized, open communication was practiced, and individuals were trained in nonviolent action. Here, one put coalitions to a test that went beyond established ideological views and political boundaries. (p. 171)

In the final analysis, the document concludes, these were the groups that left the churches in the GDR's last years and then "[set] in motion the transformational process that directly led to the political turning point [*Wende*] of fall 1989" (p. 172).

Against this background, it was presumably small comfort to the churches' defenders that not all of the parliamentarians on the Enquete commission were inclined to go quite this far in criticizing the churches for their dealings with the East German state. In a partially dissenting minority opinion to the final report, the Social Democratic members of the body presented an analysis of the church–state relationship that qualified and softened some of the majority's harsher findings.

For these participants, a major area of concern involved intimations in the document that one of the chief factors behind the churches' failure to take the dissidents more seriously was their thorough penetration by informants of the Stasi. This weakness was compounded by the inclination of at least some church representatives to treat known MfS agents as legitimate discussion partners for conducting church business. From the SPD's perspective, one did not have to read too closely between the lines to see that, on both points, the CDU majority on the commission clearly had Manfred Stolpe, the current

Social Democratic minister–president of Brandenburg, in mind in making these allegations. Provocatively, in January 1992, just before the commission began its initial hearings, Stolpe had admitted to having regular "confidential discussions" with the MfS as part of his church responsibilities. Although he denied committing any improprieties, there were persistent rumors that he had consciously worked for the Stasi as an unofficial collaborator.[21]

It may have reflected their own dissident roots that, rather than coming directly to Stolpe's defense, the authors of the dissenting opinion took pains to emphasize both the irregularity of the Stasi contacts and the misgivings they had evoked among religious circles (p. 187). But on the more important question of the MfS's influence on church policy, the Social Democrats urged their parliamentary colleagues to keep the whole issue in proper perspective. As they insisted, the evidence before the commission suggested that the secret police had managed to infiltrate almost all of the leading oppositional groups in the GDR. Yet although the Stasi's presence in the dissident community was, in their reading, "considerably higher than in the churches" and "presumably had a much greater and more burdensome influence on their political activities," it hardly seemed right that the majority report had not even brought up this side of the story (p. 185).

In addition, the Social Democrats tried to put a more favorable light on the church leadership's contributions to transforming East German society in the final years of communist rule. Notwithstanding "all of their weaknesses and mistakes, failures and anxieties," the minority opinion notes, the GDR's religious institutions had consistently been a major force in moderating conflicts between the state and the country's burgeoning dissident groups. Further, they had kept many of these opposition elements alive and therefore available for later confrontations with the SED by providing them with meeting rooms and infrastructure to sustain their activities. In this sense, it was only fair that the churches should finally get the recognition they deserved for ensuring that "independent and free-minded thought and behavior were a living reality in the GDR throughout all of the years of totalitarian rule" (p. 186).

Nonetheless, if the Christian Democratic or Free Democratic deputies on the Enquete commission recognized the validity of even these careful arguments, they did not show it. Instead of engaging the SPD's claims, the majority parties simply dismissed the dissenting opinion as a politically motivated attempt to divert attention from the churches' dubious interactions with the East German state and, above all, with the Stasi (p. 188).

A Different Stand on the Deutschlandpolitik

Because the Enquete commission found so much to fault about the behavior of the GDR's Lutheran churches in the 1970s and 1980s, one would logically have expected the body to reach similarly critical conclusions about an equally controversial chapter in the history of divided Germany: the conduct of West Germany's *Deutschlandpolitik*, or policy on national reunification, during the GDR's final decades. Like the churches, the FRG's leaders had come to see the SED as their preferred negotiating partner at this juncture in the two states' histories, and, at times, they could legitimately be criticized for having put the health and welfare of this relationship above all other concerns, including the political fortunes of the dissidents. In addition, for those eastern Germans who were convinced that their interests had been slighted in the unification process, there was a measure of poetic justice to be found in showing that the GDR's former citizens were not the only Germans who had to face up to their mistakes. Like East Berlin, it seemed that Bonn, too, would have to admit to making its share of errors over the years in dealing with the communist regime.

Commission Chair Eppelmann was especially intent on having his body make this point. As he told an interviewer on March 3, 1992, "We must be prepared to talk [not only] about the lives of the 16 million but also about the behavior of the 60 million – that is, the West Germans – at least in those cases where they directly or indirectly affected living conditions in the GDR or the behavior of those who lived there (rulers as well as ruled), either through what they did or what they did not do."[22]

Yet, even though the parliamentary commission was not lacking for members who would have been happy to take part in this critique, the final report's treatment of West Germany's *Deutschlandpolitik* is remarkably restrained in comparison to its claims about the churches – almost, although not quite, to the point of glossing over the mixed messages behind Bonn's interactions with East Berlin. Notably, this appears to have been the case not so much because the practice of Bonn's national policy in the GDR's last years was unassailable on moral and practical grounds but rather because this was one of the few issues on which western interest in the outcome of the hearings was great enough to limit the influence of the former dissidents on the commission.

To understand how the Enquete commission might have arrived at a more critical assessment than it did of the FRG's handling of the national question, it is helpful to distinguish between the basic strategy that undergirded Bonn's contacts with the SED leadership and some of the more problematic expressions of this policy along the way. On the former issue, there is nearly universal agreement that the FRG's options were highly circumscribed. Once the Berlin Wall was constructed, West Germany's leaders had little choice but to treat the East German regime as a serious interlocutor if they wanted to keep memories of a unified national culture alive in both parts of the divided nation and contribute in small but meaningful ways to "improved living conditions" (menschliche Erleichterungen) in the East. Indeed, in return for recognizing the de facto existence of a separate German state, the Social–Liberal coalition governments of the 1970s and the Christian Democratic–Liberal coalition that succeeded them in 1982 were able to make undeniable progress in reestablishing physical and emotional links between the two German populations. Beginning with the signing of the inter-German Basic treaty in 1972, millions of West Germans were given the opportunity to visit the GDR on a regular basis and to rekindle old friendships and family ties. In due course, over the ensuing years, East German authorities were gradually brought around to allow smaller, but still significant, numbers of their own citizens to travel to the West – even to the point of permitting some of the most disaffected among them to emigrate permanently to the FRG.[23]

Although West German officials could point with justifiable pride to these accomplishments, serious questions could be raised about the lengths to which they were willing to go in the 1980s to make their relationship with East Berlin work. As talks between the two German capitals became increasingly focused on mundane and practical issues, such as the amount of deutsche marks westerners were required to exchange for ostmarks upon entering the GDR, the expansion of inter-German trade ties, and the creation of sister-city partnerships, representatives of all the major parties seemed at times to be almost hyperattuned to the need to avoid antagonizing the East German regime. Hence, references to long-time shibboleths like "reunification" and the restoration of the pre-1949 national state were replaced in most politicians' speeches with less provocative appeals to "reduce the burdens of division" and to make the Germanys' borders "more permeable."

Unquestionably, of all the FRG's political parties, the opposition Social Democrats and the Greens were prepared to go the farthest in courting the SED leadership. By the mid-1980s, they were openly calling for a formal inter-German dialogue on security questions and, in the case of the SPD, for talks on "common values."[24] Some of their members even went as far as to advocate the recognition of a separate GDR citizenship and the exchange of fully accredited ambassadors with East Berlin. For its part, the Kohl government was somewhat less openly inclined than its rivals to give ground on the fundamental question of German nationhood. However, it, too, showed a noticeable readiness to move away from the confrontational rhetoric that had characterized Christian Democratic national policy only one decade earlier. Thus, when Helmut Kohl received Erich Honecker for his long-anticipated official "working visit" to Bonn on September 7, 1987, the chancellor was at pains to stress that the bulk of his conversations with the SED's general secretary would be concentrated on the "doable" (das Machbare) and not on issues that were "at the moment unresolvable."[25] In a joint communiqué the two leaders released at the conclusion of these meetings, both agreed that their governments would "[respect] each other's independence and autonomy in internal and external affairs" and proceed with "understanding and realism" in the ongoing pursuit of "practical goals."[26]

Still, for all of the concrete gains registered between Bonn and East Berlin as a result of these elite-level contacts, it is clear in retrospect that they left the Kohl government and the major opposition parties conspicuously unprepared to respond to the increasingly vociferous grassroots challenges to the SED's authority that emerged at the end of the 1980s. When the East German regime turned to punitive measures to quell rising discontent among its activist intellectuals and within the churches in the first few months of 1988 and expelled some of its most vocal critics to the West, West German politicians were practically at a loss to know how to respond. They alternately demanded that East Berlin exhibit more "tolerance and generosity" in its domestic affairs but still defended the virtues of continued close cooperation with SED authorities.[27] Similarly, when many of these opposition forces coalesced into the citizens' groups and nascent political parties – Neues

Forum, the SDP (Social Democratic party of East Germany), Democracy Now, Democratic Awakening – that were to topple the Honecker regime only a year and a half later, few of the FRG's representatives (with the partial exception of the Greens, who had long favored more direct contacts with the dissidents) could even recognize the names of the key individuals involved.

Against this backdrop, therefore, it would have been perfectly understandable if the Enquete commission's final report had contained some pointed criticisms about both the tenor and the content of Bonn's *Deutschlandpolitik*. Certainly, many of the East German oppositionists who felt left out of the FRG's strategic calculations during these years expected that their experiences and frustrations would be a central part of the body's conclusions. "We were always there," Neues Forum cofounder Bärbel Bohley complained in June 1992 shortly after the commission took up its work, "but we weren't taken seriously."[28] In the same spirit, Eppelmann lamented that West German politicians had worked so hard to ingratiate themselves with the powerholders in East Berlin when they could have reached out to other groups in the GDR. To his mind, these policymakers had come to the mistaken conclusion that "maintaining peace was more important than supporting freedom." As a result, when Honecker came to Bonn in 1987, FRG officials treated the East German dictator "almost the same way they treated the president of France or the prime minister of Britain."[29]

However, to have anticipated that the commission's findings would be driven primarily by self-critical reflections would have been to underestimate a central difference between the church–state relationship in the GDR and the practice of Bonn's national policy. Whereas the behavior of the churches under communist rule hardly constituted an "existential moment" (to quote sociologist Rainer Lepsius) for the majority of Germans who had grown up in West Germany,[30] the *Deutschlandpolitik* was an issue of much greater political sensitivity to western policymakers because of their glaring lack of preparedness for the events of 1989–90.

In the first all-German elections to the Bundestag in December 1990, claims and counterclaims about which parties had supposedly done the most or, conversely, the least to hasten the GDR's demise had played a not-so-subtle role in many politicians' campaigns for public office. Making the Enquete commission's hearings on this subject of even greater consequence, however, was that the body was slated to present its findings to parliament in 1994. This was a year most politicians were already regarding as a *Superwahljahr* ("super election year") for the FRG. In addition to national elections to the Bundestag, 18 other state and metropolitan votes were scheduled to take place over the year, including elections to all the parliaments of the new eastern *Länder*.[31] In this context, party strategists could scarcely afford to overlook the possibility that anything the commission had to say about Bonn's dealings with East Berlin in the waning years of national division might come back to haunt them in the collective judgment of the German electorate.

In this light, it is revealing that the *Deutschlandpolitik* provided the occasion for one of the most openly antagonistic partisan exchanges in the early rounds of the parliamentary debates over the Enquete commission. Willy Brandt, the éminence grise behind Bonn's opening to the East in the 1960s, had led off his remarks by cautioning his listeners about the dangers of judging the German–German record exclusively from the privileged vantage point of hindsight, and he frankly endorsed the need to make "differentiated judgments" about the subject. But then, ignoring his own advice, the former chancellor went on to single out Erich Honecker's cordial reception in Bonn for scrutiny. In 1987, he noted in an unmistakable criticism of Helmut Kohl, "one was hardly as clever as in 1989." "Otherwise," Brandt observed, "the attention that was paid the former chair of the State Council of the GDR would have been much more modest."[32]

In raising the delicate issue of the Honecker visit, Brandt most likely meant to deflect public attention from the potentially more serious criticisms that could be leveled against his own party's relationship with East Germany over the same period. But if this was Brandt's intention, his remarks seem to have had the opposite effect. Although he was not scheduled to speak at the time, Kohl angrily rose on the floor of the Bundestag to accuse his predecessor of fostering new myths about the inter-German relationship. "I do not have to explain to you," the chancellor underscored, "that out of the many decisions in my nearly 10 years in office – Herr colleague Brandt, you must know this – the decision to host the visit was one of the most difficult [that I faced]." Had Honecker been received in any other fashion, he stressed, "the visit simply would not have taken place."[33]

Rising in Kohl's defense, the CDU/CSU parliamentary leader Wolfgang Schäuble was quick to affirm that the governing coalition was not about to allow its Social Democratic adversaries to gain the offensive on the national policy. Unlike the SPD, Schäuble lectured the assembled deputies, the chancellor's party had consistently "held fast to the goal of [German] unity in freedom, even when it was criticized for being reactionary." Indeed, Kohl himself had exemplified this toughness in an "unforgettable speech" on the occasion of Honecker's visit: "Up to his fall," it seemed, "Honecker was never confronted with a more relentless [attack] upon the injustice of division and oppression."[34] Finally, even though Schäuble professed to have no interest in engaging in partisan conflict over these issues, he could not resist pointing out that "in the last phase of the GDR's history, [the Social Democrats] had committed the greatest mistakes in the *Deutschlandpolitik*."[35]

All of these conflicts are in evidence if one looks closely between the lines of the Enquete commission's final report.[36] Nevertheless, it says something for the political sensitivity of the issue that the major parties were careful not to give their rivals any ammunition that could later be turned against them. This factor helps to account for the body's noticeably more cautious handling of the national policy.

If the Kohl administration had ever been guilty of misguided judgments or miscues in its dealings with East Berlin, this would not be apparent in those sections of the report that were drafted by its deputies. So triumphal is the document's tone that one could easily come away from reading it with the mistaken impression that the ruling parties had always held the moral high ground and that the drive to German unity was preordained by the Christian Democratic–Free Democratic initiatives of the 1980s. In a section devoted exclusively to the national question, for example, we find that the governing coalition's actions were consistently defined by "clear principles" (p. 131). Its leaders' references to the goal of national reunification in public speeches and official documents were "in no way mere declarations" but "distinct statements of policy, aimed at making it clear both at home and abroad that the German question was still open, historically, legally, and politically." Furthermore, the report tells us that "the question of human rights and their denial in the GDR" was always "at the center" of the Kohl administration's interactions with the East German government as was the "unjust character of the SED regime and the unnatural nature of the division of Germany" (pp. 131–2).

If there was any respect in which the FRG's pursuit of its long-term national goals was flawed or misguided, it was – again, in the majority opinion's version of the truth – only that the governing parties' adver-saries in the SPD had failed to be equally observant of the national ideal. Hence, at times, "demands were raised in the circles of the opposition [to regard] the German question as no longer open and to examine whether the obligation contained in the preamble of the Basic Law to work for reunification should not be revised" (p. 132).

Predictably, the Social Democratic members of the commission were no more willing to allow their opponents the opportunity to get away with such charges than to give them a monopoly of virtue in their depiction of the path to unification. Yet, rather than launch-ing a frontal assault on the governing coalition's policies, as Brandt had seemed instinctively inclined to do, the SPD simply sought to use its dissenting vote in the commission report to relativize the CDU's accomplishments in the scales of public opinion.

If Kohl's administration had accomplished anything of value, we are told, this was not because of any special insight or determination on the part of the Christian Democratic leadership. To the contrary, in the opposition's view, the ruling parties had merely copied the proven policies of their Social Democratic predecessors, Brandt and Schmidt. Throughout the 1980s, it seems, "[the CDU], too, had focused on dialogue and cooperation with the powerholders of the SED-system and oriented itself to the stability of the GDR." Further, "this was a way of achieving improved conditions and greater cooperation between the states, so that through a series of small steps, one might increase the possibility that Germans from East and West could meet with each other."

Granted, at one point the minority opinion acknowledges that Helmut Kohl and others on the German Right paid more lip service than previous administrations to the "openness" of the German ques-tion. Nonetheless, the authors of this opinion immediately qualify the observation by noting that this rhetoric corresponded to "no operative policy and no concrete perspectives about unification." "This was," the document flatly points out, "more a matter of domestically oriented rhetoric that primarily caused irritations abroad" (p. 140).

In one respect, we should probably credit the Social Democratic deputies on the Enquete commission with being slightly more open to self-criticism than their counterparts in the CDU. These members were at least willing to concede (although this, too, may have been a matter of political strategizing) that one could raise pertinent questions about their party's failure, and of course that of the federal government as well, to look beyond the SED in the 1980s for possible discussion partners in the East.[37] In this respect, the minority opinion invites the reader to ask "whether and why . . . the Federal Republic gave the developing opposition movements [in the GDR] too little support and why it failed to recognize their significance." There was an undeniable disparity, the document adds, between the intensity of the talks that took place at the governmental level and the dearth of contacts with oppositional elements (p. 145).

Unfortunately, instead of using these questions as a springboard for further reflections about possible missed opportunities in the FRG's relations with East Berlin, the authors of the dissenting opinion were evidently unwilling to risk providing their opponents with embarrassing material that could someday be used against them. As a result, much like the CDU/CSU before them, the Social Democrats rested their case against their country's one-time leaders by turning to their own contributions to the restoration of German unity. According to this selective reading of the inter-German past, one could give serious consideration to the possibility that the "first phase of the [FRG's] detente policy" with the GDR (i.e., the period between 1969 and 1982, when the Social Democrats were the dominant party in Bonn) had laid the foundations for the dissident movement in the East and thereby for national reunification. Without this initial opening to the East, the document concludes, the conditions would never have been created "under which the people of the GDR were able to act in a more self-determined and politically responsible way" (p. 145).

No doubt, some truth could be found in all of these assessments of the twists and turns of the FRG's national policy, Christian Democratic and Social Democratic alike. The restoration of regular government-to-government contacts with East Berlin and the dramatic improvement in travel opportunities between the Germanys unquestionably contributed in manifold ways to the politically charged environment of summer and fall 1989. Just the same, one could hardly have blamed a skeptic for observing that the contending German parties made for strange historians.[38] Even the Bundestag's official news magazine, *Das Parlament*, could not resist a wry observation about the parliamentarians' inability to put their political interests aside in addressing the merits of the German–German relationship. "One thing was clear," the paper noted shortly after the hearings had concluded: "All of the politicians in the CDU, the SPD, and the FDP who had responsibilities in this matter acted, according to their own admission, exactly as they had to act – they were all right, and [they were] all successful."[39] Additionally, one could not miss the irony of the western parties' sudden interest in the Enquete commission's proceedings. Had their political stakes in the body's findings been less pronounced, their leading representatives might well have chosen not to become involved in these debates at all.

Mixed Emotions about the Silent Majority

Perhaps we should not be surprised by the self-serving quality of all of these interpretations of the recent German past. Was it not the logical consequence of the GDR's total collapse and the Federal Republic's emergence as the unequivocal victor in the 40-year-long contest over German national identity that those who came out on top, historically speaking, would want their own versions of the truth to triumph? "It's not unnatural at all," the commission's sole representative from the postcommunist PDS, Dietmar Keller, acknowledged when asked about the final report in June 1995. "If you use a parliament to investigate historical truth, then only those who control the [parliamentary] majority will be victorious."[40]

This circumstance also meant, however, that the report would have very little to say about the perspectives of other groups and individuals who lacked either the political passions or the electoral power required to assert their interests. Interestingly, for a document that was supposed to foster, in its own self-description, "understanding for those persons who lived and suffered under the SED dictatorship" (p. 281), this principle seems to have been borne out by the highly ambivalent stand the Enquete commission ultimately adopted on a third topic of its investigations, the ambiguous relationship between the East German citizenry and the communist authorities.

The relative passivity of the GDR population over the four decades the SED was in power was probably the closest thing to a neuralgic point for the dissidents on the parliamentary body. Aside from the workers' uprising of June 16–17, 1953, which nearly brought down the Ulbricht government before the rebellion was brutally suppressed by Soviet troops, organized expressions of discontent in the GDR were rare and largely isolated events. Up to the sealing of the country's borders in 1961, those East Germans who were most dissatisfied with their government's policies generally voted with their feet by fleeing to the West. Yet once this option was eliminated, a majority of the Germans who remained behind appear, for the most part, to have accommodated themselves grudgingly to their fate. They outwardly conformed to the public symbols and rituals of life under communist rule, such as mass parades and uncontested elections, while they kept their private grievances and complaints to themselves or confined them to a deliberately small circle of family members and friends.[41]

To recognize this point is not to deny the existence of enormous dissatisfaction with the communist system just below the surface image of societal calm in the GDR. This popular discontent finally manifested itself by exploding in the demonstrations and street protests of October and November 1989. Still, from the perspective of the tiny handful of oppositionists who had been willing to stand up to the regime much earlier and who had sometimes paid a heavy price for expressing their convictions, one had to pose the question that had already been raised in a related way about the Lutheran hierarchy and the practitioners of the *Deutschlandpolitik*: Why had it taken so long for the East German man or woman on the street to gather the internal resources to give voice to these grievances?

At least in the Enquete commission's early conceptual stages, the body's advocates seem to have wanted to make the issue of popular acquiescence in the SED's policies a major focus of their investigations. "Why was it the case," Eppelmann wondered aloud, only a few weeks before the Bundestag had approved the commission, "that hundreds of thousands of GDR citizens took part in [officially sponsored] street demonstrations on May 1 or on October 7, the GDR's founding day, to cheer those who had imprisoned them for 30 years? Why did 98 percent of elementary students become members of the Young Pioneers, [the equivalent of the National Socialist] Cub Scouts Union [*Verband der Staatspimpfe*]? And why were 85–95 percent of all state employees members of the FDGB [Free-German Trade Union Federation] when almost everyone knew the association had little to do with trade unions?" "Was it simply," he added with a tinge of sarcasm, "because they hoped to get cheaper vacations?"[42]

Likewise, in the parliamentary debates of March 1992, the eastern Social Democratic deputy, pastor, and last foreign minister of the GDR, Markus Meckel, advised his colleagues that the commission would only succeed at its self-appointed task if it convinced average eastern Germans that it was in their interest to ask probing questions about their behavior under the old regime. "When did we simply make mistakes?" he inquired. "[On the other hand,] where and how did we allow ourselves to get caught up in this system? When were we cowardly and opportunistic?" Meckel conceded that cowardice and opportunism were not exactly "punishable offenses" in the Federal Republic, and, no doubt, he would not have liked to see such common human failings understood in these terms. But in his estimation, this qualification did not preclude addressing the unspoken complicity of much of the GDR's population in the communist regime's offenses. "How great was the pressure [to conform] in everyday life?" he queried. "Who really believed that what they were doing was right? When must we instead speak of betrayal?"[43]

However, although these sorts of issues may have been uppermost on the minds of the Enquete commission's organizers when they began their investigations, it is striking how little the final report has to say about them. It was assuredly not for want of interest that the view "from below" failed to play a major role in the document's conclusions. When this perspective could be equated with the hardships of citizens who had been directly victimized by the SED's policies, the commission had no difficulty addressing the subject. Over 2 years of proceedings, the body's deputies heard testimony from scores of individuals – teachers, journalists, artists, students, and pastors – who faced formidable odds in leading fulfilled lives under authoritarian rule and, in many cases, made substantial sacrifices to remain true to their convictions.[44] In a section of the final report devoted exclusively to these stories, the reader is reminded – in a stereotypical German way, we might add – of the "duty" of all citizens to "honor the victims of the [communist] system and to ensure that their suffering is not forgotten." Moreover, this particular obligation is held to apply above all at a time "when memories of the horrors of the fallen dictatorship are weakening in the face of an undifferentiated 'GDR nostalgia'" (p. 229).

Yet the problem with emphasizing these heroic themes, as some commission staff members candidly admitted after the final report was released in June 1994, is that this approach left very little room for insight into the daily trials and experiences of the less courageous but more typical East German citizens with whom Eppelmann and

Meckel had originally been concerned.[45] One possible reason for the document's scarce attention to the subject is that the parliamentarians were wary of having to pay the political and electoral price of providing a potentially less-than-uplifting message about the behavior and motivations of a significant segment of the GDR's citizenry. Accordingly, if one could not relate much that was positive about the East German population, there was something to be said for the principle of not saying anything at all.

In this vein, there seems to be a generous dose of mixed emotions in everything the final report has to convey about everyday life in East Germany. "Oppositional activity was widespread [in the GDR]," the document proclaims in a bold assessment at one point. "But," the report then qualifies, "it was often conjoined with loyal behavior toward the regime, including a mentality of servility" (p. 211). Or in the same spirit, we are informed that "[f]or a large number of people in the GDR, oppositional activity in daily life, on the one hand, was constantly alternating with accommodation and at least partial collaboration with the SED regime on the other" (p. 212).

Then, too, if we examine these manifestations of dissenting behavior closely, it is revealing that the report describes them in even less impressive terms than the meager forms of resistance with which the commission was willing to credit the Lutheran churches. At least the churches could be lauded for having provided shelter and occasional moral support to the SED's diverse critics. In contrast, one has to wonder about putative acts of "oppositional behavior and resistance in daily life" (to cite one of the report's subsections) that went no further and were no more threatening than "the rejection of the regime's official terminology (for example, one said 'the Wall' instead of 'antifascist protective wall'); the deliberate reception of western media and the spreading of information received through them; [and] the reading and distribution of forbidden or officially undesirable literature" (pp. 211–12).

At the same time, an equally weighty factor that may have kept the commission's members from offering a fuller portrait of the East German population was their desire to avoid taking any stand that would seem to present the communist system as anything less than an undifferentiated evil. As Alliance '90 activist Gerd Poppe would later caution the Bundestag, even to imagine that there was something positive to be said about the SED's legacy was to risk trivializing its offenses.

This would be like making, in Poppe's portrayal, "the cannibalistic system of Emperor Bokassa I the measure for judging the so-called first socialist democracy on German soil."[46] As a consequence, if average East Germans had moderately intelligible or even partly understandable reasons for going along with the governing regime's policies (from simple loyalty to the place of their birth to rational calculations about maximizing their social and economic well-being), this would not be apparent to anyone reading the final report.[47]

Quite the contrary, in almost a parody of Václav Havel's characterization of the numbing impersonality of late communist rule (see Chapter 1), there are very few shades of gray in the document's depiction of the East German order. The report describes the relationship between state and society in the GDR almost entirely in terms of domination. We are told that the SED "deformed the life of every individual person and the entire society" (p. 5). It used its cadre of disciplined and dutiful members to penetrate "all areas of state and society," from the media to all aspects of popular culture, the economy, and the entire educational system (pp. 22–4). Additionally, it drew upon the omnipotent presence of the Ministry of State Security ("the shield and sword of the party") to effect "the complete suppression of freedom of opinion and the free exchange of political views in the GDR" (p. 29). At some points, suggestively echoing the rationale that some jurists originally employed to justify the Wall trials, the report comes just short of equating the SED's rule with the Nazi dictatorship preceding it.[48] "The SED dictatorship, too," it proclaims, "like [its National Socialist predecessor] was a system that ideologically, politically, and organizationally subordinated the individual and society to the monopolistic claims of the party" (p. 282).

No doubt, much of the attractiveness of this position, both for the former dissidents on the commission and for the western representatives of the major parties, lay in the need they all felt to combat the electoral advances of the reform communist PDS in the East. In this sense, one can appreciate why they would have been attracted to the idea that the principal lesson of the commission's hearings was that nothing of value could ever be salvaged from the communist period. But in taking this stand, the deputies may have inadvertently given the SED's successor a political toehold it need not have possessed. By continually reinforcing in the public mind, in this and in other forums, the PDS's connection with the GDR era, the deputies seem to have provided the party's leaders with an invaluable electoral opportunity. They could define themselves, in effect, as the natural representatives of all the easterners whose memories of the past were not as clear cut.

Dietmar Keller took this approach in framing the PDS's response to the commission's final report. In an exhaustive 28-page dissenting opinion, Keller emphasized that the GDR's long history could not be reduced to a matter of who had supported or, conversely, opposed the SED regime. Nor, it seemed in Keller's view, would one come any closer to the truth by depicting the past in such black and white terms. To treat the GDR as nothing more than a dictatorship, he argued, "[was] to simplify it and to reduce it to a state of repression." In fact, "as a state and society, the GDR was also a state that had provided for its citizens' needs [*Vorsorgestaat*] and that was united by a specific 'we feeling'" (p. 250). Interestingly, Keller was willing to concede that four decades of communist rule had not been without significant blemishes. In his estimation, there had unquestionably been "victims and perpetrators, mistaken policies, breakdowns, and crimes." But more to the point, to Keller's way of thinking, the GDR had been "a daily history of millions of people, whose personal happiness and sorrow, sense of security and well-being, conflicts and protests, public presence and withdrawal into private 'niches' could not be verified through any archival sources" (p. 251).

Keller stuck to this perspective in defending his party's dissenting opinion before the Bundestag on June 17, 1994, the forty-first anniversary of the workers' uprising. It was an insult, he insisted, to suggest that the GDR had been nothing more than "a lifelong prison sentence" for its inhabitants. Instead, he reflected, in terms that could be easily transferred to many of his compatriots: "This was my own life story. I couldn't decide where I was born. I grew up with the belief that there was a social alternative, that there were other answers to history. I admit this. I admit to still believing this today."[49]

To say the least, Keller's image of life in the GDR was overblown and excessively romantic. Still, it does not take much imagination, nor in this writer's opinion any sympathy with his position, to see how this more flattering depiction of the GDR's former citizens could be exploited to serve the PDS's political ends on the national level. In fact, in the lead-up to the Bundestag elections of October 1994, the reform communists' greatest electoral advantage was arguably their ability to portray themselves as political moderates. According to their mythology, they were not hardened defenders of a brutal and unforgiving dictatorship, as the dissidents and the establishment parties might have preferred, but instead sympathetic representatives of all of the complex and uncertain feelings that were bound up with the eastern German transition. "My biography does not begin in 1989," affirmed one of the party's most popular campaign slogans. Others emphasized the PDS's ostensibly common fate with the eastern populace's struggle to get out from under the FRG's thumb. By capitalizing on this image, the party reminded voters, to cite the judgment of one observer, that "both they and the candidates [had] shared worthwhile lives before the *Wende*."[50]

By the same token, whenever the establishment parties attacked the PDS, much as the Enquete commission appeared implicitly to have done in its assessment of the GDR record, they seemed to call into question the integrity of eastern German voters as well. Like the PDS itself, few of those persons who had lived in the GDR could claim that they were bringing unblemished or exemplary personal histories to the project of national unification. But perhaps also like the PDS, most seem to have felt that supererogatory personal attributes should not be required features of equal citizenship in the Federal Republic anyway.

In any case, if there were remaining doubts about the connection between one's characterization of the East German past and the shifting political sympathies of the eastern electorate, these were swiftly overcome by the results of the *Superwahljahr*. In successive state elections in Saxony–Anhalt, Thuringia, Saxony, Brandenburg, and Mecklenburg–Vorpommern, the PDS succeeded in dramatically increasing its share of the vote over its previous showings in December 1990, by 7.9, 6.9, 6.3, 5.3, and 7 percent, respectively. In all these cases, the party challenged the SPD for the second position in the state parliaments; in Brandenburg, it actually attained this objective.[51] Yet easily the most surprising event of the year was the outcome of the October 1994 elections to the Bundestag. The PDS was returned to parliament with a greater margin of support in the East than it had garnered in the first all-German election 4 years earlier. Whereas 11.1 percent of eastern German voters had cast their ballots for the reformed communists in 1990, the party won the support of 19.8 percent of the eastern electorate in 1994 as well as four direct mandates from Berlin's eastern districts.

As a result, on the basis of proportional representation, the PDS was able to defy scholarly predictions of its imminent demise and send 30 deputies to the new Bundestag.[52]

Revisiting East Germany's Difficult Past

Would fewer eastern voters have supported the PDS if Germany's mainstream parties had sought to empathize deliberately with their eastern compatriots and done a more effective job imagining what it had been like to make tough moral choices under a dictatorship? It is impossible to answer such a question with certainty. In any case, the character of the Enquete commission was only a small symptom of a general disposition and not the cause of the PDS's successes. Nonetheless, it is revealing that the issue was on the minds of many Bundestag members in the spring of 1995 when the German parliament debated proposals for renewing the Enquete commission for a second round of hearings.

One critic of the body's previous focuses, the eastern German Social Democratic leader Wolfgang Thierse, worried openly that his party had seriously underestimated the psychological and emotional connections many easterners still felt to their former lives in the GDR. "We must be willing to promote a differentiated and just consideration of this history," he underscored in a June 1995 press release that was devoted to identifying a future agenda for the commission. "[This would be] one that is suited to highlighting the many decent biographies that were lived under a false system and that will provide the commission with the chance to give appropriate weight to the achievements and experiences of the people of the GDR."[53] In particular, Thierse recommended that the Bundestag broaden the scope of its inquiries to include matters of direct personal concern to Germans on both sides of the old national divide. Among these, he included the manifold social and economic problems that had arisen from the rush to national unity since 1990. In Thierse's view, such a focus on common concerns would not merely help many eastern Germans to feel more equally a part of the national agenda. By identifying mistakes and misguided judgments that could not be simply dismissed as "consequences of SED policy," he reasoned that one could also counteract the current tendency in the Federal Republic to present a unidimensional perspective on the German past.[54]

In this instance, the reader should not miss the import of Thierse's observation. The fact alone that he, and other deputies like him, could make such a proposal demonstrated that there was nothing *essentially* wrong with utilizing the Enquete commission as a medium for taking the moral pulse of the East German experience. In other words all along, the parliamentarians could have used the body's investigations to present a more nuanced assessment of the GDR's history. If only they had not been driven by countervailing political and ideological concerns!

Nevertheless, when the renewed commission was finally approved by the Bundestag in the summer of 1995, it is telling that correctives, such as those that Thierse had in mind, were barely reflected in the new body's mission. Admittedly, it said something about the effect of the 1994 election results on their thinking that the commission's mainstream defenders were not above making a few obligatory bows to the sensitivities of their eastern listeners. For example, they evidently needed no prodding to declare that the body's earlier "political and moral condemnation of the SED dictatorship" had "nothing to do with condemning the persons who were subjugated by it." To the contrary, anyone could see that "the Germans in the GDR had been made to bear the heaviest burden of Germany's postwar history."[55] However, two persistent factors seem to have kept the commission's attention centered primarily upon the sorts of issues that had dominated the first round of hearings.

As in the 1992–94 period, commission members remained adherents of the idea that their purpose was not merely to disinter the truth about the not-so-distant past but also to utilize this record to instruct their fellow Germans how they should, and should not, act in the future. Indeed, a majority of deputies continued to worry about the electoral successes of the PDS. To their way of thinking, the election results confirmed the need for the Bundestag to take more aggressive steps to combat the temptation still felt by many easterners to relativize the offenses of the communist era. "We still need to deal with this problem of GDR nostalgia in the new commission," Eppelmann reflected at the time. "Of course, no one wants to admit that they've lived under the wrong ideas for 50 years."[56]

From this perspective, the risk of offending the GDR's former citizens was easily offset by the benefits that were sure to accrue to German democracy by the commission's attention to the moral lessons of the past. One only had to maintain a sharp distinction between the liberal conception of the good life that had been upheld in the first commission report and the illusory utopia that had once been championed by the SED (and, by implication, by its successors in the PDS). "We'll do it whether the majority of eastern Germans want it or not," a staff member emphasized.[57]

Second, electoral calculations continued to play a central role in the parliamentarians' reasoning. Was this not predictable? The Christian Democratic and Free Democratic representatives on the commission did not have to read very closely between the lines to see that pleas, like those Thierse was making, that they redirect their attention to the political and economic trials of unification were much more than innocent calls for a sympathetic epistemology. Had they chosen to adopt a more explicitly self-critical approach to the post-1990 period, many figured, they would have played right into the hands of their Social Democratic rivals. Presumably, the latter forces would have been happy to score points with eastern voters by finding fault with the policies of the Kohl government after unification.[58]

As a result, the governing coalition used its majority status on the Enquete commission to ensure that the body's future assignments would not be appreciably different from those of its first session.[59] As approved by the Bundestag, under the rubric of "overcoming the consequences of the SED dictatorship in the process of German unification," the renewed body was to remain primarily focused on the consequences of policies pursued in the pre-1989 period and upon issues (e.g., the structural deficiencies of the GDR's planned economy, the militarization of its society and culture, and the persecution of dissidents) that could be readily attributed to the SED alone. In addition, in what amounted to an admission of their determination to present the German people with the victor's view of history, the governing parties voted along with the SPD to reduce the size of the new commission from its original 16 voting members to a total membership of 11. This seemingly insignificant decision had the effect of relegating the PDS to an observer status on the reconstituted body, thereby depriving the party of the right to vote on the commission's second report when it wrapped up its hearings in late spring 1998.[60]

Had the new Enquete commission been slated to defend its findings in any other year, it is conceivable that the influence of partisan politics on its deliberations would have been somewhat less pronounced.

However, like 1994, 1998 was again a national election year in the Federal Republic. As a consequence, we can hardly be surprised that, in this case as well, the body was beset by the ingrained ambivalence of its predecessor.

On the one hand, as in the first Bundestag investigations of the GDR, there is no doubting the significant contributions the commission's hearings and expertise represented to future scholarship on East German communism and, to a lesser extent, the early dynamics of national unification. Over a 3-year period, from June 1995 to June 1998, the commission's members met in 24 public sessions, heard testimony from 292 individuals, and accepted expert opinions from 160 others. In the process, they compiled more than 13,000 pages of information on subjects as varied as the apparatus of repression in the GDR, the environmental impact of the regime's economic policies, the management of the socialist factory, and the diverse types of educational institutions in the country.[61] On some counts, such as the body's treatment of the attitudes and orientations of the East German citizenry ("Everyday life in the GDR and in the new *Länder*"),[62] the scholarly assessments of these subjects may have compensated for some of the shortcomings and lack of nuance in the first commission's findings. Yet, on the other hand, when we consider the renewed commission's more public final report, it is telling that the parliamentary deputies still seem to have been driven by the mixed motivations of the first Enquete commission. Hence, many of their conclusions read more like contending campaign platforms than thoughtful inquiries into the East German past.[63]

For example, when the conservative and liberal majority parties on the commission underscored the "catastrophic balance sheet" of economic conditions in the former GDR that had led them to establish "a free-market economy [in the East] without any 'ifs' or 'buts'" (p. 59), the Social Democrats seemed almost too happy to use their dissenting vote in the final report to portray the policies of the governing coalition in an unfavorable light. The Kohl administration, it seemed, had long ignored the SPD's advice that it adopt a more gradual and measured approach to the transition from centralized planning mechanisms to a capitalist economy. Furthermore, the ruling parties had supposedly failed to heed the warnings of their own experts about the risks of moving too quickly to unify the two German currencies or of exposing East German industry to competition from western firms: "This was basically an ideologically determined decision for a purely abstract economic policy that failed to take into account its probable consequences in reality" (p. 62). The Social Democrats also showed that they could rub it in. Apparently, they concluded, the Union parties had forgotten that even the Christian Democratic father of the German economic miracle, Ludwig Erhard, regarded "pragmatic transitional arrangements" as unavoidable (p. 82).

For their part, the majority parties were just as inclined to use the final report as a political weapon against the SPD. In a section devoted to "divided Germany in divided Europe," the Social Democrats (and the Greens as well) are characterized as little more than unwitting accomplices in the GDR's long campaigns for international recognition. It "corresponded to the wishes of the SED," the document informs us at one point, that West Germany's opposition parties were increasingly inclined in the 1980s to treat the GDR as a foreign country, no different from any other. For this reason, the majority opinion adds, it is no wonder that East Germany's leaders tended to "prefer the SPD as a discussion partner" (p. 287). Yet from the critics' perspective, this dubious status meant that the Social Democrats were left in a precarious bargaining position when they should instead have been making tough demands of East Berlin. Because the SPD's leaders were so eager to ingratiate themselves with their East German interlocutors – in part, the report pointedly observes, to pursue selfish electoral gain – they tended to downplay "unpleasant themes" such as human rights in their discussions with the SED and to "conduct [instead] a form of visitational diplomacy that rarely acknowledged the dictatorial character of the GDR regime."

Against this background, it was to Germany's good fortune, the report's authors conclude, that the governing parties at the time (i.e., the CDU/CSU and FDP) had remained true to the more demanding, original spirit of German–German negotiations that had been initiated under Chancellors Brandt and Schmidt. These two politicians had properly respected those agreements and treaties that were in effect with East Berlin. But to their credit, and in stark contrast to later trends in the SPD, they had refused to remain quiet about their "dissent over basic principles" with the communist government (p. 287).

In a partial exception to these partisan exchanges, the establishment parties on the Enquete commission were willing to concede that some more pressing issues were at stake in their investigations. For example, in their treatment of the theme of daily life in the GDR, they devoted

2 full days of hearings to the difficulties many eastern Germans were experiencing in adapting their ways of thinking and acting to the norms of everyday existence in the Federal Republic. "Since their experiences are not any worse but only different from those of western Germans," the majority opinion acknowledges in its comparatively brief (15-page) assessment of the topic, "most of the GDR's former citizens have no reason to regard their earlier lives as 'lost years.'" "In most respects," the authors add, "they led perfectly normal lives and thus have no reason to exclude this period from their own biographies" (p. 195).

If only the members of the commission had decided to follow up on this theme! Formally, there was nothing to prevent them from doing so. Nonetheless, aside from a handful of oblique references to different cultural norms in the East – to ordinary easterners' greater expectations about the state's role in society and to their high regard for such "secondary virtues" as work, discipline, and love of homeland (pp. 195–6) – the final report provides little insight into the factors that contributed to these "normal lives" in the GDR. It also fails to provide us with a better understanding of the key values and principles that were lost in the transition to a unified German state.

It may be that after 6 years of hearings and deliberations this outcome was prefigured by an institutional process that was geared to produce little in the way of positive findings about the period before 1989 (because of the dissidents' influence) and little that was negative about the time thereafter (because of the majority parties). Undoubtedly, the partisan character of many of the commission's investigations had a heavy role in these results. As one staffer lamented, "parties are institutions that cannot admit they've made mistakes."[64] But, this would be another way of saying that the commission's work would only be as true to the historical record as allowed by the sound instincts and determination of the politicians who led it. For all of the advantages the body brought to its inquiries and that the FRG in general had over other countries, there was no guarantee that this approach would be a better vehicle for coming to terms with Germany's complex past than the others we have considered.

A Better Commission?

Before concluding this chapter, it is worth asking whether a differently structured investigation of the East German past would have led to a more desirable outcome. At the outset of this chapter, it was mentioned that some of the early proponents of a public reckoning with the GDR's offenses, like Schorlemmer and Thierse, flirted briefly with the possibility of creating tribunals in the East to allow victims and perpetrators to explore together what really happened under SED rule. The idea quickly foundered on the problem, presumably, of ensuring due process to persons accused of wrongdoing. But what if Bonn had somehow managed to embrace the tribunal concept despite its flaws?

At an historical juncture when self-described truth commissions were springing up throughout the world, it is easy to understand the attraction of such an undertaking. In particular, if Germany's leaders would have put the views and experiences of the participants squarely at the center of their investigations, the chances of piecing together a more accurate and finely tuned picture of the dictatorial past would have been accentuated.

By all accounts, this was true of the first examples of these investigations in Latin America, the 1984 Sabato commission report on persons who had disappeared in Argentina (*Nunca Más*) and, 7 years later, the Rettig commission report of the Chilean National Commission on Truth and Reconciliation.[65] Looking over these commission reports a decade later, one is immediately struck by their chilling specificity. Each is based on the lengthy testimony of thousands of victims; each attends in minute and painstaking detail to the causes and conditions of repression; and each is committed to identifying the fate of tens of thousands of abducted, murdered, or "disappeared" citizens. Notably, the Sabato commission, which exposed depths of brutality previously unknown in Argentina, also made a point of identifying perpetrators by name. For this reason, it played a major role in the convictions of the five military commanders in December 1985 (see Chapter 2).

Likewise, when considering the proceedings of the even better-known South African Truth and Reconciliation Commission (TRC), one is taken by the size and intensity of the enterprise. In much less time than the Germans had, the TRC's three committees (on human rights violations, reparations and rehabilitations, and amnesty) held more than 50 public hearings at locations throughout the country; they accepted more than 20,000 statements from the families of victims and the survivors of unlawful arrests, kidnapping, torture, and other forms of abuse; and they received over 7,000 amnesty petitions.[66] However, what stands out most about these proceedings, in large part because of the promise of amnesty in exchange for most truthful confessions, is the utter candor with which government officials and members of the security forces admitted to unspeakable acts of violence.[67]

Nonetheless, despite the potential appeal of such approaches for the German confrontation with injustice, we should not overlook an essential difference between these three cases and the FRG's options. The Argentine and Chilean governments had to contend with extraordinarily unstable conditions in their respective transitions to civilian rule, and even then, there was no guarantee that the military would remain committed to democracy; in Argentina, these circumstances eventually led to a presidential pardon for the convicted junta members. In South Africa, the TRC was itself the product of a carefully negotiated compromise between the defenders of the apartheid regime and their victims. In effect, the one side offered amnesty, and the other, truth. In contrast, the FRG pursued multiple forms of retrospective justice, the Enquete commission being only one of them.

This difference may provide an important clue to the limitations of the parliamentary body. Perhaps it did not matter that much that Bonn failed to adopt a more engaging approach to truth telling, such as the tribunal concept, because Germany was not wanting for analogues to other states' truth commissions. Clearly, the trials of the GDR's former leaders and the border guards provided highly publicized forums for open discussions about the East German record. At a different level, the opening of the Stasi files to ordinary citizens' inspection presented a deeply personal opportunity for self-enlightenment. In this sense, although the Enquete commission could have done a better job in bringing East German reality to life, it is conceivable that this body's shortcomings were due to something more than the political quarrels of its members. The commission's deficiencies may also have arisen because some of its potential functions were already covered by other forms of retrospective justice.

5

Corrective Justice

RETURNING PRIVATE
PROPERTY

On March 4, 1992, Detlef Dalk, a 48-year-old eastern German city councilor, took his life in protest against what he perceived to be an egregious example of victor's justice along the road to national unity: the reopening of millions of western German claims to lost houses, commercial enterprises, farms, and parcels of land in the former GDR. Only his "'public' death," Dalk wrote in a letter to Chancellor Kohl just before his suicide, would suffice to dramatize the injustice signified by Bonn's acquiescence in a massive transfer of property holdings from East to West. "We have a new society," he lamented, "which has been placed right before our noses. It is not a bad society, but it is not 'ours.' We are no longer even asked."[1]

In his desperate gesture, Dalk gave voice to a mood of foreboding and helplessness in eastern Germany that was quite understandable under the circumstances.[2] When the first spontaneous protests against the SED regime broke out in October 1989, few observers would have had any idea that property ownership would soon become one of the most bitterly contested issues of the postcommunist era. For the most part, the eastern German people had not had to deal in any serious fashion with the matter of private property for more than four decades. Similarly, the great majority of their western counterparts had long since abandoned any realistic expectations of regaining lands and businesses they had lost over the years of national division.

Yet once it became clear that the two German states would soon be reunited under the auspices of the Federal Republic, hopes were immediately awakened, both in the West and in the East, of correcting these wrongs and of returning all expropriated or illegally acquired holdings to their original owners. The East German government was by no means insensitive to these pressures. In one of its last formal acts, on September 23, 1990, the Volkskammer passed a law on the "settlement of open property questions" (or Property statute).[3] Under these auspices, over the next 2 years, more than one million claims for restitution were to be filed on a staggering 2.5 million different types of eastern German property.[4]

Given the enormous scope of this undertaking, as well as its necessarily invasive character for everyone who stood to lose their homes, apartments, dachas, or garden plots in the course of its implementation, there may have been nothing officials could have done to convince Dalk and thousands of other East Germans like him of the FRG's good intentions. However, the authorities were not oblivious to the concern. Arguably, more than any of the other cases of retrospective justice we have considered in this book, the authors of the property settlement were acutely aware of the need to justify their decisions in a manner that made sense against the backdrop of the region's history. In a much publicized joint declaration of principles "on the settlement of open property questions" that Bonn and East Berlin hammered out on June 15, 1990, and that was later included as an attachment to the Unification treaty, the two Germanys pledged to return illegally acquired property to the greatest extent possible to its original owners.[5] But, in the same document, they also expressed their determination to achieve a "socially acceptable compromise" among the diverse claimants to ownership in both states that would take into account the specificities of the German past.

In some respects, this attempt to provide a balanced response to the property problem acted as a restraining force on federal policymaking. Both the joint declaration and the Property statute reflect the influence of western *and* eastern German interests in the negotiations. The settlement was truly a "child of two fathers."[6] Also, in large part because of the Volkskammer's insistence that Bonn respect legitimate transfers of property rights under GDR law, the document includes notable exceptions to the principle of "natural restitution," that is, the notion that expropriated property should automatically be given back to its original owners.[7] As a result, the number of properties actually taken from easterners over the 1990s turned out to be much lower than critics of the policy initially feared.[8] Further, with the passage of time and the acquisition of experience, lawmakers proved willing to modify their practices in ways that directly benefited the eastern economy.

For example, they made it easier for private investors to acquire businesses and land-holdings considered essential for the region's economic development.

Nevertheless, the impulse to think and act historically may ironically have been a source of some of the most abiding grievances about the property settlement. This proved to be the case not only for eastern Germans who were to lose much of the security they had possessed for decades under socialism but for significant numbers of westerners as well who would find their expectations of restitution frustrated in pursuing claims to ownership.

Unlike the other types of retrospective justice examined in this study, such as the Wall trials or the hearings of the Bundestag's Enquete commission, property officials enjoyed the comparative advantage of being able to identify relatively clear-cut violations of preexisting laws in making their decisions about the fate of contested properties. Still, what made their investigations unique was not merely that they proposed to use the past as a guide to effect justice in the present. At almost exactly the time the Volkskammer was passing the Property statute, it is worth noting that Czechoslovakia's new democratic government was enacting equally radical legislation to return illegally expropriated property to its original owners. Yet, unlike the Czechs and Slovaks, who feared the consequences of trying to restitute property losses for the period before the communists came to power in 1948 and who also limited themselves to the restitution of businesses and landholdings already in state hands, German decision makers concluded that they could not confine their judgments to instances of GDR-era wrongdoing alone.[9]

Many of the injustices they hoped to correct had transpired either well before the SED came to power in 1949 – under the Nazi dictatorship or, subsequently, during the 4 years of Soviet occupation – or in the months immediately following the communist regime's collapse in 1989. For this reason, the authors of the property settlement insisted that social peace would be ensured only if every exchange were evaluated in the context of the legal order in which it took effect. Yet this was one case in which the historical record was not the most unequivocal guide to justice. Because the approach invariably led them to endorse different legal remedies depending on which Germany they emphasized (the return of property in some cases but the maintenance of the status quo in others), officials were bound to alienate some claimants no matter how carefully they acted.

The Narrow Choices behind the Property Settlement

The most important thing to understand about the form Germany's property settlement ultimately took is that the FRG's options were never as great as either its leaders desired or its critics imagined. In retrospect, it might appear as though the nation's long-term interests would have been better served by avoiding the property issue entirely or at least by choosing a less divisive approach to the problem (such as the payment of monetary compensation to the first owners) than was implied by the emphasis on restitution. However, as both East and West German officials quickly realized in their initial discussions of the issue in January and February 1990, one could not easily ignore the arguments for returning many properties and possessions to their original owners.

Certainly, this was a self-evident truth to many members of the governing coalition in Bonn, including the then state secretary (and later justice minister) Klaus Kinkel and the leadership of the Free Democratic Party.[10] In making the case for restitution, these politicians could appeal to a long-standing tradition of strong property rights in Germany.[11] In fact, the principle was enshrined in the Basic Law: "Property and the right of inheritance shall be guaranteed" (Article 14[1]).

There were also plenty of people in both parts of Germany who could vividly remember how they or their families had lost houses, lands, and other valuables in one or another period of German tyranny since 1933. This lent an air of urgency to these property claims. Under National Socialist rule, some had property taken from them as a prelude to their internment in concentration camps. In many cases, they or their relations had then regained these holdings when they were liberated by American and British troops after World War II. But in a new round of injustices, they were to lose them again as part of the Soviet occupation government's land reform campaigns of 1945–49.[12] Similarly, following the GDR's founding, thousands of people were forced to give up their properties and were resettled to other parts of eastern Germany in late May 1952 when East Berlin abruptly decided to secure its westernmost borders by creating a no-man's-land along its boundary with the FRG. In the middle of the night, families were removed from their homes with little time to pack their possessions. Subsequently, equally brutal inroads on the rights to property were made between August and September 1961 to clear a path through the center of Berlin for the construction of the Wall.

Following the barrier's erection and the consolidation of the SED's authority in the 1960s and 1970s, it may appear as though the East German government adopted a less explicitly antagonistic approach toward those persons who still held private property. Yet for most citizens, the essence of the regime's earlier policies remained unchanged. Over the years, in a practice known as "cold expropriations," the state effectively compelled apartment owners to abandon their properties by keeping rents on buildings so low that they could not afford to comply with municipal safety and sanitation standards. Likewise, government officials routinely coerced would-be émigrés to the Federal Republic into selling their homes and estates at below-market prices as a condition for expediting their applications.[13] Even after the GDR's implosion in 1989, many eastern Germans feared that members of the old SED *nomenklatura* would perpetuate these wrongs by using their connections and insider knowledge to buy up the best properties in downtown Berlin and in prime residential areas like Kleinmachnow and Teltow.

Under these conditions, as participants in the inter-German negotiations have confirmed, it would have been unimaginable for Bonn to have declared its determination to resign itself to the status quo as far as property questions were concerned. The wounds of the past were simply too many and too deep to ignore.[14] Further restricting the FRG's freedom of maneuver, federal officials recognized with regret that they could not buy their way out of the property problem by offering only monetary payments to the original owners in the place of restitution.

This point requires some elaboration. In view of enormous tensions that were to be generated between eastern and western Germans, one can understand why observers would later regard this decision as one of the great missed opportunities in Bonn's unification strategy.[15] Clearly, there was a notable precedent for taking such a step. In the early 1950s, the fledgling West German government had provided offset payments to ethnic Germans who had fled political persecution in the East. These funds would eventually play an important part in the country's postwar recovery. Then, too, 40 years later, in the early 1990s, similar arrangements were being debated in countries like Poland, Bulgaria, and Hungary whose governments did not want to hazard the risks of restitution. For example, the Hungarian parliament adopted a plan to grant indemnification vouchers to the victims of illegal expropriations under its predecessors.[16]

Still, as attractive as compensation might appear in hindsight, there were serious political and social obstacles in 1990 that stood in the way of giving priority to the approach. For one, it was by no means evident to decision makers which segment of the German population they should ask to bear the financial burden of any compensation plan. In the 1950s, the bulk of the offset payments the FRG made to expropriated landowners had been paid for by contributions to a fund from Germans who had been fortunate to reclaim lost possessions and real estate after the war. In 1990, however, a comparable undertaking (Schäuble estimated the minimal cost at 8 billion deutsche marks, although later assessments were considerably higher[17]) could only have been financed out of the pockets of *western* German taxpayers. In the eyes of skeptical politicians, such an arrangement was equivalent to asking the victims of injustice to reimburse themselves for their own losses – a step which, they believed, would amount to a "second expropriation."[18]

Additionally, it was also unclear, as subsequent developments would confirm, whether these same western claimants would have been satisfied with just any form of compensation. If the Federal Republic's past record was any indication, both in its handling of the claims of the Jewish victims of Nazism and of the needs of German nationals escaping postwar communist oppression, the German government could not realistically be expected to pay current market prices for lost property. This fact alone was a bitter pill for the former owners, but it was even harder for them to swallow amidst the inflated promises and high expectations of national unification. Under conditions in which one could easily foresee a flood of western investment capital into eastern Germany and a corresponding rise in property values, it hardly made economic sense for the original owners to favor compensation when they could earn even more money by reclaiming their holdings and selling them themselves.

Finally, federal authorities had to consider that, in certain respects, a precedent for returning property to the original owners had already been established by, of all political actors, the GDR's last communist government. This was ironic in view of the outspoken opposition to the property settlement that was to spread throughout eastern Germany. The Modrow regime had decreed on March 7, 1990, that over 11,000 semiprivate firms that had been nationalized by the Honecker government in 1972 could be reclaimed by their former owners in exchange for payment of a nominal fee.[19] There was nothing substantively wrong with this decision, also known as the "Modrow decree," because the earlier expropriations had followed on the heels of years of state-induced intimidation and credit starvation. However, the fait accompli had the effect of forcing German officials to face up to some looming contradictions among their core principles. One property expert, Ernst Niederleithinger, later framed the awkward choices before the Kohl administration in the following query: "Should [Germany's] democratic parties and government now put themselves into the position of saying [the Modrow decree] was all a mistake and, therefore, the returned property should be turned back to its earlier condition? Or should they instead represent the view, in clear violation of the [Basic Law's] commitment to equal treatment, that this particular settlement could not be applied to other cases of expropriation?"[20]

In view of Bonn's constrained options, the decision to extend the logic of the Modrow decree to other unresolved property questions was not the only controversial move the FRG's leaders could have made. No matter what stance they took, it seems, they were likely to offend someone in one or the other part of Germany.

Nonetheless, it says something for their sensitivity to the history behind these circumstances that federal officials acknowledged that they could not act as if the GDR had never been a separate country.[21] As Schäuble explained in his memoirs, writing only one year after unification, it would have been foolhardy had he or his colleagues assumed that the only interested parties in a just property settlement were the former property owners in the West. To his mind, one needed to include in this equation the many other Germans in the East "who, years and even decades earlier, had in good faith and trust in the continuity of their legal order acquired property and building rights on previously expropriated pieces of land." To have failed to take into account their legitimate concerns, Schäuble reflected, "would have been to burden the unification process . . . with tremendous additional social tensions."[22]

Just how Bonn could address these interests while paying heed to westerners' demands that it observe the constitution's strong property principles was, of course, a major challenge for anyone who aspired to maintain a semblance of intellectual coherence and consistency in the property settlement. But in the interest of helping Germans on both sides of the national divide feel equally a part of the undertaking, policymakers demonstrated that they were prepared to make at least three general types of exceptions to the policy that very loosely became known as "the priority of restitution over compensation."

First, in a telling admission that some historical developments were too ingrained in existing institutions and ways of acting to undergo further modification, the western signatories gave in to East German and, implicitly, Soviet pressures by agreeing in the joint declaration of 1990 to exclude from restitution all properties seized during the Soviet Union's land reform and nationalization campaigns of the late 1940s.[23] This decision would become a source of fierce controversy in the FRG because it seemed to apply an unequal and apparently arbitrary standard of justice to those West Germans (and their descendants) who had been the major losers during this tumultuous period in postwar German history. However, in view of the massive social dislocations that would have been entailed by reopening claims to nearly a third of the agricultural holdings in the GDR, or roughly eight million acres of land, it is hard to imagine how any other decision would have been socially or politically feasible.

Second, in an intriguing concession to the historical reality of the GDR, the western authors of the property agreements gave their blessings to exempting all holdings from restitution that had been acquired in, what they termed, "an honest manner (*in redlicher Weise*)" under the old East German state. Technically, the West German civil code's emphasis on the acquisition of property in good faith could have threatened tens of thousands of easterners with the loss of their properties if it turned out that these holdings had once been illegally expropriated from refugees or other victims of SED policy. But thanks to this innovation in German law, which said a lot for Bonn's willingness to see things from the perspective of those who had lived under dictatorial conditions, current property holders were provided with a somewhat lower threshold for justifying their claims to ownership.[24] They merely had to show that they had lawfully purchased their homes under GDR law or that they had received the right (*dingliches Nutzungsrecht*) to build houses on state-owned property. As property experts pointed out, this was not so much a matter of caving in to East German demands as recognizing undeniable facts about the East German experience. Thus, rather than asking the region's population to abide by legal norms it had not experienced for over 40 years (even more, if one included the Third Reich), western officials were only saying that their compatriots should be judged by a standard they could reasonably have observed at the time: "the formally existing legal order of the GDR and [whether they had] behaved correctly in light of this legal order" (Property statute, §4 [2]).

Third, in a final exception to the priority of restitution, the western signatories expressed their determination to resolve outstanding ownership disputes in a manner that served the common good of all citizens, even if this entailed keeping some contested properties in the same hands. For its proponents, this precept was not only compatible with the Basic Law's commitment to basic property rights, but it corresponded to an expressed feature of the law: "Property imposes duties. Its use shall also serve the public good (Article 14 [2])." To this end, the joint declaration excepted a distinct class of cases from restitution (e.g., apartment buildings, kindergartens) because their return would have been contrary to the broader interests of the community. In these instances, original owners were assured of some form of financial compensation for their losses, but only if they had not been adequately compensated by the GDR.[25]

For like reasons, and again with West German support, the drafters of the Property statute included several provisions in the law that were specifically intended to promote economic growth in the new *Länder* by removing major obstacles to private investment. In line with this goal, which was reinforced by the passage of the Law on Special Investments in the GDR, the drafters of the Property statute gave investment opportunities priority over restitution in cases in which investors could satisfy state and local authorities that they would generate new jobs in the East, promote the construction of new housing, or otherwise improve living conditions in the region.[26]

None of this is to deny that strong property principles remained the default mode for resolving the majority of claims disputes. For example, the joint declaration obliged Bonn and East Berlin to work together to return thousands of properties and businesses the East German state had held in trusteeship and, in many cases, improperly administered since the flight of millions of the GDR's citizens to the West in the 1950s.[27] Also, the two regimes agreed to nullify all exchanges and contracts that could be shown to have resulted from "unfair machina-tions" (*unlautere Machenschaften*) during the period of communist rule such as exchanges based on corruption, deceptive business practices, or the abuse of state power. And, in accordance with past *West* German policy, the Property statute extended this principle to Jewish claimants and other victims of Nazi persecution whose houses and land-holdings had been illegally confiscated between 1933 and 1945.[28]

Just the same, German authorities were not eager to have the pro-perty question become a new flash point between easterners and west-erners. In fact, during the Bundestag debates over the Unification treaty, Schäuble advised his colleagues against pushing the issue overly hard. There were "some things in history," he noted, "that one [could not] undo – war, division, injustice, and dictatorship; one [could not] undo every instance of injustice on a point for point basis." Schäuble admitted that his government's remedies for this situation would not always please everyone in every respect. Yet in view of the contending interests at stake, the agreements the Kohl administration had struck with East Berlin were as good as anyone could have expected. "In the final analysis," Schäuble affirmed, "after more than 40 years of divi-sion, the most important thing is to secure the present and the future of our German fatherland. This goal is even more important than any reckoning with the past."[29]

The Challenge of Implementing the Property Statute

Naturally, in view of the vast scope of the task before them, not even the most ardent supporters of property revision would have assumed that this undertaking could be accomplished overnight.[30] From the first, it was evident to everyone involved that it would take time to assemble the professional staffs needed to implement the Property statute. By the late 1990s, the Berlin-based Federal Office for the Settlement of Open Property Questions (or BARoV) and the six state offices and over 220 local offices that were created to investigate and adjudicate con-flicting claims would have over 5,200 employees. All of these agencies had to be built from the ground up. This enormous task not only ne-cessitated locating personnel with the appropriate administrative and legal skills to fulfill these functions, but officials also required ongoing retraining and adaptation to keep pace with the law itself. In the first 5 years of its existence, the Property statute alone underwent eight major revisions, which is nearly twice the rate at which the West German Offset-payments law had been amended in the 1950s.[31]

In addition, the challenge of reviewing millions of claims to lost property was slowed by the need for continual coordination among the claims offices themselves. Had Bonn really possessed the neocolonial ambitions that critics accused it of exhibiting in the early stages of unification, one might have expected the German government to channel all property-related decisions in a top–down manner through the federal claims office in Berlin. But, as the agency's employees were quick to stress, the BARoV was "a tiger without teeth."[32] With the exception of claims involving the holdings of the former SED party organization, the federal agency enjoyed little more than an advisory role in the implementation of the Property statute. Instead, to an even greater degree than with the screening of suspected Stasi informants (a process that at least allowed for the centralization of basic information in the offices of the BStU), the primary responsibility for redressing property disputes was dispersed among the *Länder* and lower municipal agencies.

In many cases, this situation meant that the way the law was applied from state to state was shaped by the diverse settings in which decisions were adjudicated. Some states, like Saxony and Mecklenburg–Vorpommern, were more efficient than others in recruiting the personnel required to review conflicting ownership claims. Others, in contrast, had to contend with unusually complex legacies of injustice. This was especially true of many of the claims on former Jewish land-holdings and businesses in and around Berlin. Even the lines of administrative accountability varied from state to state. In Saxony, central authority was invested in the Ministry of Labor and Economics; in Saxony–Anhalt, in the justice ministry; and in the other *Länder*, in the ministries of finance.[33] Further complicating matters, local land offices in Berlin operated with a significant degree of managerial autonomy from their titular superiors at the state level.[34]

From the practitioners' standpoint, however, the greatest obstacle to the expeditious resolution of disputes was the extraordinary expenditure in time and effort that was required to make sense of the competing claims before them. The scope of the undertaking is reflected in a typical claims official's having to pass judgment on the following questions for every contested claim: (1) the extent to which the application for restitution or compensation had been filed in conformity with the law

(Was it submitted before the relevant filing deadline? Did it address the appropriate issues? What sections of the property statute were applicable?); (2) the "history" of the property in question (To what extent could ownership claims be substantiated? How had control over the property been lost? What evidence had the current property holder provided that acquisition had been "honest" [*redlich*]); and finally, (3) the fate of the property itself (Was it to be returned to the original owner? Or was the claimant only entitled to compensation for his or her loss?).[35]

Finding the answers to these questions was not easy. After all, the leaders of the SED had not operated under the assumption that they would need to prepare the German people for national reunification – at least not under capitalist auspices.[36] As a consequence, the registration of land titles and related obligations in GDR times had often been carried out in a sloppy and haphazard fashion. In many instances, large sections of property registers were inked out or pages removed to conceal information about original ownership rights. In others, entirely new registers had been created to simplify the multiple divisions and subdivisions of properties that had taken place after their initial expropriation.[37]

Accordingly, claims officials frequently had to sort their way through cases in which multiple claims to ownership could be made, apparently legitimately, on a single piece of property. Consider the following example. It was not unheard of for one group of claimants to demand the return of part of a given landholding on the grounds that its members had been unfairly compensated for losses incurred during the SED's nationalization campaigns in the early 1950s. At the same time, a competing group would lay claim to another section of the same property by arguing that it had been illegally expropriated after its former owners had fled political persecution in the GDR. Simultaneously, ownership of the entire property could be called into question by the heirs of Jewish victims of Nazi "Aryanization" policies.[38]

In this regard, one can understand why the officials charged with putting the property settlement into motion were subsequently inclined to define the success of their mission in quantitative terms.[39] Indeed, if one looked only a few years down the road and focused on the straightforward fulfillment of statutory obligations, the results of these efforts were encouraging. By early 1994, despite the doomsayers' prophecies, federal, state, and local agencies had together managed to resolve one-third of the 2.7 million property claims of all types that had come before their offices.[40] By fall 1995, they had settled over half of those (or roughly 2.2 million claims) that specifically involved disputes over real estate.[41] One year later, this number had risen to nearly 70 percent.[42]

Property officials also brought the same matter-of-fact perspective to the related task of stimulating private investment in the eastern *Länder*. The last word has yet to be written about the degree to which unresolved property questions contributed to the ex-GDR's manifold economic difficulties in the early 1990s.[43] There can be no doubt that uncertainties about ownership in the East clouded the economic atmosphere for some western business persons. Still, even if Bonn and East Berlin had never raised the issue of restitution, potential investors would have had to worry about numerous other obstacles to the region's economic development. These included the wildly fluctuating value of many of the properties that interested them and the countless hazards bequeathed to the German nation by decades of socialist mismanagement such as widespread environmental contamination.[44]

In any event, German decision makers acted as though the pursuit of corrective justice could not, in every instance, be allowed to stand in the way of economic growth. On March 31, 1991, in the first of the revisions to the Property statute, the Bundestag passed legislation to increase the availability of properties considered integral to the eastern German economy. Although this incentive had been assured formally by the Unification treaty's Law on Special Investments, it had become apparent that the fulfillment of the original statute was impeded by a time-consuming review process in which local property officials were required to certify investors' claims to provide jobs and housing. The revised statute, the extraordinarily named Law on the Removal of Obstacles to the Privatization of Businesses and the Promotion of Investments, eased these procedures for properties already in the hands of government agencies by doing away with the certification process entirely.[45] It also turned over much of the legal competence to dispose of contested real estate to local officials and to the massive trust agency, the *Treuhandanstalt*, that had been formed in 1990 to oversee the privatization of state enterprises in the GDR.[46] Although the new law did not specifically rule out restitution and would not in any case have applied to the Soviet expropriations of 1945–49, it nevertheless reaffirmed the parliament's concern for promoting a healthy investment climate in the East. Claimants who preferred restitution over compensation were required to prove that their use of the property in question would provide equivalent economic benefits to the region.[47]

Here, too, if the ability of claims authorities to live up to the stated goals of the statute was used as the measure of success, the results of these innovations were striking. By September 1996, officials could boast that over 70 percent of all business-related disputes in the East had been settled.[48] In fact, the Removal of Obstacles law and other major revisions to the Property statute (such as a decision by the Bundestag to extend the claims deadline for private investors through the end of 1995) were such integral parts of the federal government's commitment to a pragmatic resolution of the property conflict that commentators began to speak as though an entirely new principle had taken hold in Bonn, the "priority of investment over restitution."

Nonetheless, despite politicians' confident assertions that the German people would soon be able to put the conflict over land and homes behind them, little could be done to overcome persistent feelings among easterners and westerners alike that the property settlement itself was intrinsically unjust. This was not at all because claims officials were unable to provide solid historical evidence to back up their decisions. In their handling of the four distinct legal orders covered by the Property statute (the National Socialist dictatorship, the Soviet occupation regime, the four decades of SED rule, and the three transitional governments of the GDR's final year), they were practically hyperattentive to these questions. Rather, a more interesting, if unintended consequence of their efforts to take these different legal cultures into account was that they frequently found themselves seeming to apply one standard of justice to the victims of one era of expropriation but quite a different standard to those who lost property in another.

The Legitimacy of Jewish Claims

To understand the predicament represented by the many different German property orders in the twentieth century, it is helpful to begin with an example far removed from the injustices of the GDR era, that is, the crimes committed against property holders under the Third Reich. If ever there was a case of injustice Bonn could not ignore, it was this one, however intractable it may sometimes have seemed.

On the one hand, the Property statute's inclusion of the victims of "racial, political, religious, and ideological" persecution for the period between January 30, 1933, and May 8, 1945, as potential subjects of restitution and compensation was bound to produce its share of critics if only because a half century or more had elapsed since many of the offenses the law was seeking to correct. Especially in the case of the Jewish victims of National Socialism and their heirs, who constituted the majority of claimants in this category and a significant share of the total property claims in some parts of eastern Germany (e.g., up to 25 percent in Berlin), it was enormously time-consuming to locate the properties in question. Entire cities had been rebuilt as a result of the devastation of the Second World War, and, over the intervening years, once familiar streets, buildings, and other landmarks had vanished. Adding to the trouble, few of the original owners were still around to reacquire their lost homes and land. Because many claims were therefore filed by relatives who would probably never return to their ancestral homes or by impersonal organizations acting on behalf of the victims, such as the Jewish Claims Conference, some commentators were quick to conclude that the benefits of redressing these wrongs were easily outweighed by the heavy costs they represented to social peace.[49]

On the other hand, even with the passage of time, it is difficult to imagine how lawmakers could have entertained any other policy toward the Jewish victims of National Socialism. The precedents for returning property in these cases were very strong. In the immediate postwar period, all of the Western allies had adopted statutes in their respective zones of occupation that restored confiscated buildings, real estate, bank accounts, and other possessions to their original owners. Following the FRG's founding in 1949, these measures then became defining features of Konrad Adenauer's commitment to atone for "the base acts perpetrated in the name of the whole German people." True, the chancellor's motives were not completely altruistic. By emphasizing restitution and reparations, he may have hoped to deflect attention from his government's decision to refrain from making criminal trials or purges of former Nazi officials a central feature of its *Vergangenheitsbewältigung*.[50] One way or the other, beginning with the signing of the Luxemburg agreement of September 1952, the Federal Republic made billions of marks in indemnification payments to the individual victims of Nazism and to the state of Israel. In July 1957, the

Bundestag passed the Federal Restitution Law, which provided the legal framework for redressing over 700,000 property-related claims over the ensuing three decades.

In this light, the Kohl administration needed no new legal rationale for assuming the same obligations for eastern Germany. In particular, advocates of the property settlement maintained that the resolution of these claims was necessitated by the Basic Law's commitment to equal treatment (Article 3 [1]). Given the SED's failure to address the restitution issue adequately after the war, a policy that was later complemented by scarcely disguised anti-Semitic programs in the 1950s, the return of illegally expropriated property in eastern Germany was unavoidable. To property settlement supporters, it was a matter of completing the process of moral reparations that had already been successfully carried out in the other half of the divided nation.[51] Thus, Jewish victims who had been unable to realize their demands for justice during the more than four decades of communist dictatorship in the GDR would finally be able to take advantage of the rights and privileges that had long been a commonplace in the West.[52]

Once again, however, in responding to these injustices the federal government was not acting in a vacuum. For one thing, the GDR had set much of this process of restitution in motion. On April 12, 1990, under de Maizière's leadership, the Volkskammer had finally adopted a declaration of responsibility in its part of Germany for the persecution of the Jewish people under National Socialism. Symbolically, this step was to make up for the communist regime's years of official neglect of the Holocaust.[53]

Then, too, even the manner in which reparations claims were to be assessed was based upon precedent – in this case on a principle established four decades earlier by western Germany's three occupation authorities. In a fashion subsequently reviewed and declared constitutional by the FRG's courts, Great Britain, France, and the United States had sought to take into account the unique historical circumstances under which many land-holdings and houses had changed hands under National Socialism by beginning with the assumption that all Jewish property lost in the period was the result of persecution. This step allowed them to shift the burden of proof required to resolve ownership disputes in these instances away from those Jewish claimants who were seeking restitution and to place it squarely on the shoulders of the current property holders.[54]

In taking this step, the allies and later German policymakers did not mean to suggest that everyone who professed to be a victim of Nazi persecution was automatically entitled to regain their lost holdings. To have gone this far would have been tantamount to depriving the current tenants of many properties of their own constitutionally guaranteed rights of ownership. Rather, the objective was to induce claims officials to treat all property exchanges occurring during this unstable era in German history with a greater than normal degree of skepticism.

In the implementation of the Property statute, this principle was spelled out as follows: For cases involving the period between January 30, 1933, and September 14, 1935, when one could maintain that there was still a predictable rule of law in Germany, current property holders could defend their claims to ownership merely by showing that they or their relations had acquired the property in question at a fair and appropriate market price. But for the period thereafter, beginning with the enunciation of the "Nuremberg laws" on September 15, 1935, and culminating in the Nazis' wholesale persecution of the Jews and other groups, the official test of ownership was more severe. In these instances, current property holders could only retain their holdings if they demonstrated that they (or their relations) had made every reasonable effort to respect the interests of the former owners in the midst of the chaos engulfing the country.[55]

In actuality, some quite prominent disputes involving Jewish claimants during the 1990s did not result in restitution because current property holders were able to meet these relatively stringent tests of legal ownership. For example, in one closely watched case, a Potsdam administrative court ruled in mid-December 1996 that Peter Sonnenthal, a principal heir to the Berlin industrial fortune of Max and Albert Sabersky, was not entitled to several sizable plots of land in the area of Teltow–Seehof because, in the judges' opinion, all of these properties had changed hands under circumstances that could be considered fair and normal business practice in 1934. Sonnenthal and other heirs immediately appealed the decision.[56]

Still, it is easy to see why those who were intent upon acting on the property question would have needed little persuading that National Socialist injustice was an instance in which one had to look beyond the offenses of the GDR era alone. Indeed, the Property statute included a "priority principle" (§3 [2]) according to which individuals who had been the first to be subjected to unlawful expropriation were given preferential treatment over all other claims. By itself, this approach made good sense in view of the different legal orders in the nation's past. Yet the authors of the property settlement almost immediately seemed to contradict themselves when they sought to let history be their guide in another era of injustice, the Soviet expropriations of 1945–49. This time, notably, in view of the other types of retrospective justice we have considered, the primary losers were not on the eastern side of the inter-German border but in the West.

... but the Irreversibility of Soviet Expropriations

Reasonable people will likely continue to disagree about the extent to which any event in the past century can be equated with the crimes of the Holocaust. Notwithstanding this caveat, the massive expropriation of land-holdings by the Soviet Military Administration in Germany (SMAD) in the first few years after World War II would qualify as a grave instance of injustice. Under the pretext of engaging in "land reform" in their occupation zone, Soviet authorities undertook the sweeping and, in many cases, brutal confiscation of nearly one-third of the landed property of the area that would eventually become the GDR. Some of the occupation regime's measures were directed against identifiable war criminals and former Nazi leaders and their sympathizers. Others were directed against the Prussian nobility, or Junkers, even though most representatives of this class had been killed during the war or in its immediate aftermath. But in numerous other cases, ordinary citizens became the targets of expropriation merely because their land-holdings were deemed extensive enough, in Marxist terms, to have contributed to the system of monopoly capitalism and reactionary politics that gave rise to fascism. In effect, anyone possessing over 100 hectares of land (roughly 247 acres) in the years after August 1945 was eligible for inclusion in this category. Often with little more than an hour to pack their belongings and with little hope of ever being compensated for their losses, thousands of landowners were deprived of farms and estates that had been passed down through families for generations. Many were then forcibly resettled to other parts of the Soviet occupation zone – ostensibly so they would not get in the way of Moscow's land measures.[57]

It was thus with shock and indignation that many former owners and their heirs received word that the signatories of the joint declaration of

1990 had decided to exclude all of these properties from restitution and to make this principle a binding feature of the Unification treaty. From their predominantly western German vantage point, the protection of private property rights was a fundamental and uncompromisable element of the FRG's status as a *Rechtsstaat*. Therefore, for Bonn even to appear to sanction the Soviet Union's actions was directly contrary to the guiding spirit of the rule of law. One commentator summarized the point succinctly: "*Ex iniuria ius non oritur*" ("justice cannot be made out of injustice").[58]

As the reader will have anticipated, the former owners and their advocates lost no time in arguing that the failure to return their lost holdings was an outright violation of the Basic Law's commitment to equal protection. How, they wondered, could the German government avoid blatant self-contradiction if it agreed to return properties from one period of its history (i.e., the era of National Socialist injustice between 1933 and 1945) but then failed to guarantee the same constitutional rights to the victims of Soviet injustice in the years immediately thereafter?

Adding fuel to these arguments, the critics could marshal evidence to suggest that Bonn had made its fateful decision less out of a thirst for justice than on the, in their view, morally problematic grounds of political expediency. From the moment the property question emerged as a major subject of discussion between the two German governments in early 1990, the GDR's representatives had advised their western interlocutors that they would refuse to consider any postunification arrangement that included a revision of the Soviet land reform properties. For members of the Modrow government, this was practically a matter of faith. They regarded the land reform period in quasi-theological terms as marking the definitive break from centuries of reaction and the advent of a more progressive era in German history.[59]

It cannot have helped the FRG's credibility in this dispute that there was additional evidence that Bonn caved in to pressures from Moscow in its handling of these matters. When the multinational "two-plus-four" negotiations on the restoration of full German sovereignty began in February 1990, Soviet negotiators appeared, to many observers, to link their readiness to come to a settlement directly to the Kohl administration's acceptance of the finality of the postwar property regime. This view was expressed in a frank statement by the TASS news agency on March 27, 1990. It advised that "any eventual attempts to contest the rights of current land-holders and of other property in the GDR that had once been acquired with the consent of the Soviet [Union] and as a result of its decisions . . . would be absolutely unacceptable."[60]

If there was any remaining doubt, however, about the weight of expediency in Bonn's calculations, this would seem to have been overcome by the flat pronouncement of East Germany's freely elected de Maizière government that the land reform properties were "not open to negotiation."[61] Unlike their predecessors, the new prime minister and his colleagues could not have been accused of harboring the same sentimental attachments to Marxist ideology. Instead, they simply seem to have believed that the reopening of the status of millions of acres of landed property in the GDR would precipitate widespread social unrest. Many of the current occupants of these properties, as one-time expellees and refugees from Poland, Czechoslovakia, and other eastern parts, had been the immediate beneficiaries of the expropriations of 1945 and 1946.[62] Further, despite the SED's collectivization drives of 1952 and 1960, they still retained formal legal title to these holdings. Hence, it was only natural, the GDR's last government emphasized, that these claimants have their rights to ownership confirmed.

Given the sensitivity of these issues and the intense polarization they generated between East and West, it is not surprising that the FRG's role in this part of the property accord was soon the subject of an important test before the FCC. In suits filed before the court shortly after the signing of the Unification treaty, 14 former landowners argued that the German government had exceeded its authority in amending the constitution (Art. 143 [3]) to exclude the land reform properties from restitution. The new article, they argued, violated Article 79 (3), which prohibited amendment of the Basic Law in a way that would infringe certain fundamental values.[63] Nevertheless, although the court recognized that some compensation was owed to those whose property was expropriated in 1945–49 – though not necessarily at full market value – the first senate ruled against the complainants' demands for restitution, essentially upholding all of the central features of Bonn's stand on the land reform properties.[64]

By itself, this decision was significant because of the instant solace it offered to the tens of thousands of eastern property holders who had feared they would be the ultimate losers in this dispute. These were undoubtedly the people Schäuble had in mind when he observed that the property question was not only a vital concern to aggrieved westerners but also to residents of the former GDR who had acted in the good faith that their country's legal system would remain in place to protect their interests. But for our purposes, it was how the court came to this judgment that was most revealing of the tricky position in which it found itself in seeking to explain, in effect, why one of these competing demands for corrective justice should get preference.

One section of the court's ruling was bound to be disquieting to the former landowners in any case because it had little to do with justice per se. This involved the degree to which West German negotiators had been motivated by considerations of *Realpolitik* in their discussions with Moscow and East Berlin about the status of the contested properties. Notably, the court did not dispute the factual basis of this argument. Relying upon oral testimony from Klaus Kinkel, Germany's recently named foreign minister, and State Secretary Dieter Kastrup, the judges concluded that political expediency had, in fact, played a major role in Bonn's calculations. Yet instead of jumping from this evidence to the conclusion that federal authorities had acted improperly by acceding to Soviet and East German demands, the judges argued that the FRG's representatives had simply done their best in difficult circumstances to realize a constitutionally prescribed goal – national unification. Without the attainment of this objective, they opined, no property settlement at all would have been conceivable. In this sense, because the eastern parties had consistently maintained that "the chance to restore the unity of Germany could not have been taken if their conditions were not accepted," the court found Bonn's behavior to be perfectly consistent with the Basic Law.[65]

In another section of their ruling, the justices appealed directly to the historical context under which the expropriations had taken place. They used this perspective to cast doubt on the Federal Republic's competence to sit in judgment on the Soviet occupation regime in eastern Germany. As the court explained, "[t]he question of whether somebody is entitled to a specific legal interest can only be answered with respect to a concrete legal order."[66] In this instance, the justices found that Bonn's ability to define this order was obscure at best. Although West Germany had long considered itself to be, in the sense of the Basic Law's original preamble, responsible for the German nation in its entirety, one could, in the court's opinion, raise serious doubts about whether its claims to jurisdiction in the East were equal to those of the Soviet Union at the time of the expropriations. During that period, the justices pointed out, the Basic Law did not even exist. In contrast, Moscow was the closest thing to a sovereign authority in eastern Germany by virtue of its rights as an occupation power. For this reason, the court determined that the Soviets were best positioned to decide the operative legal norms in the territory under their control, including those governing the uses and distribution of property.[67]

Subsequent commentaries have made much of the fact that the high court's decision was far from being a model of legal clarity and consistency, and it also bore signs of having been hastily drafted.[68] For example, the judgment is vaguer than one would desire about the nature and extent of Soviet sovereignty over eastern Germany, leaving open the possibility that the expropriations could have violated existing international law on military occupation. Further, in portions of the judgment, the court seems to have gone to extreme lengths to steel itself against reminders of the indignities and harms inflicted under Soviet occupation. In one passage, aptly characterized by one critic as "astonishing,"[69] the court seems blithely to dismiss the complainants' argument that they were being deprived of their right to restitution, almost to the point – remarkably, we might add – of endorsing the SMAD's definition of its revolutionary objectives. "It is part of the essence of such a change in the social order," the judges cooly assert, "that little or no compensation will be paid because otherwise the anticipated social upheaval would come to naught."[70]

In all probability, Germany's highest court would have chosen more judicious language had it been commenting on the property claims of the victims of National Socialist policy. Still, the more compelling question to pose is, Was the court applying a different standard of justice in insisting that the land reform controversy be assessed in the light of the specific legal order in the Soviet occupation zone between 1945 and 1949? In this case, there is good reason to conclude it was not.

As we have already seen, even though the burden of proof was reversed in the FRG's handling of the victims of Nazi oppression, the outcome of many of these disputes over earlier offenses was dictated by the lower courts' interpretations of the historical conditions under which contested properties had changed hands. Particularly for the first years of National Socialist rule, when it was easier to defend the existence of a functioning rule of law in Germany, there were numerous cases when the grounds simply did not exist for restitution. Similarly, one can say that the high court was making the same argument for the Soviet period. As morally reprehensible as the SMAD's policies had been, they nonetheless had the binding force of law.

As will be discussed in the next section, it was more than slightly ironic that this reliance upon preexisting legal standards would provide more hopeful grounds for the return of properties lost in the period after the GDR's founding in 1949. Yet even for these cases, the FRG's willingness to take another regime's legal structures seriously would still give rise to some seemingly glaring instances of injustice. This is nowhere more apparent than in the fate of many properties that were expropriated in 1961 to allow for the construction of the Berlin Wall.

Vying Responses to GDR-Era Injustice

In view of the preceding controversies, the casual observer of German property policy for the 1949–89 period may understandably wonder whether Bonn was not more interested in satisfying the demands of claimants from the GDR era than in the misfortunes of the victims of Soviet policies. As we have suggested earlier, another contested part of the Property statute, albeit one mainly disputed by easterners, was its provision for the return of property (or, minimally, the payment of some measure of compensation) to persons who had lost homes and land-holdings as a result of political persecution by the SED, "cold expropriations," and various other forms of shady or unfair business practices. However, to imagine that this stance simply bespoke a greater sensitivity to the crimes of East German socialism would be to neglect a more revealing point about the property settlement. The GDR was not only a different legal order from that of the Soviet zone of occupation but one for which it was significantly easier for Bonn to justify claims for corrective action. As a consequence, policymakers' room for maneuver was much greater than it had been for the immediate postwar period.

One reason for this difference will be immediately apparent to the reader. More convincingly than in the pre-1949 cases, federal authorities could argue that their ability to act upon instances of injustice under SED rule was consistent with their long-standing claim to speak for the interests of all Germans. When millions of East Germans were forced to flee the GDR in the 1950s because of unpopular political views and unwelcome class backgrounds or as a result of the SED's campaigns to hasten the transition to socialism, the FRG had not hesitated to extend to them all of the benefits and protections of the Basic Law. They were automatically considered full citizens of the Federal Republic by virtue of their common German nationality. Accordingly, it made sense to think that Bonn should immediately seek to rectify the wrongs they had suffered (so-called *Teilungsunrecht* or "division-related injustice") now that the artificial separation of the German people had been overcome.

More important, decision makers could take advantage of the fact that many of the offenses in question, such as the expulsion of citizens living along the inter-German border in 1952, had taken place in violation of the GDR's own laws. Suggestively, in view of the SED's policies to come, the right to private property was formally guaranteed by both East German constitutions of 1949 and 1968, and an elaborate code of laws had governed the manner in which these holdings could be transferred from one party to another. For example, like most modern states, the East German government reserved the right to expropriate private property when it was needed to serve the common good, such as the construction of public buildings and highways. Yet even this prerogative was not meant to be exercised irresponsibly; the constitution specified that owners should be appropriately compensated for their losses. Similarly, the East German penal code, like its West German counterpart, contained numerous provisions that supposedly protected citizens against abusive state practices and other "unfair machinations," such as corruption, duress, and deception.[71]

An immediate advantage of these statutes was that they put former property owners in a position in which they could theoretically argue, much as prosecutors were to do during the Wall trials, that the GDR had violated its own laws in depriving it citizens of their holdings. Thus, if they had not been adequately compensated for land lost as a result of, say, the GDR's Construction law of 1950, which facilitated the rebuilding of many war-ravaged city centers, or the National Culture law of 1970, which provided for the creation of a countrywide system of recreation parks and resorts, they could readily appeal to East German statutes to buttress their claims. In any case, many original owners complained that Bonn's assessment of the extent of these losses was insufficient to cover the difference between the original value of their holdings and the property's much higher market value after unification. In some cases, such as the prime real estate in the vicinity of Berlin's Potsdamer Platz, the value of these holdings had nearly doubled. But unlike the former owners in the dispute over the Soviet land reform properties, these claimants could take comfort in knowing that some legal avenues were available for pursuing their grievances.

Other remedies were potentially available to the thousands of East Germans who, in various ways, had been coerced and cajoled over the years into selling their homes and possessions when they applied for official permission to emigrate to the West. Quite frequently, people who were subjected to these pressures were given no time to reach their decisions and rarely had any say over the final price at which their holdings were sold. For these reasons, it was at least debatable whether property obtained in this manner should be considered an honest acquisition under GDR law. A lot depended on how the property's subsequent owners had received title to the holding.

A slightly less obvious but no less important benefit of this recourse to preexisting standards was that German policymakers were thereby freed from the onerous – indeed, impossible – challenge of having to resolve all of the property-related injustices that had taken place over the history of the GDR. German administrative courts were at pains to emphasize the point, noting that the negotiators of the property settlement had never envisioned a complete revision of the eastern property order. Such an attempt would not only have been impractical in view of the breadth and depth of the GDR's transformation under socialism, but it would also have been incompatible with Bonn's and East Berlin's avowed aims of arriving at a viable compromise among the diverse claimants in the two parts of Germany.[72]

Nonetheless, as sensible as it may have seemed to confine claims for restitution and compensation to explicit violations of GDR law, some legal analysts were careful to point out that this selective manner of dealing with the past came at a potentially high cost. In the many instances when the communist regime had already provided one-time owners with what it judged to be appropriate levels of compensation for their losses, its successors in the FRG were under no further obligation to redress property owners' claims after the attainment of national unity.

This contradiction became painfully apparent in the early 1990s when many of the original owners of properties along the path of the old Berlin Wall (including those in the area of Potsdamer Platz) sought to regain title to their now immensely more valuable holdings by arguing that they had been unjustly expropriated under the GDR's National Defense statute of September 20, 1961. In making these demands, the claimants stressed that the measures surrounding the Wall's construction were fundamentally different in moral terms than the Construction law or the National Culture law. Klaus Kinkel's successor in the Justice ministry, Sabine Leutheusser-Schnarrenberger, came to their defense on this point in 1994. "The expropriations [that served the erection] of the Wall and barbed wire," she declared, "were nothing short of symbols of the regime of injustice of the former GDR and the division of Germany."[73] For that matter, the claimants themselves emphasized that the primary beneficiaries of restitution in this case would not so much be the haves of German unification, the presumably better-off citizens of western Germany, but instead the have-nots of eastern Germany who had lived along the barrier's perimeter and remained in their country after 1961.

Nevertheless, although justice seemed to dictate that the interests of these Germans be addressed through the return of their properties, lawmakers were reluctantly forced to concede that the communist regime's most conspicuously immoral act could not be undone in any meaningful sense. In the majority of these cases, the former property owners had already received compensation for their losses. As a result, the return of their holdings was precluded.[74] The FRG's reliance upon East German norms apparently gave its leaders no other choice but to live with the status quo.

Ambiguities of Drawing the Line

In light of these difficulties, it must have appeared paradoxical to policymakers to find themselves immediately mired in the opposite sort of controversy when they sought to establish a cutoff date, or *Stichtag*, at which GDR law could no longer be utilized to justify the honest acquisition of property. In itself, a decision of some sort was unavoidable. At some point, property officials had to agree upon a date at which the norms of the Basic Law would supplant those of GDR law. Then, too, a point of demarcation was necessary from a practical standpoint as well. At an early stage in their discussions, both eastern and western German negotiators had recognized that the crumbling SED regime no longer had the authority to back up its own laws. As we have suggested, the GDR's representatives worried that former party bosses and apparatchiks would take advantage of their previous positions and political connections to snap up many of the most valuable pieces of property – "filet pieces," as they were called – still in government hands. On the western side, the FRG's representatives were sensitive to apprehensions among the original owners that so many contested properties would change hands before October 3, 1990, that the priority of natural restitution would be rendered meaningless.

As in the other aspects of the property settlement, one can be sure that any decision lawmakers reached on the point at which one period of German history ended and another began would produce an abundance of disappointments. From the perspective of the former owners, the later the date, the greater was the likelihood that existing injustices would be reinforced and new wrongs would be generated. But for even greater numbers of easterners, in contrast, a *Stichtag* that was set too early would have the effect of generating a different sort of injustice. Thousands of ordinary East German renters and leaseholders would be deprived of the opportunity to purchase houses and land-holdings from the state they had occupied and maintained for decades. In fact, in the last days of the Modrow regime, in March 1990, the assembled parties in the Volkskammer anticipated this dilemma by enacting a special statute, the Sale law (*Verkaufsgesetz*), which accorded the eastern German population precisely this right. In short course, local land registries were overrun by a storm of anxious eastern tenants eager to secure title to upwards of 500,000 pieces of real estate. Many were rewarded with their properties.

Given the circumstances, one can understand why these same tenants reacted with disbelief and horror when they learned that the authors of the Property statute had set the official *Stichtag* at the earliest conceivable date, October 18, 1989, the day of Honecker's fall from power.[75] For those who had thought they could improve their station in life by moving, literally, from one Germany to the next, the disqualification of all of the purchases resulting from the Sale law and other related provisions was a terrible blow. It was, as one observer has expressed in a play on the word *Stichtag*, a "stab in the heart" (*Stich ins Herz*) for anyone who believed his or her deeds should be evaluated according to the only legal system he or she had known for 40 years.[76]

In defense of their position, lawmakers explained that they had chosen the date of Honecker's resignation because it marked the decisive point at which the transition to a new social and economic order had begun in the East. Naturally, the officials cautioned, East German citizens deserved to be judged in the light of their country's laws. But, they added, this principle made sense only as long as that system of laws was fully in effect.

The logic behind this argument may have been impeccable, but it is hard to avoid the conclusion that, in at least two respects, it was applied in an unnecessarily rigid and restrictive manner.[77] First, the lawmakers' attempt to use GDR history as the medium for setting the threshold date seems on closer inspection to have been curiously ahistorical. To be sure, with the benefit of hindsight, we can see that Honecker's departure marked the first in a series of key events that would culminate in the country's collapse and pave the way for unification. But on October 18, 1989, these facts were apparent to almost no one. When Egon Krenz replaced his former mentor as general secretary of the SED on that date, most East Germans, and especially the leaders of the civic groups that had brought the ruling party to its knees, still viewed their country's best prospects in terms of a thoroughgoing reform of the existing communist system. Only in later weeks – notably, after the opening of the Wall on November 9 – did the topic of German unification emerge as a subject of public speculation, and this occurred only sporadically at first. It was not until November 28, 1989, more than a month after the date of the announced *Stichtag*, that Helmut Kohl broached a cautious, long-term program for restoring national unity. Yet even this plan was to be based at first on the elaboration of certain unspecified "confederal structures." Indeed, a clear picture of German unity would only begin to crystallize with both East Berlin's and Moscow's grudging acquiescence in January 1990.[78]

For these reasons alone, it seems inappropriate for Bonn to have expected that East Germany's citizens would have any more insight into their country's future than the decision makers most intimately connected with the inter-German relationship. In fact, as commentators on the legality of the cutoff date have pointed out, the prospect of a completely different property order in eastern Germany was not really clarified until June 14, 1990, when the two German governments signed their joint declaration on unresolved property questions.[79] Would not a later *Stichtag* have been better?

Second, even if the announced cutoff date had made better sense from an historical standpoint, there was no reason for the FRG's leaders to have applied it as rigidly as the Property statute required. The joint declaration as well had used October 18, 1989, as a threshold date, but only for establishing a juncture at which subsequent property exchanges were to be, in the document's terminology, "scrutinized."[80] In this case, the concept of honest acquisition remained fully in effect. If, on the one hand, claims officials determined that a piece of real estate had changed hands as a result of the corrupt practices or political machinations that had been feared of SED *Bonzen* (party bosses) during the GDR's last days, the exchange could be nullified immediately. On the other hand, if the current occupants of a property had made an honest effort to purchase a house or apartment they had inhabited for years, they would at minimum have been given the chance to defend their claims.

To its credit, the Bundestag sought to address these issues in later amendments to the Property statute. A revision of the law on July 14, 1992, protected property holders from the threat of restitution and gave them the opportunity to purchase contested holdings (at approximately half of their current market value) if they fell into any one of three categories: if they had made the attempt to acquire title to these properties before the cutoff date, if they would turn the property to beneficial commercial purposes, or if they had already made significant material improvements to the property. Likewise, with the Property Adjustment law (*Sachenrechtsbereinigungsgesetz*) of September 21, 1994, the parliament provided additional safeguards for individuals who had previously obtained easements to houses or other forms of property without gaining title to the land on which these buildings were situated.[81]

Nevertheless, although such refinements in the law would help to protect the interests of some property holders, it is easy to understand why they were too few or were introduced too late to ease the anxieties of thousands of other claimants. These parties sensed, with good reason, that they had become caught between incommensurable periods in German history.

The Enduring Burden of Multiple Pasts

In short, when Detlef Dalk committed suicide in 1992, he gave voice to a deeply felt and largely understandable sense of dissatisfaction in the East about the consequences of the property settlement. Yet this sentiment cannot be attributed simply to a failure by the FRG to take eastern German interests into account in the architecture of the Property statute. There were elements of compromise at almost every stage of negotiation. Nor can it be said that western Germans were merely imposing an arbitrary victor's justice on the citizens of the former GDR. Whether in different ways or to differing degrees, the issue took its toll on Germans in both parts of the nation, and it spoke to the difficulty of pursuing corrective justice in the unusual circumstances of having to contend with multiple German legal orders.

This problem was raised anew in late 1992 and early 1993, when the conservative parties in the Bundestag broached a plan for making compensatory "settlement payments" to the former owners of the Soviet land reform properties much like those the fledgling West German state had paid to refugees in the early 1950s. As we have seen, the Constitutional Court had required some degree of compensation in its landmark 1991 decision, though it left the amount open. What made the Bundestag's overture especially controversial, however, was the parliamentary majority's proposal that these payments be used to buy back portions of the land reform holdings themselves. According to the plan's advocates, this step was perfectly consistent with the spirit of the joint declaration because, in their view, there was no real contradiction between recognizing the irreversibility of the Soviet expropriations, on the one hand, and furthering the constitutional right of all Germans to purchase property, on the other.[82] However, many former GDR citizens were outraged at the proposal, finding it to be nothing short of a cynical attempt to undo one of the few significant eastern gains in the property agreement. Also, because much of the land in question would have been unavailable to the large cooperative associations that had succeeded the GDR's collective farms, the parliamentarians' actions seemed to be unequivocal proof of Bonn's determination to destroy one of the last positive remnants of socialism in the East.[83]

In fact, the bitter conflict that ensued over this issue eventually led the Bundestag to adopt a modified compromise agreement in September 1994. With the Compensation and Equalization Payments law, the former owners of land reform properties were allowed to forego the settlement payments to which they were entitled in exchange for the right to purchase moderately sized parcels of agricultural and forest land that had previously been in state hands. It is important to note that this privilege was structured in such a way as to preserve two distinct aspects of the status quo. The first rights of purchase were to go to those individuals, in the East or West, who were best prepared to put their acquisitions to immediate economic use; above all, this provision was designed to favor the current lessees of farm property and the agricultural cooperatives. At the same time, the new statute imposed significant limitations on the amount of land would-be purchasers could acquire for speculative purposes alone.[84]

At first blush, one might have expected this agreement to have all of the elements of a lasting quid pro quo. Although neither of the two parties to the dispute had gotten exactly what it wanted, could one not say that significant progress had been made in addressing one of the great anomalies of the postwar era? However, the adoption of this optimistic perspective would be to overlook the vastly different understandings that still prevailed in eastern and western Germany of what had occurred in the 1945–49 period. As a result of this psychology, the two sides concentrated their attention as much upon what they stood to lose from the new statute as upon what they stood to gain.

As far as many eastern land-holders were concerned, Bonn was only extending to them something they deserved in any case: the right to determine the economic future of their own part of Germany. They believed they already possessed this right by virtue of the region's unique experience with socialism after 1945. Thus, in their eyes, the FRG's concessions to the old landowners were a flagrant denial of these conditions.

In contrast, because many western claimants still refused to accept the legality of the Soviet expropriations, they tended to view the Bundestag compromise as yet another demonstration of Bonn's readiness to sell out their interests. The amount of the settlement payments, many thought, was still much too low to represent adequate compensation for their actual losses. Furthermore, most regarded the parliament's conditions on the acquisition of property in the East as blatant violations of the constitutional guarantee of equal treatment. Indeed, these critical sentiments reverberated throughout the upper echelons of the Kohl administration. In early December 1996, a new justice minister, Edzard Schmidt-Jortzig, shocked his colleagues when he seemed to break ranks with the official line by proclaiming that justice would only be achieved when the land reform properties were returned to their original owners.[85]

Similarly, much the same battle over contending views of the German past took place over the FRG's efforts in the mid-1990s to extricate itself from the embarrassing position of seeming to condone the expropriations of properties along the former Berlin Wall. As we have seen, the Property statute prevented claims officials from returning these holdings if the original owners had already received appropriate compensation for their losses from the GDR government. But in July 1996, the Bundestag bowed to popular pressure to underscore the unjust circumstances behind the Wall's erection by passing legislation that was meant to provide the next best thing to full restitution. Under the statute, original owners were given the right to purchase their lost properties at 25 percent of their current market value, excepting only those holdings that were required for pressing public needs. In these latter cases, the federal government agreed to take on the burden of compensating the one-time owners at 75 percent of the properties' market value.[86]

Here, too, one could easily have concluded that Bonn had found a "balanced compromise" (to quote chancellory spokesman Friedrich Bohl)[87] between conflicting interpretations of the historical record. At last, the victims of the Defense statute of 1961 would be allowed to recover their previous holdings at, by all accounts, extremely favorable prices. Or, failing this option, they would at least be entitled to receive compensatory payments far in excess of those available for other expropriations under SED rule. In the same motion, the FRG would save face among its citizens by taking a strong stand on one of the most heinous acts in GDR history.

Yet once again, one's conception of whether this represented a just solution was directly related to the position taken on the East German past. Far from receiving universal acclaim, the new law was roundly assailed by opposition deputies in the Bundestag for being, in their words, a "cynical, improper, and unjust" attempt to legitimize the GDR's actions retroactively.[88] The only appropriate response to the measures of August 13, 1961, the critics contended, was to return to the original owners that which had been wrongly taken from them. In fairness, one could not ask anything of them in return.

At the same time, conversely, constitutional experts did not hesitate to point out that the statute raised difficult questions about the norms the German government had previously used to distinguish legitimate from illegitimate expropriations under SED rule. If confiscations

under the Defense law were now to be considered at least partially re-
mediable, who was to say that similar injustices could not, and should
not, be identified in the implementation of comparable East German
legislation, such as the Construction law of 1950? And if this was the
case, what was to become of the FRG's already well-established reliance upon preexisting law as the measure for adjudicating property
conflicts over the 40 years of the GDR's existence?[89]

None of this is to say, of course, that in these and other instances
claims offices and courts were unable to work out satisfactory solutions to many of the ownership disputes that pitted Germans against
one another, both between the two parts of the formerly divided nation
and within eastern Germany itself. In fact, as officials gained experience in addressing property questions and as the Property law itself
underwent successive revisions and fine-tuning throughout the 1990s,
the issue gradually lost the sense of immediacy that originally made
it appear to be one of the prime impediments to national unification.
Nevertheless, as much as German policymakers may have hoped to put
this contentious aspect of their past finally behind them, their grappling
with such deeply rooted historical problems suggests that a satisfying
solution to the property conflict would remain permanently beyond
their reach.

6

Conclusion

A MANAGEABLE PAST?

Had the proponents of an aggressive policy of retrospective justice in unified Germany been looking for symbolism, they would have been pleased with two events that occurred virtually 10 years to the day the Berlin Wall was opened. On November 8, 1999, the fifth senate of the Federal Court of Justice in Leipzig rejected an appeal by former SED politburo members Egon Krenz, Günter Schabowski, and Günther Kleiber to have their August 1997 convictions overturned for their roles in the shooting deaths at the border. According to the presiding judge, Monika Harms, the lower court in Berlin had properly found that all the defendants had been key, behind-the-scenes decision makers in the system that facilitated the killings. Thus, it was appropriate that they finally began serving the sentences for their crimes.[1]

Then, on November 9, 1999, a decade's worth of wrestling with the wrongs and injustices of the GDR era seemed to be given definitive legitimation when the Bundestag chose Stasi files commissioner Joachim Gauck to represent the interests of eastern Germany's civil rights activists at the anniversary celebrations over the Wall's fall. In his address before the Berliner Reichstag, Gauck acknowledged that the transition to a unified German state had not always been easy, especially for the handful of idealists who, like himself, had evinced the guts and moral wherewithal in the fall of 1989 to take their case against dictatorship into the streets. Many "had dreamed of paradise," he noted ironically, "and woke up in North Rhine–Westphalia," the western *Land* where Bonn was located. Still, Gauck reflected, the activists' determination "to put so much pressure on the old ruling elite that its walls could no longer be maintained" had brought the Federal Republic something their western German cousins could only dream about, the "historical gift" of having made a revolution in the name of freedom on their own. This moment, and not the later attainment of national unity, was the real point about the events of 1989, and, Gauck seemed to imply, recognition of this achievement should remain a hallmark of his government's policies.[2]

Just below the surface, however, there were good reasons for wondering whether the symbolism behind these developments was really an illusion. For one thing, it was telling that Gauck's inclusion in the Wall ceremonies was largely an afterthought. Only after intense pressure from prominent representatives of the civil rights movement had the Bundestag's Council of Elders finally agreed to add an activist's name to the event's more mainstream speakers' list, which already included George Bush, Mikhail Gorbachev, the FRG's new Social Democratic chancellor, Gerhard Schröder, and Kohl. By virtue of his calm, self-assured profile as head of the BStU, Gauck undoubtedly seemed like a safe choice.[3]

More significant, by the end of 1999, one could hardly say the issue of coming to terms with the GDR's past was anywhere near the center of the Schröder government's policies. As eastern issues came into play, the country's new ruling coalition of the SPD and Greens was primarily concerned with the more concrete and present challenge of reconciling the imperatives of national unification with pressing macroeconomic priorities: how to maintain high levels of "solidarity" payments to the eastern *Länder* and combat long-term unemployment in the region while living up to the coalition's pledges to cut federal spending, overcome institutional paralysis, and stimulate productivity throughout Germany.[4] In this light, it probably said something for the political mood of the time that, when the Federal Court of Justice issued its decision in the politburo case, several prominent figures from across the political spectrum – Hans-Ulrich Klose (SPD), Hans-Christian Ströbele (Greens), Peter Gauweiler (CSU), and even Rainer Eppelmann (CDU) – urged judicial authorities in Berlin to grant Krenz and his associates an immediate pardon lest festering tensions between the two parts of Germany be further aggravated and the GDR's former leaders be transformed into martyrs.[5]

No doubt, much of this flagging interest in the FRG's reckoning with the East German past occurred because the principal vehicles for accomplishing the task had by and large completed their missions as the 1990s drew to a close. On September 30, 1999, the *Staatsanwaltschaft II*, the special prosecutor's office in Berlin charged with investigating major instances of GDR-government criminality, closed its offices. Over the decade, it had considered more than 22,000 possible offenses (out of a total of 62,000 investigations nationwide) and recommended criminal indictments in 1,065 cases.[6]

Also by this time, Gauck had announced his intention not to stand for a third term as overseer of the Stasi holdings (he had been reappointed to the position in 1995). Interest in reviewing personal MfS files remained surprisingly high among both eastern Germans and growing numbers of westerners; by May 1999, more than 1.3 million such requests had been satisfied.[7] However, the use of the records as a tool for administrative screening was tapering off by decade's end. In its fourth Activity Report in 1999, the BStU reported that monthly requests for information from public agencies had declined by about 35 percent.[8] Tentatively, Gauck and others broached the idea of eventually transforming the Stasi archives into a center for historical and journalistic research.[9]

By this juncture as well, the Bundestag's experiment with retrospective justice, the Enquete commission on the "history and consequences of the SED dictatorship," was largely a distant memory for most Germans. The body had wrapped up its second, much less publicized round of hearings over a year-and-a-half earlier. The same point could be made about the German property settlement. By late fall 1999, federal and state officials could claim to have resolved upwards of 92 percent of all private property disputes.[10] On November 23, in fact, the Federal Constitutional Court seemed to cast a definitive, final word on the subject with a ruling on the contested cutoff date (*Stichtag*) – October 18, 1989 – by which properties must have been acquired under East German law to be considered legitimate purchases. In rejecting a complaint by the state of Brandenburg about the constitutionality of this early threshold date, the high court essentially fixed in stone one of the most abiding controversies in the inter-German debate over property rights.[11]

Yet there was a greater cause for concern at this point. This was that after years of fits and starts, missteps, and advances in the pursuit of retrospective justice, many Germans – from well-placed politicians, to commentators in the press, to the ordinary man or woman on the street – had lost sight of the point behind the FRG's long attempt to come to terms with the record of communist rule in East Germany.[12]

Indeed, when the last person involved in the Wall shootings was jailed for his crimes and the country's public bureaucracies were finally purged of the worst Stasi offenders (and, unfortunately, some lesser offenders as well), one could still pose the same questions about the Federal Republic's actions that had been the stuff of fierce debate in 1990. Was the price unified Germany had to pay in terms of added strains and irritations between the two German populations worth the benefits of attempting to rectify the abuses of an era that was, by all accounts, much less horror filled than the Third Reich? Or, conversely, would the FRG's leaders not have been on more solid ground had they simply chosen to draw a "thick line" between a dismal and eminently forgettable period in their national history and the political opportunities of the present?

At first glance, the cases presented in this book appear to provide ample ammunition for the skeptics who took the latter position. The jurisprudence behind at least some of the Wall trials – including, arguably, that which had led to the convictions of Krenz's two politburo associates, Schabowski and Kleiber – was sometimes questionable. On occasion, these judgments may well have led to misunderstandings in the East about the meaning of the rule of law in a *Rechtsstaat*. Then, too, the hunt for Stasi collaborators had sometimes been conducted in a manner that failed to live up to Gauck's and the BStU's high ideals about the appropriate uses of the MfS files. The German public may have been left with the altogether false impression that more easterners had been involved with the Stasi than was actually the case. Likewise, as we have seen, the findings of the Bundestag's Enquete commission were far from free of the political and ideological biases its organizers had hoped to avoid in a bipartisan parliamentary investigation. Last but not least, we would be hard pressed to identify another aspect of Bonn's reckoning with the GDR that contributed to more tensions and misunderstandings between easterners and westerners than the property settlement.

Nonetheless, there are three good reasons for resisting the temptation to write off the FRG's policies as merely misguided or discordant notes along the path to unification. First, it is crucial not to overstate the room for choice that was available to the Federal Republic's leaders in acting upon the East German record of wrongdoing. In fact, in many of the cases we have considered in this study, Bonn's options were limited as a result of earlier decisions by *eastern* officials in the rapid succession of governments attending the GDR's fall. Although there were many occasions when western policymakers would have preferred to look beyond the SED's offenses and focus only on the present, this stance was not always a viable option for them.

Second, as difficult as the pursuit of retrospective justice was, one should not underestimate the federal government's ability to pursue its policies in a manner basically compatible with healing wounds between Germans and promoting social peace. To a great extent, as we have seen, Bonn's success in the endeavor depended upon its leaders' readiness to take East German conditions into account in making their decisions.

The final reason for giving due recognition to the FRG's actions is the broader significance of this example of retrospective justice. Far from being merely a passing episode in twentieth-century German history, the way Bonn dealt with the GDR's legacy – which was, in many respects, a more manageable past than that of National Socialism – is likely to have important implications for how Germans think about themselves in the years to come.

The FRG's Constrained Options

Because of the FRG's overwhelming economic and institutional advantages over the moribund GDR, it is easy to fall into the trap of assuming that Bonn simply foisted its desire for retrospective justice upon the people of eastern Germany after the signing of the Unification treaty. Some historians would apparently have us believe that this was the deciding factor behind the GDR's fate.[13] Yet, as this book has demonstrated, the relationship between the two parts of the German nation in East Berlin's waning months was considerably more complex. Western authorities were capable of acting with much greater subtlety and self-restraint than (to quote historian Herbert Butterfield's famous warning) to "gloat over the defeated, count their trophies, commemorate their achievements, and show how righteousness [had] triumphed."[14] In many respects, far from forcing their ideals upon their hapless counterparts, policymakers actually responded to political agendas and demands for retribution that had initially been generated in the East. In this sense, despite the appearance that the FRG's leaders could dictate the main terms of the German–German relationship, they did not believe that eastern interests could be ignored.

The Wall trials are such an example. They were, of course, conducted by the courts of unified Germany, but many of the precedents for using legal mechanisms to redress injustice were first established by the East German regime. As we have seen, when Egon Krenz took over the SED leadership after Honecker's fall from power, he attempted to use the GDR's legal system to buy time for his government. In late October 1989, the regime created a commission to investigate accusations of police brutality against rights activists and demonstrators. Shortly thereafter, it invited prosecutors to look into the possibility of charging Honecker and others with misconduct in office.

When we consider these actions more than a decade later, it is clear that the Krenz government was primarily interested in using such legal forays to cement its tenuous grip on power. Nevertheless, we can also see that the more the regime and its successors, under Modrow and de Maizière, availed themselves of this avenue, the more the law came to be regarded in the public consciousness as an appropriate vehicle for overcoming the mistakes of the past and establishing a new political order.[15] Technically, the West German architects of unification could have chosen to overlook the rising number of accusations leveled against Honecker and his associates over the ensuing months. Yet, when the charges grew in August 1990 to include the crime of "instigation to commit murder" for the shootings at the inter-German border, Bonn had to contend with a new dynamic, that is, the possibility that it would permanently alienate many easterners who expected that their demands for justice would finally be taken seriously. Then, too, inaction would have raised awkward questions about a basic pillar of the German Rechtsstaat, that is, the notion that no individual was above the law. As a result, when the competence to investigate these cases was transferred to the public prosecutor's office in Berlin after October 3, 1990, the authorities' discussions centered not so much on whether proceedings should be carried out but instead on a more mundane matter: Which of the many charges against the GDR's former leaders could be brought into line with West German statutes?

Likewise, German officials faced constrained circumstances in weighing their response to the two major controversies surrounding the uses of the Stasi files. The first matter, the disposition of the files themselves, was in many ways an explosive issue because of what these records symbolized for hundreds of thousands of citizens whose lives had been adversely affected by the secret police's activities. As we have seen, after the storming of the Stasi's Normannenstraße headquarters, politicians and rights activists were by no means in agreement about what should ultimately be done with these remnants of the apparatus of surveillance. Some believed the MfS's records should immediately be made available to the victims. In contrast, others protested that the opening of the files would provoke havoc in the East – "murder and manslaughter," to quote Prime Minister de Maizière.[16] Or at the very least, it would result in the documents' misuse by foreign intelligence agencies, journalists, and various unscrupulous parties. It was for this reason that overzealous activists made the fateful February 1990 decision, which they later regretted, to destroy the electronic indexes to the MfS holdings. This step was followed by the ministry's foreign intelligence division, the HVA (*Hauptverwaltung Aufklärung*), which succeeded in gutting most of its own records by June 1990.

Still, there was one proposition on which most participants in the debate over the secret police files could readily agree. Whatever fate was to befall the records, they firmly believed that this decision should be made by the GDR's citizens alone. Dissident Jens Reich captured the popular mood in the fall of 1990 as rumors spread that West Germany was planning to move the files out of the GDR for permanent storage in the federal archives in Koblenz. "This is our dirty laundry and our stink," he declared, "and it is up to us alone to clean it up."[17]

In this light, the Stasi Records law (StUG), which the Bundestag enacted in December 1991, must be seen as something more involved and, in this writer's view, more intriguing than merely a western imposition on an unwitting population. In many respects, the decision to regularize the uses of the files was a natural outgrowth of sentiments and expectations that had already come to fruition in the East by the spring of 1990. As early as April 1990, the news weekly *Der Spiegel* found that 86 percent of the East German citizens it surveyed wished to retain the right to examine their personal Stasi dossiers.[18] In this spirit, in the summer of 1990, the Volkskammer drafted a provisional law on the "protection and uses of the personal records [of the MfS]," which was to guide the two Germanys in their final negotiations over the subject. Bonn initially balked at the idea of including the document in the Unification treaty, but many of the parliament's stipulations nevertheless worked their way into both Schäuble's and Krause's negotiations over the accord and into subsequent agreements. These included the proviso that the files should remain on eastern German territory, that some as yet unclarified rights of access to these holdings should be provided to regular citizens, and that strict controls should be placed on their use by intelligence agencies. Many of these stipulations eventually found their way into the StUG as well.

In much the same fashion, western officials found their choices circumscribed by the second issue of consequence surrounding the MfS records, their utilization for vetting public- and private-sector employees. As was suggested earlier in this study, some prominent politicians, including Chancellor Kohl and then-Interior Minister Schäuble, would have been content to play down this particular use of the files. In particular, they worried that these measures would further aggravate the already tense political atmosphere in the East. As will be indicated shortly, they may have also been apprehensive about records in the MfS archives surrounding their own behavior over the years of separation.

Yet here, too, western policymakers were confronted with a series of eastern faits accomplis that dramatically narrowed their options on the Stasi question. One of the formative events in the region's transformation, the Volkskammer elections of March 1990, was shaken by revelations that key figures from the dissident movement, like the Democratic Awakening cofounder Schnur and the eastern Social Democratic leader Böhme, had long been covert informants of the MfS. As these discoveries became more and more frequent, the parliament bowed to public pressure to screen its ranks for Stasi IMs. It then followed up on this initiative by turning its attention to the state ministries and other government agencies. The Volkskammer even made a point of including a provision in its draft law to allow the secret police holdings to serve this end. From this juncture onward, Bonn's use of the files to review potentially every German politician and civil service employee in the East was again only a matter of acting on precedent.

Notwithstanding these pressures, the most intractable issue on which the FRG's leaders found their hands tied was the bitter contest over property rights in eastern Germany. As the property topic surged to the forefront of discussions between Bonn and East Berlin in early spring 1990, even the casual observer of German affairs would have sensed that the attempt to devise just and equitable solutions to millions of unresolved claims to land-holdings, dwellings, and other forms of real estate in the East were destined to precipitate bad feelings and lasting conflicts on both sides of the national divide. The persistent dilemma for western policymakers, however, was that, on many counts, they could not have avoided tough decisions of some kind on these questions. In reviewing the eastern landscape, they not only had to decide whether to uphold some key property-related decisions of the GDR's last governments, which was a large enough challenge by any measure, but also had to factor into their calculations some well-established precedents of their own.

In East Germany, months before unification, West German officials had to contend with strongly held feelings about the final form the property settlement would take. Representatives of both the Modrow and de Maizière governments were adamant in opposing any arrangements that would have led to reassessing or redrawing the Soviet expropriations of the 1945–49 period. Furthermore, they insisted – more reasonably, in this writer's opinion – that recognition be given in an eventual property statute to transactions that had taken place lawfully or otherwise been carried out in an "honest manner" in GDR times.

Naturally, in crafting their responses to this situation, western politicians and judicial officials still enjoyed substantial leeway in determining which of their counterparts' demands would be acceptable to them, both politically and legally. But even with this freedom, it was never a realistic option for them to do nothing. This appears to have been especially true of their response to the final acts of the Modrow regime. Although there were some matters on which policymakers could agree to revisions of the status quo without stirring up much controversy – as was generally the case with the last communist government's decision to return over 11,000 semiprivate firms to their original owners – they were destined to step into the crossfire between easterners and westerners on other matters. This situation arose again over the cutoff date the Kohl administration adopted for property transfers under the Modrow government's Sale law.

Just the same, even if the FRG's leaders had somehow managed to reduce their responsiveness to eastern German demands, they could not have ignored preexisting West German policies on property. As we have seen, from Adenauer's chancellorship onward, the governments of the preceding 40 years had established powerful precedents for returning – or, minimally, paying compensation for – real estate and land-holdings that had been unlawfully expropriated from Jewish citizens and other minorities at the height of the Third Reich. In light of the GDR's widely acknowledged failure to provide for an adequate accounting of these crimes, western policymakers were logically bound to extend the same protections to the eastern victims of National Socialist rule. In fact, the Basic Law's commitment to equal treatment seemed to require this step. But of course, once the FRG's representatives began to move down one path of restitution, the likelihood grew that they would invite further controversy by reawakening questions about property-related injustices in other periods in their nation's history.

In contrast, as the reader will already have surmised, the one form of retrospective justice on which West Germany's leaders seemed to have the greatest latitude in setting priorities was the Bundestag's quasi-historical Enquete commission on the GDR. Had they so desired, they probably could have rebuffed their compatriots' demands for a formal parliamentary inquiry into the East German past or perhaps even muscled through a narrower interpretation of the communist record. Yet despite the FRG's advantaged position, this particular initiative was, if anything, one of the easiest eastern demands for the government to support. Revealingly, this was not so much the case because of a passionate commitment to the cause of truth telling in Bonn; few western officials seemed to have any reason for thinking the body's hearings would ever touch their lives, either positively or negatively. Rather, as long as the parliament's investigations did not violate accepted notions of fairness and due process – as some critics had feared of the early "tribunal" proposals – and as long as they were not explicitly targeted at the West, officials could give their blessings to the undertaking as a sign of simple goodwill.

On Judging the Past in the Right Way

German policymakers also had to wrestle with a second issue of consequence. Even in those instances when they believed they had no choice but to act on the GDR's offenses, they still needed to justify the pretension to sit in judgment on the behavior of another regime. As we have seen, when this issue was framed in abstract moral terms, the two sides to the debate seemed to give Bonn almost no room for maneuver at all. Predictably, the advocates of retrospective justice would rally around the idea that the rectification of the SED's abuses was a moral obligation to the victims of dictatorship as well as a prime opportunity to integrate a disenfranchised segment of the population into the body politic. On the other side, the policy's fiercest opponents had no hesitation in condemning these measures as new injustices and needless impediments to the easing of inter-German tensions.

As we have found, however, in the four different types of retrospective justice considered in this book, the choices before Germany's leaders were rarely this stark. Few of the skeptics went quite so far as to maintain that anything Bonn did to address the concerns of the victims would be wrongheaded and misguided. Most could agree that victims of grievous indignities and harm under the communist regime were owed some type of affirmation. Many also recognized that in extreme cases, some form of corrective action was allowable. At the same time, even the most ardent advocates of retribution and related measures generally admitted that there was a limit to the *Rechtsstaat*'s capacity to repair the wrongs of a state that no longer existed. Provocatively, Schäuble acknowledged in his 1991 memoirs that he had consistently advised his colleagues "to concentrate [only] on the worst cases of actual guilt and not on trying to work through the 40 years of GDR history in all its details." He had also urged them "to err on the side of generosity over self-righteousness."[19]

However, even with the leeway to develop policy within these boundaries, federal authorities faced no inconsiderable challenge. Above all, they had to prove to the doubters that one could fit moral and legal categories that made sense in the liberal–democratic Federal Republic into the very different political conditions that had prevailed in East Germany.

In this context, the potentially good news for the Kohl administration was that the pursuit of retrospective justice was partly an empirical problem. To hold people accountable for their past behavior or to make a credible case for redressing the old order's offenses, German judges, politicians, parliamentarians, and civil servants essentially had to demonstrate that the GDR was something more than the clichéd image of the *Unrechtsstaat*. This meant showing that it had not been an authoritarian black hole in which every meaningful distinction between right and wrong was obliterated and in which its citizens had no chance of making responsible choices. In fact, as has been noted, officials were able to devise some persuasive responses to this challenge throughout the 1990s.

Again, the handling of the Wall trials is a case in point. The jurisprudence in these proceedings underwent a significant shift over the 1990s as judges and prosecutors wrestled with the implications of appearing to hold their eastern German counterparts to a moral standard that superseded many of their previous laws and practices. For some jurists, the advantage of bringing a higher law to bear on the communist record was that doing so afforded them the chance to move quickly and decisively to rectify injustice. But as others realized, this strategy, when pursued in isolation, had the disadvantage of seeming to hold former East German party members and officials accountable to an ex post facto norm of conduct.

For this reason, judicial authorities increasingly turned to preexisting East German statutes for additional evidence of why wrongdoers, like the border guards, should have been aware of the fundamental impropriety of their actions. Without exactly abandoning Gustav Radbruch's appeal to natural law, this recourse to historical context offered authorities a way around the constitutional prohibitions on retroactive legislation. By emphasizing the specificity of crimes under the communist regime, it also provided them with an attractive alternative to the assumption of collective guilt in East Germany. Some GDR citizens, the policymakers seemed to say through the medium of the trials, would have to admit to their crimes under the old order. However, this judgment did not apply to everyone for the simple reason that wrongdoing was specific and individualizable. This was precisely the spirit of then-Justice Senator and later Federal Constitutional Court President Jutta Limbach's pronouncement that the SED's abuse of power had not been a natural catastrophe at all. It was a "mosaic of individual deeds committed by responsible persons" (see Chapter 2).

In this spirit, on November 19, 1997, the criminal chamber of the Berlin state court finally convicted one of the two guards originally responsible for the killing of the two East German children at the Wall in March 1966; the other guard had died before the proceedings could begin. In coming to its judgment, the court reasoned that the defendant, who had used a Kalashnikov machine pistol to fire over 40 shots at one of the victims, must have known that his actions could lead to the taking of a life. Although he claimed he had no intention of killing anyone – and, he insisted, would not have fired had he known his targets were children – he was fully aware that he was only supposed to use appropriate means in preventing escapes. These could not have included the decision to employ automatic weaponry. Still, as in earlier instances, the judges took mitigating circumstances into account in sentencing the former guard to a year and 8 months probation for his role in one of the shootings. Although he had violated the law "at its core," the court reasoned in his favor, much like Judge Tepperwein had done a half decade earlier, that he had been at the bottom of the GDR's decision-making hierarchy on border security and also that he had made a full admission of his misdeed.[20]

This is not to say that it was easy for Germany's courts to find an appropriate balance in determining which offenses from the GDR past they would prosecute and, conversely, which they would pass over. The desire to establish an ideal picture of guilt in the Wall trials, from the highest echelons of the National Defense Council down to the lowliest border guards, at times led judicial authorities to undertake criminal prosecutions in cases for which the historical evidence of culpability was obscure and ambiguous. Every time they took this step, they risked conveying a mixed message about the rigors of the rule of law to the eastern populace.

Evidently, this temptation to press the legal system to its limits, and perhaps beyond them, was still in evidence in spring 2000 as the FRG entered the tenth year of unification. At this juncture, prosecutors began legal proceedings against the remaining members of the SED politburo (Herbert Häber, Hans-Joachim Böhme, and Siegfried Lorenz), who, by virtue of their comparatively good health, could still be tied to the Wall shootings. (Earlier proceedings against Kurt Hager, Erich Mückenburger, and Horst Dohlus had been halted in 1996 for health reasons; the first two individuals had subsequently died in 1998.) Technically, as in the convictions of Krenz, Schabowski, and Kleiber, one could say that all the defendants had a moral connection with the shoot-to-kill orders. As members of the party's preeminent policy-making body, prosecutors maintained, they must have known what was transpiring at the inter-German border. However, what one missed in these charges was explicit attention to the differing degrees of responsibility that each figure bore in the leadership.

Once again, as in the early stages of the first politburo trial (1994–97), the defendants were charged not so much for what they did but for what they did not do. Yet, here too, although the original indictment specifically accused the politburo members of committing "manslaughter through neglect" (*Totschlag durch Unterlassen*) for failing to humanize the border regime, prosecutors gave no indication of wanting to investigate whether any of them had contributed to an amelioration of the conditions at the inter-German border. One candidate for such a differentiated approach would have been Häber, the long-time director of the SED central committee's "West division" (for relations with the FRG), who had suddenly been appointed to the politburo in May 1984 and then was summarily ejected from the party leadership only 18 months later. Arguably, no individual in the SED had been more responsible than Häber for the improvement of relations between East Berlin and Bonn in the 1980s, a period that included Honecker's visit to the FRG and manifold opportunities for inter-German travel by ordinary citizens. Nonetheless, when Häber was finally brought to trial in May 2000, observers assumed that guilty verdicts in his and his colleagues' cases were virtually predetermined by the outcome of the preceding politburo trial.

Yet to the surprise of many, the Berlin regional court demonstrated that it was, arguably, more sensitive than some of its predecessors to the centrality of historical conditions in assessing the culpability of the accused. On July 7, 2000, it freed all three of the defendants. In Häber's case, the presiding judge, Hans Luther, emphasized that the evidence was conclusive. In contradiction to the prosecution's charges, the SED's former expert on the West had clearly gone to great lengths (to use Häber's own words) "to organize the relationship between the two Germanys . . . in such a fashion that no one would ever again need to climb a wall in order to act on his right to freedom of movement." But in contrast, the judge employed more guarded language in describing the decisions about Böhme and Lorenz. Here, the historical record was more complicated. Rather than trying to improve conditions at the inter-German border, Luther contended, the two defendants "simply took no action at all, nothing more and nothing less." In his view, one could not convict them of active involvement in the Wall killings, as the courts had previously done with Krenz, Schabowski, and Kleiber, for neither had taken part in politburo decisions about the border regime. Still, he left one question tantalizingly open (their legal obligation to have humanized the SED's policies) by deeming the matter of "manslaughter through neglect" an issue more properly interpreted by the Federal Court of Justice. On this basis, Berlin prosecutors planned to appeal the two acquittals (though, interestingly, not that of Häber) directly to the higher court. [21]

Somewhat less surprisingly, at the same time the courts were wrestling with these issues, their critics were continuing to decry the trials' purposes. Notably, the calls that were mounted in late 1999 for pardoning Krenz, Schabowski, and Kleiber achieved a tangible form in mid-January 2000 when the Berlin Senate used its executive powers to free the former chief of the Berlin Wall border guards, Klaus-Dieter Baumgarten, once he had served half of his $6\frac{1}{2}$-year sentence. By itself, the decision was perplexing. Few persons in the East German decision-making hierarchy had been more intimately associated with the Wall killings than Baumgarten. Moreover, the Senate's rationale in taking this particular step was unclear. Certainly, it was debatable whether the pardon would contribute in a positive way, as its proponent, Saarland politician Erwin Seel maintained, to "greater understanding [between the two parts of Germany] and the internal unification of our people."[22] Who could say whether an abrupt reversal of policy would increase public confidence in the rule of law or just undermine it by causing even greater confusion? In any case, this decision and the prospect of related measures to come was, at minimum, weighty testimony that the West's relationship with eastern Germany was far more complex than that suggested by many critics' exaggerated depictions of the FRG's motivations.

Similarly, the creation of the BStU and policymakers' subsequent recourse to the secret police files as instruments of bureaucratic screening cannot be characterized as either undiluted victories for the proponents of national unification or, conversely, as unmitigated failures. Rather, on the basis of the evidence reviewed in this book, one can only conclude that it would be impossible to cast a single, unambiguous verdict on the impact of these processes.

From a positive perspective, many of the anxieties that had been expressed about the MfS holdings as the GDR was imploding in early 1990 would appear, in retrospect, to have been misplaced. Once authorities knew what was in the ministry's records and understood how they were organized, they were able to establish that fewer of the GDR's citizens had been compromised by the secret police than was initially feared. Just as important, it would become clear that citizen activists like Gauck and Rathenow were not engaging in wishful thinking when they speculated that the opening of the Stasi's archives could have a beneficial and perhaps even liberating effect on the thinking of ordinary easterners. Provided they were utilized with circumspection and care, the records would help to demystify the secret police's hold on East German society. With the same precautions, the files could also aid officials in drawing necessary distinctions between those citizens who had seriously violated public and private confidences in colluding with the MfS and other easterners whose failings had been fleeting and inconsequential.

Nonetheless, the abiding uncertainty was how the files would be deployed in the vetting process. As we have seen, despite initial doubts to the contrary, the BStU was able to make a solid circumstantial argument for treating the Stasi's holdings as generally reliable sources of information for screening. Indeed, if there was a lesson to be gleaned from the nearly 1.6 million private citizens between January 1992 and May 1999 who took advantage of the Gauck agency's facilities to determine whether they had a Stasi file (or the roughly 200,000 of those who were still anxiously waiting at decade's end for the agency to process their applications), it was that many Germans implicitly subscribed to this position.[23] They believed there had to be some truth value to the files.

In addition, authorities could make an equally persuasive argument about the import of using these records in a manner that respected the rights of the individuals involved and that reflected, in the same breath, skepticism about the motivations of an organization that had been dedicated to instilling distrust and confusion among its citizens. For the most part, in responding to the millions of requests for information by various public and private agencies, the BStU seems to have worked within these boundaries. If anything, German administrative and labor courts showed even greater sensitivity to these concerns. By the mid-1990s, judges were routinely raising questions about the evidentiary hurdles for Stasi complicity and urging their colleagues to take mitigating factors into account in assessing employment suitability.

Yet despite their good intentions, the one thing the advocates of screening could not guarantee was that even-handed standards were applied at every other stage of the search for MfS informants. By statute, the Gauck agency was forbidden from taking a stand on the significance of the files under its purview, and the courts were restricted to post hoc rulings on judgments made by others. As a result, the most consequential decisions about culpability were often reached at the intermediate stages of this process (in *Länder* governments, police departments, local school boards, and private corporations) for which the standards for assessing employees' past conduct were the most volatile and unpredictable. In these cases, it really mattered whether these bodies were attentive to context. Sometimes, their rulings appeared sensible and defensible. But in many other cases, as we have found, the interpretation

of guilt and innocence varied widely across the political spectrum, depending upon the state or municipality in which one found oneself.

There was little policymakers could have done at the national level
to remedy this problem. In the treatment of public officials, the constitutional allocation of powers of appointment and dismissal to the
Länder meant that a truly comprehensive form of coordination would
have been unrealizable. But naturally, this feature of German democracy came with a price. The pointed message Gauck and other activists
wanted to convey about eastern involvement in the Stasi was, at best,
mixed. No matter how hard they tried to sell the residents of Germany's
western states on subtle distinctions between tolerable accommodation
and intolerable overaccommodation or, for that matter, no matter how
many stories they collected of individuals who had stood up to the
threats and temptations of the MfS, observers would continue to take
every revelation of complicity as proof that the Stasi had corrupted all
human relationships in the GDR.

Similar ambiguities were presented by the politically motivated findings of the Bundestag's Enquete commission. The body's organizers began with noble intentions, but there were important respects in which
their parliamentary inquiry was negatively influenced by conflicting
political agendas. For example, when they needed to render a judgment on the survival strategies of the Lutheran churches, the former
dissidents on the commission were content to use the body's investigations as a pretext for depicting their own activities before 1989 in a
favorable light. For many of the same reasons, when the body surveyed
the *Deutschlandpolitik*, its western members suddenly became interested
in the GDR and rushed to defend their partisan views on the topic. Yet
neither side needed any coaching to arrive at correspondingly bleak
conclusions about the behavior of the East German populace under
SED rule. Both were inclined to indict the GDR's citizens for their
less than heroic qualities.

Still, to recognize these shortcomings is not to maintain that the
deputies of the Enquete commission were incapable of reaching historically balanced judgments. As participants in an enterprise that was
at least as well-organized and lavishly funded as their Latin American
and South African counterparts, they not only had the capacity to
address a broad range of historical concerns, but their freedom of maneuver was arguably much greater than that which had been enjoyed
by either the criminal courts in the Wall prosecutions or the advocates

of civil service screening. In this respect, they could have provided a more sensitive portrayal of the East German experience had only this been their inclination.

For example, one can sympathize with the desires of many easterners to use the public spotlight of the Bundestag to vent their frustrations with those policies of the Lutheran church hierarchy over the 1970s and 1980s that seemed oriented toward maintaining the status quo in East Germany. However, there is no reason the parliamentarians could not simultaneously have given these same church leaders greater credit for their role in fostering the protected niches in which opposition to the communist regime first germinated and later flourished. Had they taken this stand, the deputies could have painted the eastern German populace as a whole in a more favorable light rather than seeming to confine all serious interest in meaningful change to a noble but nonetheless numerically insignificant group of dissenters.

Similarly, the GDR's citizens might not have appeared quite so pusil- lanimous in making the most of their lives under socialism if western parliamentarians had been more candid about the miscues and judg- mental errors in their own government's policies on the national ques- tion. In responding to the challenges of division, it seems that actors on both sides of the German border – western politicians as well as eastern church leaders – had made mistakes. Few participants could honestly claim to have anticipated the events of 1989–90 or to have been ade- quately prepared to act upon subsequent developments. But of course, although they had sometimes made ill-informed decisions, this did not preclude Germans of either background from leading honorable and responsible lives after unification.

Indeed, it was not history per se that kept the Enquete commission from living up to its full potential but all too often the conscious politi- cal choices of its members. One of the body's particularly glaring binds was that its electorally minded deputies need not have played as easily as they did into the hands of the PDS. In this and in other pub- lic forums, they probably would have better served their long-term interests had they pushed for a less stereotypical assessment of the sources of stability and discord under communist rule, but, the desire for short-term political advantage appears to have gotten the best of them.

Most likely, for several reasons we have considered earlier, includ- ing the unusual nature of the German transition and the existence of alternative means of pursuing retrospective justice, the Bundestag inquiry would never have lived up to the emotional intensity and deeply revelatory character of the Chilean or South African commissions. Still, there was little that one could term irretrievably flawed or futile about this particular attempt to come to terms with East Germany's legacy. The key to achieving modest success in the endeavor was for the politicians and officials who were directly involved in the process to engage the past in a convincing and historically credible way.

In contrast, as was pointed out in the introduction to this book, there are times when the greatest impediment to justice lies not with the intentions of decision makers but with the pliability of the historical material with which they operate. We have encountered one case in this study in which officials seem to have faced up to an unwinnable battle – the attempt to devise a just and politically tractable solution to the millions of competing claims to private property in the East.

In this matter, the dilemma for the advocates of a comprehensive property settlement was not the matter of interpreting East Germany's history correctly. For the most part, claims officials were capable of retracing the circumstances under which properties had changed hands in the 57 years between 1933 and 1990. With time and effort, they could use extant records to verify thousands of cases of "honest acquisition" in the East and to identify corresponding violations of the former regime's laws. However, there was one outcome claims officials could not guarantee. This was that their prescriptions for resolving disputes would take the same form for the four or five vastly different property orders in Germany since Hitler. As a result, whether these officials were dealing with the victims of the Nazis' policies in the 1930s, large landowners and other farmers who suffered expropriation under Soviet military rule in the late 1940s, or property owners who lost valuable real estate owing to the Berlin Wall's construction in 1961, rival claimants were destined to accuse them of invoking arbitrary and illegitimate norms of remediation.

This was the reaction to the FCC's rejection, in November 1999, of Brandenburg's complaint about the cutoff date for property purchases in the GDR's waning months. As was suggested in Chapter 5, the high court probably would have been better advised to have set a later threshold date for such transfers than October 18, 1989, the day of Honecker's ouster, because national unification did not become a certainty until several months later. Nonetheless, even if a later date would have represented a more accurate statement about the conditions East Germans faced as their country fell apart and might thereby have served to smooth over sizable differences among diverse segments of the region's population, this move would not have solved the conflict over land and homes. One way or the other, the court still had to set a definitive line demarcating two periods in modern German history. In this case, far from resolving the controversy, a later date would have only created new problems. Even greater numbers of original owners would have felt cheated out of their holdings, whereas many of the current occupants of these properties would have maintained that the settlement had not been generous enough.

This logic apparently came into play in the popular response to the FCC's 1999 ruling. As the Berlin daily *Berliner Morgenpost* editorialized shortly after the judgment was handed down, it was not enough that the court had deemed the early threshold date to be a fair compromise between the two sides to the debate. Both would continue to "feel themselves to be unjustly treated and would have doubts about [the efficacy of] the *Rechtsstaat*." The one side would only see what it had lost from the decision, whereas the other would resent being compelled to make additional sacrifices to retain what it had already acquired. Accordingly, it is difficult to imagine that a satisfactory resolution of the property conflict would ever be found.[24]

GDR Wrongdoing in Perspective

Against this backdrop, one cannot take for granted the German government's fortunes in acting on any instance of injustice in the GDR. Just the same, for anyone with a passing familiarity with the decades of impassioned debate over the crimes of Germany's first dictatorship, National Socialism, one point will already be evident. We have been using a markedly different idiom in this book to characterize Bonn's policies in the 1990s. Historians of the Third Reich have frequently bemoaned the difficulty of coming to grips with the extent of Hitler's tyranny and concluded, on this basis, that the enormity of the Nazis' deeds will continue to elude the full understanding of participants and scholars alike. As Hannah Arendt expressed so well, this is the nature of radical evil. "All we know," Arendt advised,

> is that we can neither punish nor forgive such offenses and that they therefore transcend the realm of human affairs and the potentialities

of human power, both of which they radically destroy wherever they make their appearance.[25]

Yet how different has been the FRG's reckoning with Germany's more recent experience with dictatorship! In its much more straightforward, even mundane terms, one gets the impression from Bonn's approach that at least some of the darker moments of SED rule can be overcome.

To be sure, in broaching this claim, we do well to acknowledge the limitations upon any government's ability to master a fractured past in any complete sense. We can also appreciate the challenges a regime faces in helping citizens down the tortuous path of confronting national responsibility for acts of brutality, inhumanity, and betrayal. In this respect, no matter how grandiose a politician's claims, the work of retrospective justice is never truly over.

To cite one issue, we might agree without hesitation that there was little in the GDR's history that was remotely comparable in magnitude to the Nazi death camps or to the Hitler regime's systematic extermination of ethnic and religious minorities. But this qualification does not mean that we must discount or downplay the difficulty, for both perpetrators and victims alike, of acting upon the GDR's record of wrongdoing. As Günter Schabowski confessed about his government's actions (see Chapter 2), every fatality at the Wall – especially, one might add, every lost child – will continue to represent a heavy moral burden on the souls of the policymakers who orchestrated the killing machine at the German–German border. Likewise, even if the Stasi's methods of intimidation and coercion pale in comparison with the atrocities of National Socialist organizations like the Gestapo, we should be careful not to underplay the damage done to countless human relationships by the unseen machinations and intrigues of East Germany's secret police. For that matter, we should resist assuming that these harms can be easily or quickly repaired – even by opening the MfS's files to its victims or by dismissing informants from public employment. For these reasons, the GDR's comparatively more modest offenses will still require decades of debate, discussion, and agonizing self-appraisal before the generations that experienced them find the resources to put their memories behind them.

Nonetheless, our survey of Germany's most recent experiment with retrospective justice suggests that the GDR past, although not really masterable, has at least turned out to be a manageable burden. In this regard, before concluding this study, we must confront a related question about unified Germany's policies. What significance should be attached to the fact that, in less than a decade's time, the country's leaders made so much more headway over so many different issues than had either of its predecessors, in Bonn or East Berlin, with the offenses of the Third Reich?

In part, this question exposes a seemingly insurmountable asymmetry between these two periods of modern authoritarianism.[26] Does it matter in the imperfect scales of human justice that the Federal Republic was able to address the GDR's abuses more quickly and with greater ease than the more heinous crimes of National Socialism? Certainly, the German people faced a unique challenge in the aftermath of World War II in having to come to terms with the monstrous crimes that had been committed in their country's name and by many of their fellow citizens. Still, in this writer's view, the disparity between Arendt's "radical evil" of the Nazi era and the admittedly more mundane evil of East German communism is not as compelling a problem as it may seem at first glance.

First, if one is dealing with incontestable instances of wrongdoing, such as the Wall shootings, it should not matter that the offenses of one regime are significantly more grievous than those of another. After all, injustice is injustice. Regardless of their lesser intensity or lower quantity, the state-sponsored crimes of the sort perpetrated by the GDR still cry out for some form of corrective action from a democratic successor.[27] Moreover, on the basis of the evidence we have considered in this study, and despite the claims of some critics, we have seen that one should resist the temptation to stereotype the FRG's responses to the SED's offenses. Whatever their merits, Bonn's actions were far from reckless or one-dimensional.

Second, even if one concedes that the Nazis' crimes against humanity will continue to demand a special form of acknowledgment and atonement in the twenty-first century by virtue of their uniquely horrific character, there is no reason to think that the thoroughness with which German officials dealt with the later communist dictatorship should detract from this task. Indeed, Bonn's successes in acting upon the more manageable record of GDR-era injustice may serve as a potent reminder of how much farther Germany's leaders, now in the restored capital of Berlin, must go in contending with Hitler's legacy. Given the variety of political, legal, and administrative responses the

SED's offenses have called forth, one can reasonably expect German officials to be even more resourceful and deliberate in focusing citizens' attentions upon the remaining lessons to be learned from the experience of National Socialism.

Of course, even if policymakers succeed at striking the appropriate balance in their response to the twin periods of German authoritarianism, this will not be their only challenge. Most likely, they will also need to confront a glaring asymmetry between the steps many eastern Germans took after unification in grappling with diverse aspects of their country's history since 1933 and the comparative indifference and lassitude of their western counterparts on these questions. We have encountered ample evidence of this problem throughout this book. For example, although federal officials had the opportunity to do so, they took few steps to implement Stasi screening procedures in the western *Länder*. Similarly, the Enquete commission was reluctant to face up to the shortcomings and miscalculations in Bonn's *Deutschlandpolitik*.

Nevertheless, as astute observers of German politics, from Jürgen Habermas to Fritz Stern, were to caution throughout the 1990s, the issue of fairness and balance is deeper than the inability to apply one or another type of retrospective justice with consistency.[28] The principal dilemma for those who want the GDR's former citizens to feel more fully a part of their new homeland is that they alone, the people of eastern Germany, were forced to shoulder the burden of two separate eras of dictatorship. Not only did they have to endure greater hardships during the devastated nation's reconstruction after World War II, but they suffered by themselves through the debilitating consequences of Soviet occupation and their inability, until 1990, to act upon the right to "free self-determination" (to quote the Basic Law's original preamble). Consequently, if they are not to be punished anew for the fate of having been born in the wrong place, it is logical for them to expect their western counterparts to hold their own actions up to the same high moral standards that were previously applied to the GDR.

In this regard, we may consider it a wry form of poetic justice that western Germans did not have to wait long before they were given the opportunity to test this maxim. At almost exactly the moment the Federal Court of Justice was confirming the politburo verdicts and the German people were celebrating 10 years of freedom from the Wall, the predominantly western leadership of the CDU was rocked by a series of revelations that some of its key personnel had, for years, consciously engaged in violations of the Bundestag's party finance laws. On November 5, 1999, the CDU's former treasurer, Walther Leisler Kiep, became the first Union notable to admit that he had illegally funneled a million-mark gift from a German businessman into the party's coffers in 1991. For months thereafter, the Christian Democrats were engulfed in successive waves of accusations and counteraccusations about clandestine campaign contributions, kickbacks for shady business dealings, and secret Swiss bank accounts.

Granted, this was not the first time a shadow had been cast over the FRG's one-time governing party for illicit financial activities. In the so-called Flick affair of the early 1980s, several prominent party officials (including Leisler Kiep) were revealed to have hidden millions of deutsche marks of corporate campaign contributions in dummy bank accounts in an attempt to evade heavy tax burdens. Still, this most recent scandal was made all the more difficult for the CDU to surmount because of Helmut Kohl's role in the affair. The ex-chancellor stubbornly refused to own up to his full responsibility in the affair or to divulge the names of the sources of the illegal contributions. Thus, when the Bundestag formed a special committee to look into the matter and the prosecutor general's office broached the heretofore unthinkable possibility of charging Kohl and others with malfeasance, it was not surprising that some party faithful moved swiftly to recapture the moral high ground by distancing themselves from the "chancellor of German unity." Angela Merkel, the CDU's general secretary and one of the few easterners to have found a place in the Union leadership, used the pages of the middle-of-the-road *Frankfurter Allgemeine Zeitung* to announce that the party's future could only be built "on the foundation of truth." In this spirit, she urged her fellow Christian Democrats to move on to a post-Kohl era.[29]

Had this been the extent of the controversy, it is conceivable that the analogies critics were soon to draw between this supposedly "western" scandal and the East German regime's much greater offenses would have been muted. To be sure, at least one parliamentarian, Werner Schulz, a Green deputy from Saxony, sought to draw parallels between the CDU's transgressions and the SED's total disregard for public accountability. To his mind, "this kind of secrecy and obsession with power, this mentality of keeping quiet and looking away," bore a striking resemblance to the operational style of the politburo.[30] But for the time being, a majority of the Christian Democrats' opponents seemed satisfied with simple *Schadenfreude*. They merely emphasized the respects in which the party's financial irregularities would knock some of western Germany's biggest names off their high moral pedestals and expose them to be, after all, mere mortals. "We are now a bit more equal," the eastern German essayist Monika Maron mused about her compatriots as word of the CDU's misdeeds spread. "Even better," she added, "we now know that we were always a bit more equal."[31]

However, a more direct German–German dimension was soon to be added to the outcry against the Christian Democrats. On March 28, 2000, Joachim Gauck matter-of-factly advised the Bundestag's investigative committee that the BStU would be happy to turn over thousands of pages of previously unreleased telephone conversations between top Union officials that might be useful for its inquiry.[32] For decades, it seems, the Ministry of State Security's special department for monitoring signal traffic in West Germany, the *Hauptabteilung III* had kept exhaustive records of the behind-the-scenes wheeling and dealing of personalities as varied as Kiep, his senior counsel Uwe Lüthje, the party's accountant Horst Weyrauch, and – it would turn out – Helmut Kohl. Further, the records would show that the MfS had been fully aware of the CDU's financial peccadilloes and "black accounts" since at least 1976. Making this revelation all the more embarrassing to the party, the German press subsequently recalled to the public's attention that the Kohl administration in June 1990 had summarily destroyed a collection nearly 1,000 meters in extent consisting of documents from the *Hauptabteiling III* – apparently without reviewing their contents.[33] Yet painfully for the CDU – and potentially for every western policymaker who had been subject to the Stasi's intelligence-gathering activities – over 170 meters of materials (approximately 50,000 transcripts of telephone conversations as well as thousands of reels of tape and cassettes) had escaped the shredder.

One could have predicted the contours of the ensuing battle over the disposition of these holdings, though, this time around, provocatively unlike the debates of 1990, neither side seemed to have the least doubt about the accuracy or historical reliability of the Stasi's records. On the one hand, Kohl himself was the first politician of note to denounce the use of telephone transcripts from the, in his words, "[East German] criminal regime (*Verbrecherregime*)" for shedding light on the national past. Citing the illicit character of the Stasi's activities, Kohl pointedly threatened to go to the FCC to prevent the release of any documents that impinged on his right to legal security.[34] Interestingly, several leading Social Democratic politicians – General Secretary Franz Münterfering and parliamentary speaker Peter Struck – joined the former chancellor in opposing the release of the documents in any form. No doubt, the SPD, too, feared the consequences for its reputation of any unsupervised disclosures from the MfS archives.[35] And, why should it have expected to be spared this discomfort?

But on the other hand, it was just as easy to find equally determined personalities who saw in the existence of the Stasi transcripts a chance to pay a long-overdue tribute to the eastern German people, many of whom seemed – if opinion polls can be trusted – to agree with the idea of turning the records over to the investigative committee.[36] The head of the Greens' Bundestag *Fraktion*, Rezzo Schlauch, led the charge, insisting on March 28 that his government needed to make every effort to mobilize the MfS archives to clarify the CDU's role in the finance scandal. It was unacceptable, Schlauch emphasized, for the current administration to ignore "records that concerned politicians from the old Federal Republic, since these same persons had previously rubbed their hands [in delight] over similar revelations about politicians from [Germany's] new states."[37]

In testimony to the adage about politics making odd bedfellows, Schlauch was probably taken aback when Manfred Stolpe interjected himself in support of this position. For the prime minister of Brandenburg and, so it appeared, the IM known as "Sekretär," it was self-evident that western German politicians should now be judged according to the same rigorous standards, and with the same evidentiary tools, they had freely imposed upon others. In this sense, just as easterners had "found their rights unfairly and unjustly violated for 10 years by," as Stolpe put it, "these scraps of paper," so too in his estimation was it fitting for "those who had once sat in a different chair to now endure the same treatment."[38] Even the postcommunist PDS, normally an archcritic of transitional justice in any form, jumped onto the bandwagon. Parliamentary floor leader Roland Claus expressed his party's view succinctly: "In the files, everyone is equal."[39]

Equal or not, one can appreciate that in this instance, as in Germany's other attempts to act upon the past, the legal basis for using the Stasi's records was not as clear-cut as it appeared at first glance.

We can sympathize with the temptation of many easterners to take advantage of the devices that had been so detrimental to their own reputations to scrutinize the behavior of politicians who had previously occupied the limelight in the unification process. But as commentators hastened to point out, the two types of wrongdoing were really quite dissimilar. The whole point of the Stasi Records law had been to grapple with the activities of the East German secret police and, in conjunction with the Unification treaty, to bring to light the misdeeds of the MfS's thousands of hidden agents and informers. Yet Kohl and his associates could hardly be put in the same class as Stasi IMs. As their defenders argued, they had not only played a major part in securing their nation's well-being after 1990, but, if anything, the presence of tapes in the Stasi *Zentrale* containing their conversations demonstrated that they were the victims of injustice and not its perpetrators. Therefore, even if the files confirmed that Union politicians had engaged in dubious activities over the preceding decades, one could make a compelling case for preventing the illegal transcriptions from entering the public domain. It was a matter of safeguarding the constitutional guarantee of privacy.[40]

In the months to come, the attention given to the legal status of the Stasi tapes would subside as a result of further revelations about financial irregularities involving Kohl and other CDU notables for which one did not require proof from the MfS holdings. Yet, even with these developments, the exposure of wrongdoing in the upper ranks of the CDU signified a turning point of a sort in the short history of unified Germany. After 10 years of scrutinizing the behavior of a variety of actors in the former GDR, from politburo members to disgruntled property claimants and dissident activists, and then seeking to apply legal and moral concepts that made sense in the context of a communist dictatorship, the German people were invited to speculate about a basic truth that should have been apparent to them the whole time. For all of the political, social, and economic advantages the citizens of the old FRG had enjoyed in the postwar period, they did not have a natural monopoly on personal integrity or virtue, nor was there reason to think they had been any more noble or self-sacrificing than their eastern counterparts. In this simple wisdom, there lies a germ of hope that the two parts of the nation will slowly come to know each other with a spirit of greater openness and perhaps even a mutual curiosity about their respective paths to unification.

Contending Venues of Justice

We began this book with a straightforward observation. Of all the democracies that struggled with the issue of retrospective justice in the final decades of the twentieth century, the German model of contending with a dictatorial past seems to have been the most thoroughgoing and comprehensive. Additionally, we echoed the widely shared opinion that the FRG's determination to follow through on this agenda was due in part to the propitious circumstances under which East Germany was incorporated into the Federal Republic. After October 1990, there were no entrenched elites left in the GDR to stand in the way of Bonn's actions. Indeed, in 1990 there was no more GDR. At the same time, decision makers could find advocates of some kind of reckoning with the SED's crimes on both sides of the national divide. The only question for the German government to resolve – albeit an extraordinarily complex one – was, What steps were best-suited to fulfill this goal? As we have seen throughout this book, even a powerful state's ability to act upon injustice is not an automatic recipe for doing the right thing.

With the passage of time, the converse of this proposition can be confirmed: even weak states have options. As the 1990s progressed, the FRG's leaders were not alone in their desire to act upon legacies of wrongdoing. Moreover, many new democracies did not require conditions as favorable as those in Germany to take the issue of pursuing justice after dictatorship seriously.[41]

With respect to criminal trials alone, countries as diverse as Chile, South Korea, Ethiopia, Honduras, and South Africa all found ways over the decade to hold former officials accountable for offenses as wide-ranging as the abuse of power, corruption, kidnapping, torture, and murder.[42] In much the same fashion, following a period of initial hesitancy, several of eastern Germany's ex-communist counterparts discovered that they could no longer resist popular pressures to bring some of their ex-leaders to justice. In the first half of the decade, only Bulgaria had followed the FRG's example, using communist-era laws in 1992 to prosecute health officials for misleading the public about the health hazards of the Chernobyl disaster and then, in 1993, convicting party chief Todor Zhivkov of embezzlement and mismanagement of state property. But by the middle and late 1990s, several other European states had followed suit. In 1994–95, the Albanian government used these same standards to convict several former members of the communist politburo for "crimes against fundamental human rights" and various forms of corruption. In 1999, a Romanian court sentenced two generals to lengthy prison terms for ordering their troops to open fire on unarmed citizens during protests in Timisoara one decade earlier. During the same year, the parliament of the Czech Republic voted to lift the statute of limitations on crimes committed by former public officials, and prosecutors initiated proceedings against one-time Czechoslovak Prime Minister Lubomir Strougal. By this point, even Hungarian officials normally inclined to believe that "living well [was] the best revenge" had undertaken the prosecution of soldiers involved in the killing of civilians in October 1956.[43]

Likewise, several governments in the region were eventually persuaded to take steps to deal with the secret police's impact on their societies. Although its efforts were by no means as far-reaching as the German model, Poland implemented a formal screening mechanism for using secret police records to review top politicians and government officials. In various ways, the Czech Republic, Bulgaria, and Hungary went even further, creating BStU-like agencies at which ordinary citizens and journalists could scrutinize the files for themselves and reach their own conclusions about past events.

At any historical juncture, all of these measures would have been noteworthy. Yet for much of the world, they were overshadowed by two dramatic developments in the area of international law as the century came to a close. The first was the decision by the United Nations Security Council, in February 1993 and then in November 1994, to establish ad hoc tribunals on the atrocities that had occurred as a result of "ethnic cleansing" in ex-Yugoslavia and the genocidal civil war in Rwanda. The second, in June–July 1998, was the affirmative vote of 120 different countries in Rome (out of a total of 148 participants) on a draft treaty for a permanent International Criminal Court (ICC).

By all accounts, these events will long be regarded as pivotal achievements along the path to an international human rights regime. For years, rights activists have bemoaned the slow pace since World War II at which even democratic states were prepared to learn from their mistakes. In the immediate aftermath of the war, it had been relatively easy to find governments that agreed in the abstract about the importance of protecting human rights, as evidenced in the late 1940s by the Nuremberg and Tokyo war crimes tribunals, the Universal Declaration of Human Rights, and the Geneva and Genocide conventions. Yet many of the same states stood by helplessly over the next 50 years as mass atrocities continued to be committed and even accelerated at the end of the century.[44]

Accordingly, if one were looking for rays of hope in the world, the sudden emergence of the ad hoc tribunals and the ICC seemed to indicate that the time had finally arrived when gross rights violations could no longer be committed with impunity. Indeed, the ICC treaty notably gave individual states a powerful incentive to carry out prosecutions on their own soil. Under the principle of "complementarity," national governments were granted precedence over the proposed court but only on condition that they showed good faith in redressing injustice. Otherwise, international mechanisms would be preferred.[45]

But do these developments signify that the independent efforts of countries like the Federal Republic to pursue retrospective justice in the 1990s will gradually fade in significance as a new system of international institutions and covenants emerges? From an optimist's perspective, they might. No one would deny the attractiveness of a global rights regime that is based on the principle of universal jurisdiction. At a minimum, the acceptance of such norms could make it easier for states to prosecute violators in domestic courts regardless of when they committed their offenses. Such a system could also help states to hold individuals accountable outside of their national borders as Spain's democratic government tried to do in 1999 in its ultimately unsuccessful efforts to extradite former Chilean dictator General Augusto Pinochet.

Nevertheless, it would be shortsighted to assume that international mechanisms are necessarily the ideal tools for pursuing retrospective justice or that they are, in the cautionary words of one scholar, "'magic bullets' capable of generating instant social consensus and closure."[46] For one thing, they often require more time to build legitimacy than do domestic institutions. In 1994, the international tribunal on the Rwandan genocide got off to a slow start when the country's Tutsi-dominated government voted against the initiative out of pique at the Security Council's insistence on conducting the proceedings in another country, Tanzania, and on excluding the death penalty as an option for punishment.[47] Similarly, in 1998, the draft treaty on the ICC was severely compromised as a result of demands by the United States that Security Council members be given certain veto rights over bad-faith prosecutions. Even after the signatories had made this concession, the United States, along with China, Iraq, Libya, Yemen, Qatar, and Israel, voted against the treaty.

As the German case shows, domestic approaches to retrospective justice may not only enjoy greater public confidence but also have an added advantage in the depth and breadth of the issues they can cover. Granted, there is no technical limit to the amount of evidence an international tribunal can collect, or witnesses it can call, in the prosecution of a case. Nonetheless, it stands to reason that local courts will be better suited than many external agencies to meet the challenge of reconstructing past events and administering appropriate judgments. In this vein, human rights activists may have had cause to rejoice in May 1997 when the first of the defendants before the ad hoc tribunal on ex-Yugoslavia, Dusko Tadic, was found guilty of torture, crimes against humanity, and war crimes. But, they also wondered, justifiably, how much longer the international community could be counted upon to support such proceedings. The Tadic trial alone required 120 witnesses, 7,000 pages of testimony, and a judgment of over 300 pages; moreover, it cost nearly $20 million.[48]

Then, too, national responses to state-sponsored injustice have another advantage with respect to the different types of wrongdoing they can consider. Whereas most of the international remedies being debated by 2000 were restricted to criminal behavior, domestic institutions like those we have encountered in the FRG (administrative courts, public offices, special commissions, and parliaments) seem to be equipped to handle a much broader variety of offenses. They are, literally, closer to the issues, and they are better positioned to distinguish among competing explanations of wrongdoing. In this regard, one can imagine they will have a greater ability to present a fuller picture of a dictatorial era and to offer their citizens richer opportunities to make sense of their experiences.

None of these observations should be taken to imply that the choices governments face between national and international mechanisms for dealing with legacies of injustice will be self-evident. When one is addressing massive human rights abuses on the order of ex-Yugoslavia or Rwanda, or for that matter, of the Nazi dictatorship more than a half century ago, international regimes can provide the most realistic means of restoring order and taking decisive steps to apprehend perpetrators. Conversely, as countries like Chile and South Africa have shown in dealing with equally disturbing legacies of inhumanity, local governments are sometimes better suited to sponsor controlled inquiries into the past, such as truth commissions, or to resolve divisive disputes, such as those over land, by taking corrective measures.

One way or the other, a future generation of historians should be able to appreciate fully how Germany's experiment with retrospective justice in the 1990s will fit into an emerging system of rights protection. In both its many successes and, just as important, in its mistakes and shortcomings, the FRG's attempt to come to terms with the offenses of the East German dictatorship offers an illuminating lesson of what can be accomplished if governments take the historical record seriously. They can draw on multiple options when called to deal with a fractured past, and these may include retribution, disqualification, and other forms of corrective justice.

Appendix

The German Court System

The judicial system of the Federal Republic of Germany is divided into numerous jurisdictions that reflect the country's federal structure and the diverse types of law. The majority of initial court decisions, or "decisions in the first instance," are reached in various state courts, which are entitled to apply both *Land* and federal statutes. Under this system, most minor cases are adjudicated in the hundreds of local courts (*Amtsgerichte*) spread throughout Germany. For the adjudication of more complex cases or for the review of facts and procedures in local court decisions, each state has a compartmentalized system of regional courts (*Landgerichte*) divided into five basic jurisdictions: ordinary law (criminal and civil), administrative law, labor law, tax and finance law, and social welfare law. Most of the *Länder* have corresponding appeals courts (*Oberlandesgerichte*) to review the findings of the regional courts. Most *Länder* also have constitutional courts to assess the compatibility of lower court decisions and of state law with their respective constitutions.

In conformity with Germany's federal structure, the FRG has a matching system of federal courts. These courts are divided into similar jurisdictions and are superior to the state courts. The Federal Court of Justice (*Bundesgerichtshof*), arguably the most prominent of these bodies, acts as the last court of appeals in criminal and civil matters and is largely confined to reviewing questions of law. In addition, there are other federal courts of appeals corresponding to each of the four remaining state jurisdictions, namely, a Federal Administrative Court (*Bundesverwaltungsgericht*), a Federal Labor Court (*Bundesarbeitsgericht*), a Federal Finance Court (*Bundesfinanzgericht*), and a Federal Social Court (*Bundessozialgericht*).

For constitutional questions, the Federal Constitutional Court (*Bundesverfassungsgericht*) stands at the pinnacle of this system. However, unlike the Federal Court of Justice, which comes under the supervision of the Justice Ministry, the FCC enjoys complete autonomy and independence in its activities. The high court's overriding purpose is to act as the guardian of the Basic Law by serving as the final authority on all matters of constitutional interpretation and application.

Because the FRG is a *Rechtsstaat* (constitutional state) in which the written law provides the main source of guidance for lawful behavior by both government authorities and ordinary citizens, it is no wonder that much of the FRG's attempt to pursue retrospective justice in the 1990s was framed in legal terms and, hence, frequently channeled through the aforementioned courts. The Wall trials were primarily conducted in the criminal chambers of the Berlin Regional Court and were then subject to appeal before the Federal Court of Justice. Disputes over the disqualification of former Stasi operatives were generally contested in three jurisdictions: before labor courts when they involved contractual disagreements between employers and employees, before administrative courts when they involved relations between public officials and citizens, and before ordinary courts when they involved criminal matters. Finally, disputes over property ownership and restitution were handled by administrative courts when they involved conflicts between claims offices and private parties and by ordinary courts when they involved private contractual disputes. In every case, the FCC represented the last word on the constitutionality of the laws in question and related court judgments.

For further information, see Wolfgang Heyde, *Justice and the Law in the Federal Republic of Germany* (Heidelberg: C. F. Muller Juristischer Verlag, 1994), 38–72, and Donald Kommers, *The Constitutional Jurisprudence of the Federal Republic of Germany*, second edition (Durham, NC: Duke University Press, 1997), Chap. 1.

Notes

Chapter 1

1. A useful general discussion is provided by Claus Offe, "Disqualification, Retribution, Restitution: Dilemmas of Justice in Post-Communist Transitions," *Journal of Political Philosophy* 1, no. 1 (1993): 17–44. For contrasting perspectives from the vast literature on retrospective justice, see Aryeh Neier, "What Should Be Done about the Guilty?" *NYRB*, 1 February 1990, 34, and José Zalaquett, "Balancing Ethical Imperatives and Political Constraints: The Dilemma of New Democracies Confronting Past Human Rights Violations," *Hastings Law Journal* 43, no. 6 (August 1992): 1426–32.
2. For background on these cases, see the chapters by N. Alivizatos and N. Diamandouros (Greece), C. Acuña and C. Smulovitz (Argentina), and R. Mayorga (Bolivia) in *Transitional Justice and the Rule of Law in New Democracies*, ed. A. James McAdams (Notre Dame: University of Notre Dame Press, 1997). On the contrasting experiences in East Europe, see the chapters by Andrzej Walicki (Poland) and Kim Lane Scheppele and Gábor Halmai (Hungary) in ibid., as well as Helga Welsh, "Dealing with the Communist Past: Central and East European Experiences after 1990," *Europe–Asia Studies* 48, no. 3 (1996): 413–28.
3. *BZ Online* (www.berlinonline.de), 1 October 1999. On these processes, see John Borneman, *Settling Accounts: Violence, Justice, and Accountability in Post-socialist Europe* (Princeton: Princeton University Press, 1977), Chap. 4.
4. Roman Grafe, "Generalstaatsanwalt Christoph Schaefgen: 'Wenig aufbauend ist die zahlenmäßige Bilanz unserer Arbeit'," *DA* 1 (January–February 1999): 6–8.
5. Vertrag zwischen der Bundesrepublik Deutschland und der Deutschen Demokratischen Republik über die Herstellung der Einheit Deutschlands vom 31.8.1990, attach. I, Chap. XIX (A), §3 (1) (5) (2), *Bulletin*, no. 104, 877–1120, 6 September 1990. Hereafter, Unification treaty.
6. For a qualification of this point, see Gregg O. Kvistad, "Accommodation or 'Cleansing': Germany's State Employees from the Old Regime,"

West European Politics 17, no. 4 (October 1994): 52–73. On the subject of administrative reform, see Wolfgang Seibel, Arthur Benz, and Heinrich Mäding, eds., *Verwaltungsreform und Verwaltungspolitik im Prozeß der deutschen Einigung* (Baden-Baden: Nomos, 1993).

7. These measures may have seemed controversial, but they fell short of the degree of compensation to which many victims believed they were entitled. On this, see the definitive constitutional study of German unification by Peter Quint, *The Imperfect Union: Constitutional Structures of German Unification* (Princeton: Princeton University Press, 1997), Chap. 15.
8. Czechoslovakia and South Africa are two exceptions to this rule. I address them briefly in Chapter 4.
9. Offe, "Disqualification," 20–1.
10. On the absence of this zeal in the early stages of other postcommunist transitions, see Stephen Holmes, "The End of Decommunization," *East European Constitutional Review* (summer/fall 1994): 33–6.
11. To paraphrase a remark by Jürgen Habermas about the treatment of secret police informants, as cited in Lothar Probst, "German Pasts, Germany's Future: Intellectual Controversies Since Reunification," *GPS* no. 30 (fall 1993): 29.
12. See Hubertus Knabe's reflections on the limitations of West Germany's reckoning with the Nazi past, "Das schwere Erbe des Stalinismus," *taz*, 10 April 1990, 7; and for a qualification of this argument, cf. Norbert Frei, "Wider die falschen Analogien," *SdZ*, 10 March 1995, 13. Also, see Frei's *Vergangenheitspolitik: Die Anfänge der Bundesrepublik und die NS-Vergangenheit* (Munich: C.H. Beck, 1996), which is a superbly differentiated analysis of Bonn's early policies.
13. Gesine Schwan, *Politik und Schuld* (Frankfurt am Main: Fischer 1997), Chap. 5.
14. Jeffrey Herf, *Divided Memory: The Nazi Past in the Two Germanys* (Cambridge: Harvard University Press, 1997), 72–195; Tina Rosenberg, *The Haunted Land* (New York: Random House, 1995), 315–19.
15. See especially Paul M. Schwartz, "Constitutional Change and Constitutional Legitimation: The Example of German Unification," *Houston Law Review* 31, no. 4 (winter 1994): 1060–64. On the round table, see Uwe Thaysen, *Der runde Tisch: Oder wo blieb das Volk?* (Opladen: Westdeutscher Verlag, 1990).
16. Cited in Luc Huyse, "Justice after Transition: On the Choices Successor Elites Make in Dealing with the Past," *Law and Social Inquiry* 20, no. 1 (winter 1995): 55. For supportive arguments, see Eckhard Jesse, "'Vergangenheitsbewältigung' nach totalitärer Herrschaft in Deutschland," *GSR*, special issue, ed. Wolfgang-Uwe Friedrich (fall 1994): 157–71, and Christa Hoffmann, *Stunden Null? Vergangenheitsbewältigung in Deutschland 1945 und 1989* (Bonn: Bouvier, 1992).
17. Lore Maria Peschel-Gutzeit, "Zur rechtlichen Auseinandersetzung mit dem SED-Regime," *RuP* 31, no. 3 (1995): 132.

18. The broad literature on this subject will be cited throughout this book. For two provocative English language accounts, see Anne Sa'adah, *Germany's Second Chance: Trust, Justice, and Democratization* (Cambridge: Harvard University Press, 1998), which presents a skeptical perspective on the German pursuit of retrospective justice, and Borneman, *Settling Accounts*, which presents a more sympathetic view.

19. For such a politically motivated account, see the essays by representatives of the Party of Democratic Socialism, or PDS (the successor party to the SED), in Lothar Bisky, Uwe-Jens Heuer, and Michael Schumann, eds., *'Unrechtsstaat'?: Politische Justiz und die Aufarbeitung der DDR-Vergangenheit* (Hamburg: VSA Verlag, 1994).

20. Bernhard Schlink, "Vergangenheit als Zumutung," *Öffentliche Vorlesungen*, 61 (1996): 39; also, "Rechtsstaat und revolutionäre Gerechtigkeit," ibid., 3–20. Similarly, Uwe Wesel, "Plädoyer für ein Schlußgesetz," *Zt*, 13 January 1995, 3.

21. Cited in Andreas Zielcke, "Der Kälteschock des Rechtsstaates," *FAZ*, 9 November 1991, n.p. Also, see Wolf Biermann, "'à la Lanterne! à la Lanterne!'" *Spg* no. 39 (21 September 1992): 81–92. In a similar spirit, from a western perspective, see Friedrich Karl Fromme, "Nach einer Revolution Gerechtigkeit," *FAZ*, 25 July 1991, 5, and by the same writer, "Eine Probe für den Rechtsstaat," *FAZ*, 5 August 1991, 1.

22. See Peschel-Gutzeit, "Zur rechtlichen Auseinandersetzung," 131.

23. For example, Marion Gräfin Dönhoff, "Niemand kann ein ganzes Volk durchleuchten," *Zt*, 17 September 1993, 4, and Hans Schueler, "Das Recht des Siegers?" *Zt*, 12 July 1991, 6.

24. See Pastor Friedrich Schorlemmer's remarks on criminal prosecutions, in Lothar Petzold, "Wer überprüft die Gauck Behörde?" *SächZ*, 24 August 1994, 21, and Bruce Ackerman's comments on administrative disqualification in *The Future of Liberal Revolution* (New Haven: Yale University Press, 1992), 96.

25. A classic statement of this position is Hannah Arendt's *The Origins of Totalitarianism* (New York: Harcourt Brace Jovanovich, 1973), Chaps. 10–13. For alternate perspectives suggesting a more differentiated view of everyday life alongside dictatorship, cf. Sheila Fitzpatrick, *Everyday Stalinism: Ordinary Life in Extraordinary Times* (Oxford: Oxford University Press, 2000) and Robert Gellately, "Rethinking the Nazi Terror System: A Historiographical Analysis," *GSR* 14, no. 1 (February 1991): 23–38.

26. "The power of the powerless," in *Václav Havel: Living in Truth*, ed. Jan Vladislav (London: Faber and Faber, 1987), 94.

27. For accounts sympathetic to Havel's position, see Timothy Garton Ash, *History of the Present* (London: Penguin, 1999), 301, and Rosenberg, *The Haunted Land*, xvii, 399.

28. Hannah Arendt, *The Human Condition* (Chicago: University of Chicago Press, 1958), 241.

29. Cited in Telford Taylor, *The Anatomy of the Nuremberg Trials: A Personal Memoir* (New York: Alfred A. Knopf, 1992), 167.
30. See Robert Shnayerson, "Judgment at Nuremberg," *Smithsonian* 27, no. 7 (October 1996): 124–41. The difficulty of pursuing retrospective justice is confirmed by the failure to prosecute cases of genocide and crimes against humanity in the communist world such as the crimes of high Stalinism.
31. Hartmut Zimmermann, "The GDR in the 1970s," *Problems of Communism* 27, no. 2 (March–April 1978): 1–40; Gert-Joachim Glaeßner, *Die andere deutsche Republik* (Opladen: Westdeutscher Verlag, 1989), Chap. 2.
32. Cited in Wolfgang-Uwe Friedrich, "Utopie und Realität: zur Misere posttotalitärer Gesellschaften," *GSR*, special issue, ed. Wolfgang-Uwe Friedrich (fall 1994): 224.
33. See my *East Germany and Detente* (Cambridge: Cambridge University Press, 1985), 140–1, 157.
34. Charles S. Maier, *Dissolution: The Crisis of Communism and the End of East Germany* (Princeton: Princeton University Press, 1997), 29–42.
35. Relevant cases are documented in Jürgen Aretz and Wolfgang Stock, *Die vergessenen Opfer der DDR* (Bergisch Gladbach: Bastei-Verlag, 1997).
36. Wolfgang Thierse, "Schuld sind immer die Anderen," *Zt*, 6 September 1991, 13.
37. For an eastern example, see the interview with Friedrich Schorlemmer in BPA Nachrichtenabteilung, 1 December 1994, 1–2. For a western view, see Günter Gaus, "Moral nach Aktenlage," *Freitag*, 13 January 1995, 3.
38. "À la Lanterne?" *Kursbuch* 111 (February 1993): 11.
39. For a defense of this position, see Joachim Gauck, *Die Stasi-Akten* (Reinbek bei Hamburg: Rowohlt, 1991), 27–40, 89–100.
40. The issue of eastern Germans' perceptions of lower status is well documented. For example, in a survey conducted by the Emnid polling institute in late 1992, 77 percent of eastern respondents agreed that GDR citizens "[would remain] second-class citizens for some time." Sixty-six percent felt that "despite their affluence, the Germans in the West have not learned to share" (cited in *Spg* 3 [18 January 1993]: 52–62). Similarly, in a survey in Mecklenburg–Vorpommern in fall 1995, Emnid found that nearly half the state's residents thought of themselves as eastern Germans first and only secondarily as citizens of unified Germany. Also three-quarters of those surveyed felt the German government primarily served the interests of westerners (cited in *The Week in Germany* [German Information Service]), 17 January 1997, 7. For background on these attitudes, see Konrad Jarausch, *The Rush to German Unity* (Oxford: Oxford University Press, 1994), Chap. 9.
41. In a survey conducted in the mid-1990s, Elisabeth Noelle-Neumann found that 73 percent of eastern Germans polled did not feel that all citizens were equal before the law, 60 percent expressed dissatisfaction with the FRG's laws, and 72 percent felt they were not well protected by the law. See "Kein Schutz, keine Gleichheit, keine Gerechtigkeit," *FAZ*, 8 March 1995, 5.

Chapter 2

1. This case is described in Peter Schmalz, "Für Kindermord gab es Lob und Geld," *DW*, 12 April 1996, 3, and in the 1997 trial of one of the border guards, LG Berlin (523) 27/2 Js 568/92 Ks (7/97), judgment of 19 November 1997.
2. For the Federal Court of Justice's review upholding the sentence, see BGH 5 StR 55/98, judgment of 17 March 1998 (original typescript).
3. Unlike contemporary references to the *Unrechtsstaat*, which frequently draw upon Jaspers' work, Jaspers himself used the more easily translatable term *Verbrecherstaat* ("criminal state"). See *Wohin treibt die Bundesrepublik?* (Munich: Piper reprint, 1988), 21.
4. Rudolf Wassermann, "Zur Aufarbeitung des SED Unrecht," *Aus Politik und Zeitgeschichte* 4 (22 January 1993): 3. Cf. Christa Hoffmann, *Stunden Null? Vergangenheitsbewältigung in Deutschland 1945 und 1989* (Bonn: Bouvier, 1992), 287–302.
5. For an assessment of the GDR as "basically an *Unrechtsstaat*," see the article by Horst Sendler, a former president of the Federal Administrative Court, "Über Rechtsstaat, Unrechtsstaat und anderes – Das Editorial der Herausgeber im Meinungsstreit," *NJ* 9 (1991): 379–81. Also see Hans Peter Krüger, "Eine Krake im Kampf mit sich selbst," *FAZ*, 13 June 1991, 34; Lothar Probst, "German Pasts, Germany's Future: Intellectual Controversies Since Reunification," *GPS*, 30 (fall 1993): 29–30; and Claus Leggewie and Horst Meier, "Zum Auftakt ein Schlußstrich?" in *Wir Kollaborateure*, ed. Cora Stephan (Reinbek bei Hamburg: Rowohlt, 1992), 55. The last two authors do not strictly view the GDR as an *Unrechtsstaat*.
6. Eckhard Jesse, " 'Entnazifizierung' und 'Entstasifizierung' als politisches Problem," in *Vergangenheitsbewältigung durch Recht*, ed. Josef Isensee (Berlin: Duncker und Humblot, 1992), 35. For similar views, see Karl Dietrich Bracher, "Die Unterdrücker zur Rechenschaft ziehen," *Universitias* 11 (1991): 1025–28; Christian Strack, Wilfried Berg, and Bodo Pieroth, "Der Rechtsstaat und die Aufarbeitung der vorrechtsstaatlichen Vergangenheit," in *Veröffentlichungen der Vereinigung der Deutschten Staatsrechtslehrer*, no. 51 (Berlin and New York: Walter de Gruyter, 1992), 11–176; and Hoffmann, *Stunden Null?*, 247, 276.
7. Radbruch's words are cited in Uwe Wesel, *Ein Staat vor Gericht: Der Honecker Prozess* (Frankfurt am Main: Eichborn, 1994), 38.
8. A. James McAdams, *Germany Divided: From the Wall to Reunification* (Princeton: Princeton University Press, 1994), 173–4.
9. Peter Richter, *Kurzer Prozeß* (Berlin: Elefanten Press, 1993), 8.
10. To cite the chancellor: see "Interview with Helmut Kohl," *Statements and Speeches* 15, no. 12 (13 August 1992): 2. Also, see Karl Wilhelm Fricke, "Honecker unter Anklage," *DA* 10 (October 1992): 1009–10.
11. *Der Vertrag* (Stuttgart: Deutsche Verlags-Anstalt, 1991), 268.

12. To quote Kohl again: "We can't have it both ways. We can't have a bloody revolution and at the same time celebrate a peaceful revolution. If we have a system of government based on the rule of law, then the law applies to every citizen of this country even if the citizen happens to be Erich Honecker." In "Interview": 2. Also, reflecting the spirit of the time, see Schäuble's comments about limiting the scope of criminal prosecutions in *Der Vertrag*, 266–70. On these constitutional rights, see David Currie, *The Constitution of the Federal Republic of Germany* (Chicago: University of Chicago Press, 1994), 150–51, 305–28.

13. See Unification Treaty, attach. I, Chap. III(C), sec. 2, §1b(1). In one exception to the rule, at §1b(4) of the same section, the treaty permits prosecutions for acts already in violation of West German law before the date of unification. Prosecutors used this provision to justify the early trials of East German intelligence officers, arguing that German law had long treated foreign espionage as a punishable offense. Authorities also specified that West German law should be applied at the sentencing stage when its criminal code was more lenient than the East German code. See Gunnar Schuster, "The Criminal Prosecution of Former GDR Officials," in *The Unification of Germany in International and Domestic Law*, eds. Ryszard Piotrowicz and Sam Blay, in *German Monitor*, 39 (1997): 119.

14. Jörg Polakiewicz, "Verfassungs- und völkerrechtliche Aspekte der strafrechtlichen Ahndung des Schußwaffeneinsatzes an der innerdeutschen Grenze," *EuGRZ* 19, nos. 9–10 (1992): 177–8.

15. Indeed, one could argue that the existence of these moral standards in the GDR gave the laws legitimacy, and not the other way around. On the recurrent tension between positive and suprapositive norms in German jurisprudence, see Donald Kommers, *The Constitutional Jurisprudence of the Federal Republic of Germany* (Durham, NC: Duke University Press, 1989), 43.

16. Klaus Kinkel, "Wiedervereinigung und Strafrecht," *JZ* 47, no. 10 (May 22, 1992), 487.

17. Ibid.

18. On the sequencing of the trials and related themes, see Uwe Wesel, *Ein Staat vor Gericht*, 33. On the border guard trials, see Joachim Hruschke, "Die Todesschüsse an der Berliner Mauer vor Gericht," *JZ* 47, no. 13 (1992): 665–70; Polakiewicz, "Verfassungs- und völkerrechtliche Aspekte": 177–90; Antje Petersen, "The First Berlin Border Guard Trial," *Occasional Paper* 15 (Bloomington, IN: Indiana Center on Global Change and World Peace, December 1992): 1–39; Kif Augustine Adams, "What Is Just? The Rule of Law and Natural Law in the Trials of Former East German Border Guards," *Stanford Journal of International Law* 29 (1993): 271–314; Herwig Roggemann, "Zur Strafbarkeit der Mauerschützen," *DtZ* 1 (1993): 10–19.

19. Cited in Petersen: 24–5.

20. See his ruling, LG Berlin (523) 2 Js 48/90 (9/91), judgment of 20 January 1992, 136–40. Original typescript.
21. Ibid., 156.
22. Jeanne L. Bakker, "The Defense of Obedience to Superior Orders: The *Mens Rea* Requirement," *American Journal of Criminal Law* 17, no. 1 (1989): 55–6.
23. LG Berlin of 20 January 1992, 156–63.
24. Bakker, "The Defense": 55–6.
25. For forceful critiques of Seidel's reasoning, see Wesel, 33–43; Adams, 298–300; and Petersen, 38. In March 1993, the Federal Court of Justice showed its reservations with the ruling by lifting the decision against one of the defendants and suspending the sentence of another. Significantly, the court based its judgment expressly on preexisting GDR law. See the ruling of 25 March 1993 (5 StR 418/92).
26. See the regional court ruling, LG Berlin (518) 2 Js 63/90 KLs (57/91), judgment of 5 February 1992, 50–2. Original typescript.
27. *DDR Handbuch*, 1 (Cologne: Verlag Wissenschaft und Politik, 1985), 575–6.
28. For such a critique, see Peter Quint, *The Imperfect Union* (Princeton: Princeton University Press, 1997), 199–205. By the same author, see "Judging the Past: The Prosecution of East German Border Guards and the GDR Chain of Command," *RoP* 61, no. 2 (spring 1999), 303–29.
29. LG Berlin of 5 February 1992.
30. In two ways, the court differed with Tepperwein. It took issue with the claim that it was always unlawful for border guards to use "automatic fire." In the judges' estimation, both GDR border law and established state practice provided for occasions when the prevention of escape attempts had priority over human life. The court also appealed to international law in judging East German border fortifications to be incompatible with the GDR's participation in the International Covenant on Civil and Political Rights. Yet the court upheld Tepperwein's use of East German law. For the decision (5 StR 370/92), see *NJW* 2 (1993): 141–9. On the use of international law in this and other cases, see Schuster, "The Criminal Prosecution": 130–1. For a critique emphasizing that the GDR Volkskammer never enacted the international covenant into domestic law, see Quint, *The Imperfect Union*: 200–1.
31. Peter Richter, *Kurzer Prozeß* (Berlin: Elefanten Press, 1993), 8–10.
32. The imperfectly translatable German term is *mittelbare Mittäterschaft*.
33. Anklageschrift, Staatsanwaltschaft bei dem Kammergericht Berlin, pp. 770–1. I am grateful to the Berlin Prosecutor General's Office for providing me with the normally confidential sections of the indictment dealing with the "legal justification" (*rechtliche Würdigung*) of the case.
34. For historical evidence, see Peter Möbius and Helmut Trotnow, "Das Mauer-Komplott: Honecker verschärft die Teilung von Tag zu Tag," *Zt*,

16 August 1991, 13, and Wolfgang Leonhard, "Erich Honecker und die Berliner Mauer," *Kursbuch* no. 111 (February 1993): 125–31.

35. See the short version of the indictment, reprinted in Richter, *Kurzer Prozeß*, 145–51. (This version was released on 30 November 1992. The court reduced to 12 the number of charges against the defendants to simplify the proceedings.) For evidence supporting the court's reasoning, see Werner Filmer and Heribert Schwan, *Opfer der Mauer: Die geheimen Protokolle des Todes* (Munich: C. Bertelsmann, 1991), 373–94.

36. For different accounts, see Jacqueline Hénard, *Geschichte vor Gericht* (Berlin: Corso bei Siedler, 1993), 57–74; Richter, *Kurzer Prozeß*, 15–17; Erich Selbmann, *Der Prozeß* (Berlin: Spotless, 1993), 6–70; Wesel, *Ein Staat vor Gericht*, Chaps. 1, 2, 5, passim; Rosenberg, *The Haunted Land*, Chap. 8; and, for a sympathetic account penned by the wife of one of Honecker's attorneys, "On with the Show," *The New Yorker* 68, no. 11 (11 January 1993): 23–6.

37. Honecker's statement is reprinted in Richter, *Kurzer Prozeß*, 159–75.

38. See Donald Kommers, "Basic Rights and Constitutional Review," in *Politics and Government in the Federal Republic of Germany, Basic Documents*, eds. C. Schweizer, D. Karsten, R. Spencer, R. Cole, D. Kommers, and A. Nicholls (Coventry, UK: Berg, 1984), 114.

39. All charges against Stoph were eventually dropped for reasons of poor health in July 1993 followed by the dismissal of charges against Mielke for similar reasons a year later. Mielke was incarcerated, however, for his conviction in the other case. In February 1995, the FCC rejected his request for review of the conviction.

40. Honecker failed to live up to this prediction by only half a year; he died in Chile on 29 May 1994.

41. See VerfGH Beschluß (55/92) in *JZ* 5 (1993): 259–61. On the legal issues, see Klaus Lüderssen, *Der Staat geht unter – das Unrecht bleibt?* (Frankfurt am Main: Suhrkamp, 1992), 98–105. Some critics contended that the court exceeded its competence. See D. Meurer, "Der Verfassungsgerichtshof und das Strafverfahren," *JR* 3 (March 1993): 89–95; R. Bartlsperger, "Einstellung des Strafverfahrens von Verfassungswegen," *Deutsches Verwaltungsblatt* 108, no. 7 (1 April 1993): 333–49; and J. Berkemann, "Ein Landesverfassungsgericht als Revisionsgericht," *Neue Zeitschrift für Verwaltungsrecht* 12, no. 5 (15 May 1993): 409–19.

42. *SdZ*, 14 January 1993, 3; *SdZ*, 16–17 January 1994, 4.

43. Keßler's and Streletz's defense arguments are in Richter, 207–14, 222–31.

44. Bräutigam's dismissal from the case was as odd as the proceedings. The judge was not removed for reasons of political bias, as one might have anticipated, but because he sought, bizarrely, to obtain Honecker's autograph for a lay judge.

45. For the main sections of the regional court's decision (LG Berlin, Urteil vom 16.9.93 – [527] 2 Js 26/90 Ks 10 [92]), see "Urteil gegen ehem.

Mitglieder des Nationalen Verteidigungsrates der DDR," *NJ* 5 (1994): 210–14.

46. Ibid., 213.
47. Ibid., 212. Also, *SdZ*, 17 September, 1993, 1 and 4; *The Week in Germany* (German Information Center), 24 September, 1993, 1; Peter Jochen Winters, "Ein Sieg der Gerechtigkeit," *DA* 10 (October 1993): 1121–2.
48. United Press International report, 16 September 1993, 1.
49. *The Week in Germany* (German Information Center), 24 September 1993, 1.
50. BGH 5 StR 98/94 – 167/94, judgment of 26 July 1994.
51. Federal Court of Justice press release of 26 July 1994 (As: 5 StR 98/94).
52. See the ruling of 3 November 1992 (5 StR 370/92), in *NJW*, 2 (1993): 146.
53. Ibid., 144–5.
54. Cited in Joachim Nawrocki, "Für Gnade ist es noch zu früh, *Zt* 32, 13 August 1993, 3.
55. *Political Justice: The Use of Legal Procedure for Political Ends* (Princeton: Princeton University Press, 1961), 336.
56. On the constructive potential of courts in general, see Mark J. Osiel, "Why Prosecute? Critics of Punishment for Mass Atrocity," *HRQ* 22 (2000): 140.
57. *The Independent* 15, no. 7, 2 August 1992, 38–41.
58. As quoted by the Federal Court of Justice, judgment of 26 July 1994.
59. Roman Grafe, "Die Strafverfolgung von DDR-Grenzschützen und ihren Befehlgebern," *DA* 3 (May–June 1997): 377–78.
60. See "Interview mit Ernst Benda," *DA* 12 (December 1992): 1341.
61. See Ronald Dworkin, "Introduction," *Nunca Más: The Report of the Argentine National Commission on the Disappeared* (New York: Farrar, Straus and Giroux, 1986), xvii–xxii. Regardless of the government's later decision to pardon those involved, it is significant that these trials took place. See Carlos Acuña and Catalina Smulovitz, "Guarding the Guardians in Argentina," in *Transitional Justice and the Rule of Law in New Democracies*, ed. A. James McAdams (Notre Dame: University of Notre Dame Press, 1997): 93–122.
62. Dworkin, "Introduction," xxiv.
63. Sections of this judgment (36. Großen Strafkammer des Landgerichtes Berlin, 10 September 1996) are reprinted in Roman Grafe, "'Niemals Zweifel gehabt': Der Prozeß gegen die Grenztruppen-Führung der DDR," *DA* 6 (November–December 1996): 862–71.
64. Ibid.
65. For this distinction, see the interview with state attorney Bernhard Jahntz in Dietmar Jochum, *Das Politbüro auf der Anklagebank* (Berlin: Magnus Verlag, 1996), 365.
66. The indictment (25/2 Js 20/92) is printed in ibid., 135–7.
67. For Schabowski's speech, see ibid., 292–3. Ironically, Schabowski was the official who, in a rambling press conference on 9 Novermber 1989 inadvertently announced the opening of the Berlin Wall.

68. Ibid., 301, 304. On the distinction between legal guilt and moral guilt, see Karl Jaspers, *The Question of German Guilt*, trans. E. B. Ashton (Westport, CT: Greenwood Press, 1978), 31–2.
69. See, for example, the statement by the SED's last general secretary, Egon Krenz, in Jahntz, 242.
70. Ibid., 354.
71. BVerfGE, 96, 95, Beschluß des Zweiten Senats von 24. Oktober. 1996 – 2 BvR 1851, 1853, 1875 und 1852/94.
72. Ibid.
73. As is appropriate for the second senate, the chamber may have seen its charge as being confined to assessing the constitutionality of the rulings before it rather than providing specific commentary on the decisions themselves. Yet this role need not have kept the justices from addressing apparent discrepancies between their judgments and those of the lower courts.
74. BVerfGE, Beschluß des Zweiten Senats von 24. Oktober. 1996.
75. Peter Jochen Winters, "Das Urteil gegen Krenz und andere," *DA* 5 (September–October 1997): 693–6.
76. See "Der Eröffnungsbeschluß," in Dietmar Jochum, *Der Politbüro-Prozeß* (Kückenshagen: Scheunen-Verlag, 1996): 203–12.
77. Ibid., 208–9.
78. See LG Berlin, judgment of 25 August 1997, 275–7.
79. Ibid., 276.

Chapter 3

1. Stephen Kinzer, "East Germans Face Their Accusers," *NYT Magazine*, 12 April 1992, 42.
2. Silke Schumann, *Vernichten oder Offenlegen? Zur Entstehung des Stasi-Unterlagen-Gesetzes* (Berlin: BStU, 1995), 19.
3. Claus Offe, "Disqualification, Retribution, Restitution: Dilemmas of Justice in Post-Communist Societies," *Journal of Political Philosophy* 1, no. 1 (1993): 30–3.
4. Marion Gräfin Dönhoff, "Niemand kann ein ganzes Volk durchleuchten," *Zt*, 17 September 1993, 4.
5. Author's interview, David Gill, Berlin, 1 June 1996. Also see Elizabeth Pond, *Beyond the Wall: Germany's Road to Unification* (Washington, DC: Brookings Institution, 1993), 150, and David Gill and Ulrich Schröter, *Das Ministerium für Staatssicherheit* (Berlin, Rowohlt, 1991), 185–6.
6. Joachim Gauck, "Dealing with a Stasi Past," *Daedalus* 123, no. 1 (winter 1994): 279.
7. Author's interview, David Gill, Berlin, 1 June 1996.
8. In a review of the Census Act of 1983, Germany's highest court ruled in December 1983 that every individual was entitled "to decide for himself, on the basis of the idea of self-determination, when and within what limits facts about his personal life [should] be disclosed." See Donald

P. Kommers, *The Constitutional Jurisprudence of the Federal Republic of Germany* (Durham, NC: Duke University Press, 1989), 332–6. BVerfGE judgment of 15 December 1983, 65 I.

9. Geiger would soon become deputy director of the federal authority for the Stasi archives. Interview with *die tageszeitung*, 17 November 1990. In Schumann, *Vernichten*, 124.

10. For a defense of using the files to pursue justice, see the remarks of the Berlin privacy commissioner Hansjürgen Garstka, "Probleme des Datenschutzes beim Umgang mit Stasi-Akten," in *Wann bricht schon mal ein Staat zusammen!* ed. Klaus-Dietmar Henke (Munich: Deutscher Taschenbuch Verlag, 1993), 49–50. For a contrasting perspective, see Bruce Ackerman's argument that the files were "fruits of the poisonous tree" and hence devoid of evidentiary value, *The Future of Liberal Revolution* (New Haven: Yale University Press, 1992), 81–9.

11. The full title of the law is "Gesetz über die Unterlagen des Staatssicherheitsdienstes der ehemaligen Deutschen Demokratischen Republik," in BGBl, 1991, I, p. 67. For an argument that the new law failed to achieve this balance because it slighted the rights of the accused, see Ilse Staff, "Wiedervereinigung unter Rechtsgesetzen," *Zeitschrift für Rechtspolitik* 12 (1992), 462–9. Useful commentaries are Klaus Stoltenberg, *Stasi-Unterlagen Gesetz: Kommentar* (Baden-Baden: Nomos Verlagsgesellschaft, 1992); Hansjörg Geiger and Heinz Klinghardt, *Stasi-Unterlagen-Gesetz: Mit Erläuterungen für die Praxis* (Cologne: Deutsche Gemeindeverlag, 1993); and Dietmar Schmidt and Erwin Dör, *Stasi Unterlagengesetz* (Cologne: Datakontext Verlag, 1993).

12. For example, *SdZ*, 28 March 1990; *GA*, 2 April 1990, 1 and 3; *DW*, 6 April 1990, 5.

13. DW, 21 April 1990, 4.

14. *Spg*, 14 (2 April 1990), 21–2.

15. Wolfgang Schäuble, *Der Vertrag: Wie ich über die deutsche Einheit verhandelte* (Stuttgart: Deutsche Verlags-Anstalt, 1991), 273.

16. "Interview des WDR mit Bundesinnenminister Dr. Wolfgang Schäuble" (Bonn: Pressedienst des Bundesministeriums des Innern, 29 March 1990).

17. "Erst erinnern, dann vergeben. Was wird aus der Stasi-Vergangenheit?" *Zt*, 13 April 1990. In Schumann, *Vernichten*, 89–92.

18. "Akteneinsicht als Therapie," *Rheinischer Merkur/Christ und Welt*, 1 June 1990, in Schumann, 93–6. "If the statistics we have on collaborators are even half true," Rathenow noted, apparently drawing on different sources of information than Eppelmann or Schäuble, "this can only mean that: [for every successful recruit], ten or twenty times as many people did not allow themselves to be recruited."

19. One reason was that several thousand regular officers of the Stasi had been transferred to various ministries (e.g., defense, the interior) as part of the last SED government's efforts to close down the MfS.

20. *StZ*, 31 March 1990, 1, 3, 5.

21. For the agreement, see Unification treaty, attachment I, Chap. II(B), §2(2), of 31 August 1990 and Vereinbarung zwischen der BRD und der DDR zur Durchführung und Auslegung des am 31. August 1990 in Berlin unterzeichneten Einigungsvertrages, 18 September 1990, BGBl, 11, 1239, art. 1. For useful assessments of the conflicts over these agreements, see Peter Quint, *The Imperfect Union: Constitutional Structures of German Unification* (Princeton: Princeton University Press, 1997), 233–4; and Schumann, *Vernichten*, 20–26.

22. Unification treaty, attachment I, Chap. XIX(A), §3(1) (5) (2). The concept of administrative *Unzumutbarkeit* defies easy translation into English. It can also be rendered as "unsupportability."

23. Interview with *Spg* no. 52 (27 December 1993), 36.

24. Author's interviews, Klaus Richter and Gerd Bäcker, BStU, Berlin, 12 June 1996. On the principles involved, see *Erster Tätigkeitsbericht* (Berlin: BStU, 1993), 7–8.

25. Portions of the BStU report on de Maizière are reprinted in *Spg* no. 12 (18 March 1991), 41–8. Some accounts list this cover name as "Czerny," but his MfS *Findkarte* says "Czerni."

26. Some dissidents have questioned the accuracy of the information in their dossiers. See Vera Wollenberger, "Eine zweite Vergewaltigung," in *Aktenkundig*, ed. Hans Joachim Schädlich (Reinbek bei Hamburg: Rowohlt, 1993), 162. Also see David Childs and Richard Popplewell, *The Stasi: The East German Intelligence and Security Service* (New York: New York University Press, 1996), 87–8. However, my impression is that a majority of the Stasi's victims have come to different conclusions, often remarking at the chilling accuracy of the files. An eloquent account is Timothy Garton Ash, *The File: A Personal History* (New York: Random House, 1997).

27. However, outright falsifications of files appear to have been rare. In 1993, BStU department head Gerd-Dieter Hirsch reported that out of approximately 50,000 cases, there had been "perhaps three cases" in which researchers had been able to verify that a control officer clearly manipulated his IM recruitment information to achieve his quota. In "Auskünfte zur Überprüfung durch Institutionen," *Analysen und Berichte: Aus der Veranstaltungsreihe des Bundesbeauftragten*, series B, 3/93 (Berlin: BStU, 1993): 87. One year later, Hansjörg Geiger put this figure at "only about a half dozen," out of hundreds of thousands of dossiers. Interview with *blz: Zeitung der GEW Berlin*, 10 October 1994, 25.

28. Norman Naimark, " 'To know everything and to report everything worth knowing': Building the East German Police State, 1945–1949," *Working Paper*, 10, Cold War International History Project (Washington, DC: The Woodrow Wilson Center, August 1994). Interestingly, the Gestapo cultivated a similar mystique, though it, too, failed at times to live up to its omnipresent reputation. See Robert Gellately, "Rethinking the Nazi Terror System: A Historiographical Analysis," *GSR* 14, no. 1 (February 1991): 31–2.

29. See Hansjörg Geiger, "Erfahrungen mit der Staatssicherheit und ihre rechtsstaatliche Aufarbeitung," in *Eine Diktatur vor Gericht*, eds. Jürgen

Weber and Michael Piazolo (Munich: Olzog Verlag, 1995), 152, and Hirsch, "Auskünfte," 86–7.

30. For a thoughtful analysis by a BStU researcher, see Roger Engelmann, "Zum Quellenwert der Unterlagen des Ministeriums für Staatssicherheit," in *Aktenlage: Die Bedeutung der Unterlagen des Staatssicherheitsdienstes für die Zeitgeschichtsforschung*, eds. Klaus-Dietmar Henke und Roger Engelmann (Berlin: Ch. Links, 1995), 23–39.

31. Interview with "Kurt Z.," in Gisela Karau, *Stasiprotokolle: Gespräche mit ehemaligen Mitarbeitern des "Ministeriums für Staatssicherheit" der DDR* (Frankfurt: DIPA, 1992), 81.

32. Bruce Ackerman, *The Future of Liberal Revolution*, 87.

33. Cited in Bärbel Broer, "Die innere Struktur der Behörde für die Unterlagen des Staatssicherheitsdienstes der ehemaligen DDR," Magisterarbeit, Universität Hannover, September 1995, 264.

34. For a notable example, see Ian Kershaw, *Popular Opinion and Political Dissent in the Third Reich* (Oxford: Oxford University Press, 1993).

35. Author's interview, Joachim Gauck, Berlin, 11 June 1996.

36. Jochen V. Lang, *Die Gestapo* (Hamburg: Rasch und Roehring, 1990), 88–9. The Gestapo's relatively small size reflects the greater popularity of the Nazi regime in comparison with the SED. Because the former dictatorship enjoyed strong domestic support, it did not require as extensive a network of informants as the GDR. The Gestapo could also count on receiving information voluntarily from its civilian population about possible enemies of the Third Reich. See Robert Gellately, *The Gestapo and German Society* (Oxford: Clarendon Press, 1990), 135.

37. Even as late as the summer of 1991, the news magazine *Der Spiegel* and the FRG's then-justice minister, Klaus Kinkel, discussed the possibility that 25–30 percent of the GDR's population had been Stasi informants. See Kinkel's interview in *Spg* no. 33 (13 August 1990): 21.

38. Statistics provided to the author in a letter from Gerd-Dieter Hirsch, BStU, 9 April 1997.

39. On the legal definition of culpability, see Thomas von Lindheim, "Zum Begriff der Zusammenarbeit des inoffiziellen und hauptamtlichen Mitarbeiters mit dem MfS," *DtZ* 12 (1993): 358–61, and Wilfried Berkowsky, "Kündigungen wegen Stasi-Tätigkeit in der Rechtsprechung," *Arbeit und Arbeitsrecht* 4 (1996): 125–8.

40. *Die Stasi Akten: Das unheimliche Erbe der DDR* (Reinbek bei Hamburg: Rowohlt, 1991), 27.

41. Ibid., 28.

42. Author's interview, Michael Zabel, BStU, Berlin, 19 June 1996. For a description and insightful critique of the BStU's self-understanding as an exclusively administrative agency, see John Miller, "Settling Accounts with a Secret Police: The German Law on the Stasi Records," *Europe–Asia Studies* 50, no. 2 (1998): 320.

43. For example, Gauck conceded the existence of "sensationalistic witch-hunting reports," though he insisted that these were "never based on the work of the [BStU]." In "Dealing with a Stasi Past," 282.

44. Tina Rosenberg, *The Haunted Land: Facing Europe's Ghosts after Communism* (New York: Random House, 1995), 326.
45. Statistics provided in a letter from Gerd-Dieter Hirsch, BStU, 9 April 1997.
46. Diemut Majer, "Ein halbierter Rechtsstaat für Ostdeutschland?" *KJ* 25, no. 2 (1992), 157–8, fn. 32.
47. For various accounts, see *Spg* no. 21 (18 May 1992), 68–72; *Leipziger Volkszeitung*, 9 November 1995, 4; *SächZ*, 11 November 1995, 48; *Focus*, 11 September 1995, 76; and Berkowsky, "Kündigungen," 127.
48. Miller, "Settling Accounts," 318–19.
49. In contrast to the looser language of the Unification treaty, Saxony's *Beamtengesetz*, the law governing the employment of public officials, states that anyone with a Stasi past is "fundamentally (*grundsätzlich*)" excluded from such appointments. See Heinz Hillermeier, "Stasi-Mitarbeiter im öffentlichen Dienst," *Landes- und Kommunalverwaltung* 5, no. 4 (3 April 1995): 141–3. On the screening of state officials in Saxony for all connections with the former regime, including SED membership, see the remarks of State Secretary Wolfgang Nowack, as cited in Herman Schwartz, "Lustration in Eastern Europe," in *Transitional Justice*, ed. Neil Kritz (Washington, DC: U.S. Institute of Peace, 1995), 471–2. A moving and provocative account of the uses and abuses of screening in Berlin is Inga Markovits, *Imperfect Justice: An East–West German Diary* (Oxford: Oxford University Press, 1995).
50. Author's interview, Gerd-Dieter Hirsch, Berlin, 13 June 1996. Also, *DW*, 26 January 1995, 2. The same political patterns could be observed in the vetting of teachers. By June 1995, 1.22 percent of all teachers investigated in Saxony–Anhalt (out of a total of 96,000) had been dismissed for Stasi complicity, whereas in Berlin this figure was only 0.9 percent (out of 20,000) (*Deutsche Presse Agentur* press release, June 1995). In conservative Saxony, a significantly higher 1.68 percent had been fired for the same reason by October 1995 (out of 60,000 investigated), *SächZ*, 16 October 1995, n.p. On the contrasting political cultures between Saxony (and other eastern states) and Brandenburg, see Anne Sa'adah, *Germany's Second Chance: Trust, Justice, and Democratization* (Cambridge: Harvard University Press, 1998), Chap. 5, passim.
51. According to Hansjörg Geiger, in an interview with the DPA, *BM*, 11 July 1994, n.p.
52. Ibid. Also see *Zweiter Tätigkeitsbericht des Bundesbeauftragten für die Unterlagen des Staatssicherheitsdienstes der ehemaligen DDR, 1995* (Berlin: BStU, 1995), 33–5. On MfS screening in the private sector, see Uwe R. Scholz, "Kündigung in der Privatwirtschaft wegen Tätigkeit für das Ministerium für Staatssicherheit/Amt für nationale Sicherheit," *Arbeits- und Sozialrecht* 34 (1992): 2424–9.
53. One BStU section head has described this as an opportunity to "thin the ranks." Author's interview, Gerd-Dieter Hirsch, Berlin, 13 June 1996.

54. Thilo Weichert, "Überprüfung der öffentlichen Bediensten in Ostdeutschland," *KJ* 24 (1991): 472.
55. Rosenberg makes this perceptive observation in *Haunted Land*, 69–76, 320–3.
56. For example, ibid., 324–6; and *Zweiter Tätigkeitsbericht des Landesbeauftragten für Mecklenburg–Vorpommern für die Unterlagen des Staatssicherheitsdienstes der ehemaligen DDR, 1995–1997* (Schwerin: LStU, 1997), 26. Some of the *Länder* representatives of the BStU proposed to resolve this problem by taking an active role in advising accused Stasi collaborators, though such a step would probably have exceeded their statutory limits. See the reflections of Thuringia's commissioner Heino Falcke in *Tätigkeitsbericht 1993/1994* (Erfurt: LStU, 1995), 26–30.
57. Cited in Frank Lansnicker and Thomas Schwirtzek, "Der Beweiswert von Stasi-Unterlagen im Arbeitsgerichtsprozeß," *DtZ* 5 (1994): 162. For a biting critique along these lines, see Maren Brandenburger, "Stasi-Unterlagen-Gesetz und Rechtsstaat," *KZ* 28, no. 3 (1995): 357.
58. See Miller, "Settling Accounts," 320–1; and Quint, *Imperfect Union*, 239.
59. Majer, "Ein halbierter Rechtsstaat," 163, also, *Spg* 21 (18 May 1992), 68–72.
60. Abgeordnetenhaus von Berlin, *Dritter Tätigkeitsbericht des Berliner Landesbeauftragten für die Unterlagen des Staatssicherheitsdienstes der ehemaligen DDR*, 13. Wahlperiode, Drucksache 13/1395, February 1997, 8.
61. BGH judgment of 5 May 1992 – 2 BJs 15/92-5 – StB 9/92, reprinted in *NJW* 31 (1992): 1975–76. For commentary, see ibid., 162–3.
62. Cited in Lansnicker and Schwirtzek, "Der Beweiswert," 163.
63. Author's interview, Richter and Bäcker, Berlin, 12 June 1996. Also, *FAZ*, 4 November 1992, 4. Even the former SED youth magazine *Junge Welt* agreed that Fink's case was not strong. See *JW*, 17 December 1992, 2.
64. LAG Berlin judgment of 16 December 1992 – 12 Sa 32.92.
65. See LG Halle judgment of 22 June 1993; OLG Naumburg judgment of 25 November 1993; BGH judgment of 12 July 1994 – Az. VI ZR 1/94, cited in Quint, *Imperfect Union*, 240 and 429, fn. 90, and *StZ*, 14 July 1994, n.p.
66. BAG judgment of 26 August 1993 – 8 AZR 561–92.
67. LAG Mecklenburg–Vorpommern judgment of 14 August 1995 – 5 Sa 359/94. Also see LAG Sachsen–Anhalt judgment of 23 August 1995 – 5 Sa 974/94, and BAG judgment of 14 December 1995 – 8 AZR 356/94.
68. Ait Stapelfeld, "Zum aktuellen Stand der Rechtsprechung und zur Praxis des Sonderkündigungsrechtes im Einigungsvertrag wegen Tätigkeit für MfS/AfNS," 6, no. 6 *DtZ* (1995): 18.
69. BAG judgment of 28 January 1993 – 8 AZR 415/92.
70. OVG 4 S 310/95, cited in *Tsp*, 4 November 1995, 10.
71. BVerfGE (2. Kammer des Ersten Senats) decision of 28 December 1995 – BvR 2263/94, 229/95, and 534/95. Cited in *SdZ*, 29 December 1995, 1; and *FR*, 29 December 1995, 1.

72. BVerfGE (2. Kammer des Ersten Senats) decision of 14 February 1996 – BvR 944/95. Discussed in *DtZ* 11 (1996): 341.
73. BAG judgment of 13 September 1995 – 2 AZR 862/94. Also Berkowsky, "Kündigungen," 128.
74. Ibid. Also consider LAG Sachsen–Anhalt judgment of 17 May 1995 – 3 Sa 627/94.
75. *Drittes Gesetz zur Änderung des Stasi-Unterlagen-Gesetzes*, 20 December 1996. Although the courts found no problem with this revision, some eastern activists complained that the new law allowed rights violators to get away with their abuses. The Bundestag sought to appease the critics by stipulating that the revised statute of limitations would not go into effect until 1 August 1998. See BGBl, 1996, I, no. 68, p. 2026. Author's interview, Herbert Ziehm, BStU, Berlin, 23 January 1997.
76. On the sharp decline in dismissals, see *Focus*, 11 September 1995, 76; *Leipziger Zeitung*, 9 November 1995, 4; *Magdeburger Volksstimme*, 15 March 1996, 4; *Mitteldeutsche Zeitung*, 3 January 1997, 2. In the first half of the decade, as Hans-Hermann Lochen points out, officials frequently overreacted to the BStU's findings of Stasi complicity, but by the mid-1990s, the proliferation of appeals cases before labor courts made them think twice about further dismissals. "Der Umgang mit den Stasi-Unterlagen," in *Juristische Bewältigung des kommunistischen Unrechts in Osteuropa und Deutschland*, ed. Georg Brunner (Berlin: Arno Spitz, 1995), 280.
77. See Geiger, "Erfahrungen mit der Staatssicherheit," 152–3.
78. *German News Online*, 10 October 1995 (germnews@gmd.de).
79. Statistics from the Berlin State Authority for the Records of the State Security Service of the Former GDR, provided by Herbert Ziehm, BStU, Berlin, 23 January 1997.
80. Weichert, "Überprüfung," 459, 465; *Spg* no. 21 (18 May 1992), 68–72. According to Robert Gerald Livingston, from 20,000 to 40,000 West Germans worked in some capacity for the Stasi between 1950 and 1990, with 3,000 to 4,000 active at any given time. "The Quest for the Stasi's Old Files," *Los Angeles Times*, 27 December 1998, M2 and M6. Westerners were scrutinized in the case of espionage, but the StUG severely limited the access of domestic intelligence agencies to the files (see §25, StUG).
81. See his testimony on 3 April 1993 before the Bundestag's Enquete commission on the GDR (53. Session), in *Materialien der Enquete-Kommission "Aufarbeitung von Geschichte und Folgen der SED-Diktatur in Deutschland."* (Baden-Baden: Nomos Verlag, 1995) 5, no. 1: 928.
82. Miller, "Settling Accounts," 323–4; Broer, "Die innere Struktur," 241–6.
83. See Abgeordnetenhaus von Berlin, *Zweiter Tätigkeitsbericht des Berliner Landesbeauftragten für die Unterlagen des Staatssicherheitsdienstes der ehemaligen DDR, 1995*, 13. Wahlperiode, Drucksache, 13/204, February 1996, 8; and Fritz Arendt, "Die MfS-Überprüfung im'öffentlichen Dienst," eds. Jürgen Weber and Michael Piazolo, *Eine Diktatur vor Gericht* (Munich: Olzog Verlag, 1995), 159–80.

84. BVerfGE, 92, 140, decision of 21 February 1995 – 1 BvR 1397/93.
85. *The Question of German Guilt*, trans. E. B. Ashton (Westport, CT: Green-wood Press, 1978), 31–2.

Chapter 4

1. For public opinion evidence supporting the activists' concerns, see Dieter Roth, "Wandel der politischen Einstellungen seit der Bundestags-wahl 1990," *GSR* 16, no. 2 (May 1993): 291–7.
2. To quote part of a petition by activists Wolfgang Thierse, Friedrich Schorlemmer, Joachim Gauck, Wolfgang Ulmann, and Gerd and Ulrike Poppe, "Ohne Aufklärung bleibt der Makel des Versagens haften," *FR*, 17 January 1992, 11. Also, see Friedrich Schorlemmer, "Wut wird wach. Sie tendiert zum Haß und sucht ihre Opfer," *FR*, 29 October 1991, 14. For background on the tribunal idea, see Petra Bock, "Von der 'Tribunal-Idee zur Enquete-Kommission," *DA* 11 (November 1995): 1171–83. For background on the dissidents' frustrations, see Paul M. Schwartz, "Con-stitutional Change and Constitutional Legitimation," *Houston Law Review* 31, no. 4 (winter 1994): 1071–9; and Konrad Jarausch, *The Rush to German Unity* (Oxford: Oxford University Press, 1994), Chap. 9.
3. Wolfgang Schäuble, then chairperson of the CDU's parliamentary party, expressed this concern diplomatically: "If it were a matter of making judg-ments about individuals, such a tribunal would run right up against the limits of the rule of law. Were it to promote open dialogue, a tribunal might be appropriate." *SdZ*, 5 February 1992.
4. The commission's full title, in German, is *"Enquete-Kommission, 'Aufar-beitung von Geschichte und Folgen der SED-Diktatur in Deutschland.'"*
5. Deutscher Bundestag, *StB*, 82. Sitzung, 12 March 1992, 6712.
6. The testimony and expertise were later published in an omnibus 18-volume collection in the autumn of 1995 as *Materialien der Enquete-Kommission "Aufarbeitung von Geschichte und Folgen der SED-Diktatur in Deutschland"* (Baden-Baden: Nomos Verlag, 1995). Hereafter, *Materialien*.
7. Author's interview, Bonn, 12 June 1995. For generally upbeat accounts of these processes, see Timothy Garton Ash, "The Truth about Dictator-ship," *NYRB* 45, 19 February 1998, 36–40, and Jürgen Fuchs, "Mißliche Wahrheiten," *Spg* 5 (29 January 1996): 50–9. For a biting critique, see Michael Jäger, "Alles Stasi?" *Freitag*, 24 June 1994, 26.
8. See the public testimony before the twentieth session of the commission (on 30 March 1992), in *Materialien*, 2, no. 1, 150–218.
9. Bericht der Enquete-Kommission "Aufarbeitung von Geschichte und Folgen der SED-Diktatur in Deutschland," German Bundestag, 12. Ses-sion, 7820, 6. Hereafter, *Bericht I*.
10. For useful accounts, see Robert F. Goeckel, *The Lutheran Church and the East German State* (Ithaca, NY: Cornell University Press, 1990), Chap. 3;

Mary Fulbrook, *Anatomy of a Dictatorship* (Oxford: Oxford University Press, 1995), 87–106.

11. See his testimony before the commission (56th session, 14 December 1993), in *Materialien* 6, no. 1: p. 154.
12. In the often-cited words of Bishop Albrecht Schönherr. For a defense of the idea of the "church within socialism" by a leading Lutheran official, see Reinhard Henkys, "Thesen zum Wandel der gesellschaftlichen und politischen Rolle der Kirchen in der DDR in den siebziger und achtziger Jahren," in *Die DDR in der Ära Honecker*, ed. Gert-Joachim Glaeßner (Opladen: Westdeutscher Verlag, 1988), 332–53. For a critique, see Gerhard Besier, *Die SED-Staat und die Kirche* (Munich: C. Bertelsmann Verlag, 1993).
13. For details, see Goeckel, *The Lutheran Church*, 241–5.
14. Ibid., 263.
15. For this argument, see Fulbrook, *Anatomy*, 124.
16. See *Protokoll der 56. Sitzung der Enquete-Kommission*, 14 December 1993, 5.
17. Ibid., 5, 7–8.
18. For example, see the testimony before the commission on 15 December 1993 (57th session) of Eberhard Jüngel, Bishop Werner Krusche, and pastor Curt Stauss, in *Materialien*, 6, no. 1: 13–24, 150–4, and 190–8, respectively.
19. The page citations in the following paragraphs are to *Bericht I*.
20. Reinhard Henkys makes this point in a critique of the Enquete commission's findings, "Kirchengeschichte im Bundestag: Anmerkungen zu einem Teilergebnis der Enquete-Kommission," *Politik und Geschichte* 3 (1994): 450–3. Also, Rudolf Mau, "Zur Rolle der Kirchen unter der SED-Diktatur," *FAZ* 8 July 1994, 28.
21. For Stolpe's defense of these contacts, see *Spg* no. 4 (20 January 1992), 22–7. For an extensive analysis of the Stolpe case, see Anne Sa'adah, *Germany's Second Chance* (Cambridge: Harvard University Press, 1998), 189–236.
22. *DA*, 6 (June 1992): 669.
23. I have analyzed these developments in *Germany Divided: From the Wall to Reunification* (Princeton: Princeton University Press, 1993). Also see Timothy Garton Ash, *In Europe's Name: Germany and the Divided Continent* (New York: Vintage Books, 1993).
24. In August 1987, the SPD's Basic Values Commission and the SED's Academy for Social Sciences released an extraordinary and equally controversial joint document, "Conflicting Ideologies and Common Security," which endorsed a new level of discourse between the blocs. See "Der Streit der Ideologien und die gemeinsame Sicherheit," *Politik* 3 (August 1997): 1–7. On the different currents within the SPD about these questions, see Wilfried von Bredow and Rudolf Brocke, *Das deutschlandpolitische Konzept der SPD* (Erlangen: Deutsche Gesellschaft für zeitgeschichtliche Fragen, 1987).

25. See Kohl's remarks from 7 September 1987, *Bulletin* 83 (10 September 1987): 705–7.
26. Joint Communiqué between the German Democratic Republic and the Federal Republic of Germany, 8 September 1987, *Bulletin* 83 (10 September 1987): 710–13.
27. See the comments of Uwe Ronneburger (FDP), Eduard Lintner (CSU), Dorothee Wilms (CDU), Hans Büchler (SPD), among others, in Deutscher Bundestag, *StB*, 11. Sitzung, 3 February 1988, 3952–63.
28. In remarks to Stephen Kinzer, in *NYT*, 7 June 1992, L15. For more criticism, see Helga Hirsch, "Der falsche Weg: Politik von Oben," *Zt*, 28 February 1992, 3, and Reinhard Mohr, "Geschichte im Windkanal," *FAZ*, 9 November 1993, 35. For a defense of Bonn's policy, see Gunter Hoffmann's interview with Egon Bahr, "Indem ich durch diese Hölle gegangen bin," *Zt*, 20 March 1992, 19.
29. *NYT*, 7 June 1992, L15.
30. See Lepsius's testimony of 4 May 1994 (76th Session) in *Materialien*, 9: 704.
31. On the *Superwahljahr*, see "*Bundestagswahl* 1994: The Culmination of the *Superwahljahr*," special issue of *GPS*, eds. Russell J. Dalton and Andrei S. Markovits, 13, no. 1 (spring 1995).
32. Deutscher Bundestag, *StB*, 82. Sitzung, 12 March 1992, 6716.
33. Ibid., 6718.
34. Ibid., 6728. When we read Kohl's speech today, the vigorousness of this attack is, to say the least, debatable. Consider his 7 September 1987 toast to Honecker in Bonn–Bad Godesberg: "In these days, let us concentrate on what is do-able, and let us agree to put those questions that we cannot solve today in the background. Despite our differences, our practical cooperation will provide an example [for others] – in the interest of all people and in the interest of peace." *Bulletin* 83 (Bonn: Presse- und Informationsamt der Bundesregierung, 10 September 1987): 706. Also see transcripts of Kohl's private telephone discussions with Honecker and others in Heinrich Potthoff, *Die "Koalition der Vernunft": Deutschlandpolitik in den 80er Jahren* (Munich: Deutscher Taschenbuch Verlag, 1995).
35. Deutscher Bundestag, *StB*, 82. Sitzung, 12 March 1992, 6728.
36. Author's interviews, M. Jansen, 6 June 1995; B. Dove, 7 June 1995; and B. Faulenbach, 13 June 1995.
37. One reason for the comparatively greater subtlety in the SPD's positions was that the party was divided on this issue between the original practitioners of *Ostpolitik* from the West (e.g., Egon Bahr) and the easterners (e.g., Markus Meckel, Stephan Hilsberg) who were highly critical of the policy (author's interview, Bernard Dove, 7 June 1995, Bonn). Some younger western Social Democratic members of the commission shared these sentiments. For example, see Gert Weisskirchen, "Ambivalenzen der Entspannungspolitik," *DA* 5 (May 1992): 526–30.

38. Regardless of party affiliation, all of the Enquete commission's staff members whom I interviewed in June 1995 said their task would have been easier had they not had to deal with the parties, political calculations. Interestingly, although the Greens could make the strongest claim to having ties with dissidents during the GDR's final years, the party confined its minority opinion in the report to a 2-page assessment of the impact of external events on the East German opposition: Poland's independent trade union movement and the West German campaign against NATO's dual-track decision of 1979 (*Bericht I*, 146–7). Green leaders may have feared delving into their own *Deutschlandpolitik* because members had frequently called for the full recognition of the GDR and the abandonment of the goal of German reunification.

39. Peter Juling, "Alle hatten damals recht und alle hatten auch Erfolg," *Das Parlament* 46–7 (November 12/19, 1993): 11. On the November 1993 hearings on the *Deutschlandpolitik* held at the Reichstag in Berlin, see Helmut Lölhöffel, "Mythen, Chimären und Schönfärbereien," *FR*, 3 November 1993, 3. The complete record and supplementary papers and testimony can be found in *Materialien*, 5, no. 3. For reflections on this theme, see my "Inter-German Relations in Historical Perspective," *German Politics* 3, no. 2 (August 1994): 193–205.

40. Author's interview, 12 June 1995, Bonn.

41. Günter Gaus's name has come to be associated with this romantic image of East German society, which he termed "a niche society" in a popular treatment of the GDR, *Wo Deutschland liegt* (Hamburg: Hoffmann und Campe, 1983). For a critique of Gaus's argument suggesting more underlying dissatisfaction with government policy, see Fulbrook, *Anatomy of a Dictatorship*, Chap. 5.

42. See his interview in *Spg* 10 (2 March 1992): 32.

43. Deutscher Bundestag, 82. Sitzung, 12 March 1992, 6733. Sociologist John Torpey notes that Meckel's questions at least had the advantage of being formulated in the first person plural. "For [these] are questions," he argues, "best addressed from the perspective of a participant who shared, however indirectly, in the commission of the acts under consideration." See *Intellectuals, Socialism, and Dissent: The East German Opposition and Its Legacy* (Minneapolis: University of Minnesota Press, 1995), 194.

44. For example, see the testimony of 15 March 1994 (67th session), 10–178, and 16 March 1994 (68th session), 179–313, in *Materialien*, 7, no. 1.

45. Author's interviews with B. Dove, 7 June 1995; I. Drechsler, 8 June 1995; B. Faulenbach, 13 June 1995, Bonn.

46. Deutscher Bundestag, *StB*, 234. Sitzung, 17 June 1994, 20451.

47. To say that East Germans might have rationalized their lives under socialism is, of course, not to defend that system. On the dangers of romanticizing the GDR past, see Fritz Stern, "Democracy and Its Discontents," *FA* 72, no. 4 (September–October 1993): 120–1.

48. Commission members acknowledged some important differences between the NSDAP and the SED. Still, the comparison was bound to evoke strong emotions if only because many communists before and after World War II had regarded the fight against fascism as their raison d'être. For the hearings, which were held in the Reichstag on 3–4 May 1994 and included such participants as historians Karl-Dietrich Bracher and Jürgen Kocka and philosopher Jürgen Habermas, see *Protokol der 75. Sitzung der Enquetekommission*, 3 May 1995, and *Protokol der 76. Sitzung der Enquetekommission*, 4 May 1995.

49. Deutscher Bundestag, *StB*, 234. Sitzung, 17 June 1994, 20449. Although his views may seem extreme, Keller was far from a compliant mouthpiece of the PDS. Some party leaders, such as Uwe-Jens Heuer, had opposed participation in the commission because they regarded the body as an instrument of victor's justice. The delegation of a PDS deputy to the commission was only approved by a slim majority. Keller was later relegated to a secondary position in the PDS after his participation.

50. Laurence McFalls, "Political Culture, Partisan Strategies, and the PDS: Prospects for an East German Party," *GPS* 13, no. 1 (spring 1995): 56. Another insightful treatment of PDS strategy is Sa'adah, *Germany's Second Chance*, 255–71.

51. As Henry Krisch shows, part of the PDS's success was illusory. In all but one of the state elections (Thuringia), the party's share of the absolute vote decreased since 1990; however, low voter turnout elevated the reform communists into a stronger electoral position. "The Party of Democratic Socialism: Left and East," in *Germans Divided*, ed. Russell Dalton (Oxford, UK: Berg, 1996), 117–20.

52. Ibid., 120–3, and Jürgen Lang, Patrick Moreau, and Viola Neu, "Auferstanden aus Ruinen . . .? Die PDS nach dem Super-Wahljahr 1994," in *Interne Studien*, no. 111 (Sankt Augustin: Konrad Adenauer Stiftung, 1995): 1–219. For background, Heinrich Bortfeldt, "Die Ostdeutschen und die PDS," *DA* 12 (December 1994): 1283–7.

53. "Den 'Kalten Krieg' beenden – DDR-Biographien ernst nehmen," *Pressemitteilung* 887 (Bonn: SPD Bundestagsfraktion, 2 June 1995) n.p.

54. Ibid. Author's interview, Wolfgang Wiemer, Bonn, 13 June 1995.

55. For an early statement of this position, see the joint bill introduced by the governing parties and Alliance '90/The Greens. German Bundestag, 13th Session, 13/1535, 31 May 1995.

56. Author's interview, Bonn, 12 June 1995.

57. Author's interview, M. Jansen, Bonn, 6 June 1995.

58. Author's interviews with B. Dove, 7 June 1995; J. Schnappertz, 8 June 1995; W. Wiemer, 13 June 1995. Thierse's contrarian stand also reflected a personal rivalry with Enquete commission co-organizer Markus Meckel, whom he regarded as naive and dogmatic.

59. On the renewed commission's agenda, see Michael Reinold, "Die Enquete-Kommission des Deutschen Bundestages: 'Überwindung der Folgen der SED-Diktatur im Prozeß der deutschen Einheit,'" *DA* 6 (June 1996): 1014–5. Although some of the body's emphases differed slightly from those of its predecessor (e.g., "Economic, Social, and Environmental Policy"), the commission remained focused upon the *roots* of eastern Germany's problems in the GDR period.
60. Eppelmann insists that this decision was reached for financial reasons alone (author's interview, Bonn, 12 June 1995). However, everyone else I have consulted on the subject has emphasized the transparently political motivations behind the exclusion of the PDS.
61. Like the findings of the first commission, the testimony and expertise were later published in a 13-volume (7 main volumes) collection, *Materialien der Enquete-Kommission "Überwindung der Folgen der SED-Diktatur im Prozeß der deutschen Einheit"* (Baden–Baden: Nomos Verlag, 1999).
62. Ibid., 5.
63. *Schlußbericht der Enquete-Kommission, "Überwindung der Folgen der SED-Diktatur im Prozeß der deutschen Einheit,"* Deutscher Bundestag, 13/1000.
64. Author's interview, M. Jansen, Bonn, 6 June 1995.
65. Ronald Dworkin, "Introduction," *Nunca Más: The Report of the Argentine National Commission on the Disappeared* (New York: Farrar, Straus and Giroux, 1986), xvii–xxii, and *Report of the Chilean National Commission on Truth and Reconciliation*, trans. Phillip E. Berryman (Notre Dame: University of Notre Dame Press, 1993).
66. Charlayne Hunter-Gault, "Introduction," in Antjie Krog, *Country of My Skull* (New York: Random House, 1998), x–xi.
67. Krog, *Country*, 120.

Chapter 5

1. Cited in Richard Motsch, "Vom Sinn und Zweck der Regelung offener Vermögensfragen," *VIZ* 2 (1993): 41.
2. Dirk Brouër, Cornelia Ebert, Alexander von Falkenhausen, Michael Freier, Holger Matthiessen, Rüdiger Postier, Klaus Rellermeyer, and Herbert Trimbach, *Offene Vermögensfragen – ein Ratgeber* (Berlin: Rowohlt, 1995), 18–20. A widely cited popular account is Daniela Dahn, *Wir bleiben hier oder Wem gehört der Osten* (Berlin: Rowohlt, 1994).
3. Gesetz zur Regelung offener Vermögensfragen vom 23.9.1990, in BGBl, II, 1159. In Unification treaty, attach. 2, Chap. 3 (B), sec. 2. Hereafter, VermG. A useful commentary is Gerhard Fieberg, Harald Reichenbach, Burkhard Messerschmidt, and Heike Neuhaus, *VermG: Gesetz zur Regelung offener Vermögensfragen, Kommentar* (Munich: C. H. Beck'sche Verlagsbuchhandlung, 1996).
4. Birgit Schöneberg, "Die Rechtsentwicklung im Bereich der Regelung offener Vermögensfragen," *NJ* 6 (1993): 253. Most of these claims were

for various forms of real estate, land-holdings, houses, and businesses; however, other forms of property included stocks, securities, and other valuables.

5. Gemeinsame Erklärung der Regierungen der Bundesrepublik Deutschland und der Deutschen Demokratischen Republik zur Regelung offener Vermögensfragen vom 15.6.1990. In Unification treaty, attach. 3. Hereafter, GemErk.

6. *Waren Sie unlauter oder redlich? Grenzen der Restitution* (Berlin: LARoV, 1995), 17.

7. The Federal Administrative Court later upheld this principle, ruling that a "total" revision of eastern property was impossible. BVerwG, decision of 29 September 1993, *VIZ* (1994), 27–8. For analysis of the validity of GDR laws, see *Waren Sie unlauter?*, 16–17.

8. For example, Roland Czada notes that, despite hundreds of thousands of claims of illegal expropriation, claims offices returned, on average, only about 2 percent of these properties to their former owners. The remaining claims were either rejected outright or resolved through payment of compensation to the original owners. "Das Prinzip Rückgabe: Die Tragweite des Eigentums," in *Studienbrief* 4 (Tübingen: DIFF, 1998): 16. Czada also notes (at 26) that only 7 percent of the rejected claims brought before administrative courts (of which there were approximately 25,000 cases by February 1997) were overturned.

9. Property restitution was regularly debated throughout East Europe in the 1990s, but the Czechoslovak and German governments went the furthest in implementing it. On the diverse approaches to the subject, see Andrzej Kozminski, "Restitution of Private Property," *Communist and Post-Communist Studies* 30, no. 1 (1997): 95–106; Anna Gelpern, "The Laws and Politics of Reprivatization in East-Central Europe," *University of Pennsylvania Journal of International Business Law* 14, no. 3 (1993): 315–72. Outside Europe, the other instance of significant land restitution was South Africa. In 1994, its government adopted legislation to put up to 30 percent of agricultural lands into African hands within 6 years by addressing the holdings of three major parties: the state, traditional rulers, and whites. The Restitution of Land Rights Act of November 1994 set up a commission to review instances of racial discrimination extending back to 1913, recommend compensation, and facilitate land exchanges. A separate Land Claims Court was established for parties who believed the commission had inadequately addressed their claims. As an indication of the complexity of the challenge, little property had exchanged hands by 2000. See T. R. H. Davenport, *The Transfer of Power in South Africa* (Capetown: David Philip, 1998), 85–7.

10. For Kinkel's and other liberals' views, see Wolfgang Schäuble, *Der Vertrag: Wie ich über die deutsche Einheit verhandelte* (Stuttgart: Deutsche Verlags–Anstalt, 1991), 259.

11. On the concept's roots in the failed revolution of 1848, see Jessica Heslop and Joel Roberto, "Property Rights in the Unified Germany: A Constitutional, Comparative, and International Legal Analysis," *Boston University International Law Journal* 11, no. 2 (fall 1993): 245–8. On the constitutional guarantees, see David Currie, *The Constitution of the Federal Republic of Germany* (Chicago: University of Chicago Press, 1994), 290–9.

12. For this image, see Schäuble, *Der Vertrag*, 260.

13. On these subtle forms of expropriation, see Weddig Fricke and Klaus Märker, *Enteignetes Vermögen in der Ex-DDR* (Bollschweil: Verlag Dr. Grüb Nachf., 1992), 26–7.

14. To quote one participant, later president of the Berlin-based Federal Office for the Settlement of Open Property Questions (BARoV), Hansjürgen Schäfer, in *FR*, 30 September 1995, 9.

15. Bruce Ackerman makes this point in *The Future of Liberal Revolution* (New Haven: Yale University Press, 1992), 90.

16. Michael Neff, "Eastern Europe's Policy of Restitution of Property in the 1990s," *Dickinson Journal of International Law* 10, no. 2 (winter 1992): 373–4; Georg Brunner and Gábor Halmai, "Die juristische Bewältigung des kommunistischen Unrechts in Ungarn," in *Juristische Bewältigung des kommunistischen Unrechts in Osteuropa und Deutschland*, ed. Georg Brunner (Berlin: Berlin Verlag, 1995), 9–40.

17. Later estimates would be much higher. See Dirk Brouër's estimate of 150 billion deutsche marks, which includes a hypothetical figure for the value of the Soviet land reform properties, in "Einleitung oder von Ängsten und Ansprüchen," in Brouër, Cornelia Ebert, Alexander von Falkenhausen, Michael Freier, Holger Matthiessen, Rüdiger Postier, Klaus Rellermeyer, and Trimbach, *Offene Vermögensfragen*, 239.

18. Schäuble, *Der Vertrag*, 256.

19. Gesetz über den Verkauf volkseigener Gebäude vom 6.3.1990, DDR GBl, I.

20. Ernst Niederleithinger, "Restitution als Grundsatz," *VIZ* 2 (1992): 55. Also, Kai Mielke, "Der vermögensrechtliche Restitutionsgrundsatz," *KJ* 27, no. 2 (1994): 205.

21. In the view of two authorities on the property settlement, Gerhard Fieberg and Harald Reichenbach, "Zum Problem der offenen Vermögensfragen," *NJW* 4, no. 6, 6 February 1991, 323.

22. Schäuble, *Der Vertrag*, 261.

23. See GemErk, 1.

24. Author's interviews, G. Körner, 14 January 1997, and Pörschke, 16 January 1997. Also, Fieberg and Reichenbach, "Zum Problem," 327; and Mielke, "Der vermögensrechtliche," 206.

25. GemErk, §3(a).

26. VermG, §3a. Also, Gesetz über besondere Investitionen in der Deutschen Demokratischen Republik vom 9.23.1990, §1, in Unification treaty, attachment II, Chap. 3(B), sec. 1.

27. This was a particularly problematic part of the property settlement, for thousands of East German citizens who had occupied these properties and, in many cases, maintained them at their own expense over the decades were not accorded the Property statute's protections on "honest acquisition." On this shortcoming, see Quint, *The Imperfect Union*, 132–3.
28. VermG §1(6).
29. See the Bundestag debate of 5 September 1990 as cited in Dahn, *Wir bleiben hier*, 190.
30. Author's interviews, Pörschke, 16 January 1997; B. Schöneberg, 20 January 1997; H. Schäfer, 21 January 1997, Berlin.
31. S. Köhler-Apel and R. Bodenstab, "Fünf Jahre Vermögensgesetz: Überblick über die Gesetzes- und Rechtsprechungsentwicklung," *OV Spezial* 19 (10 May 1995): 310–18; Birgit Schöneberg, "Die Rechtsentwicklung im Bereich der Regelung offener Vermögensfragen," *NJ* 6 (1993): 253–7.
32. Author's interview, Körner, Berlin, 14 January 1997.
33. Hermann-Josef Rodenbach, "Die Reprivatisierung in den neuen Bundesländern," in *Juristische Bewältigung des kommunistischen Unrechts in Osteuropa und Deutschland*, ed. Georg Brunner (Berlin: Berlin Verlag, 1995), 317.
34. Author's interview, Pörschke, Berlin, 16 January 1997.
35. Author's interviews, Körner, Berlin, 14 January 1997; Pörschke et al., Berlin, 16 January 1997. Also, *Praxisfragen zum Vermögensrecht* (Berlin: BARoV, 1996).
36. See Dirk Brouër's observations in "Einleitung oder von Ängsten und Ansprüchen," in Brouër, Cornelia Ebert, Alexander von Falkenhausen, Michael Freier, Holger Matthiessen, Rüdiger Postier, Klaus Rellermeyer, and Trimbach, *Offene Vermögensfragen*, 24.
37. On the use of property registers (*Grundbücher*) to verify claims, see Klaus Rellermeyer and Cornelia Ebert, "Das Grundbuch oder kein Buch mit sieben Siegeln," in Brouër, Cornelia Ebert, Alexander von Falkenhausen, Michael Freier, Holger Matthiessen, Rüdiger Postier, Klaus Rellermeyer and Trimbach, *Offene Vermögensfragen*, 208–37; also *Spg* 41 (8 October 1990): 46–50.
38. For an elaboration, see Rodenbach, "Reprivatisierung," 319.
39. For such a justification, see Justice Minister Sabine Leutheusser-Schnarrenberger's remarks in "Bewältigung der rechtlichen Probleme der Wiedervereinigung," *DtZ* 9 (1994): 293–4.
40. *BZ*, 25 February 1994, 5.
41. *FR*, 30 September 1995, 9.
42. Press release, Bundesamt zur Regelung offener Vermögensfragen, 7 November 1996.
43. Though, for a skeptical perspective, consider Monika Prützel-Thomas, "The Property Question Revisited: The Restitution Myth," *German Politics* 4, no. 3 (December 1995), 112–27.
44. Mielke, 211.

45. Gezetz zur Beseitigung von Hemmnissen bei der Privatisierung von Unternehmen und zur Förderung von Investitionen, 22 March 1991, BGBl, I, 776. The changes were included in a revised Property statute in 1992, VermG §§3a, 6a, 6b, and 29a.
46. The history and functions of the *Treuhandanstalt* exceed the purposes of this volume. Among the vast literature, see Wolfgang Seibel, "Lernen unter Unsicherheit: Hypothesen zur Entwicklung der Treuhandanstalt," in *Verwaltungsreform und Verwaltungspolitik im Prozeß der deutschen Einigung*, eds. W. Seibel, A. Benz, and H. Mäding (Baden-Baden: Nomos, 1993), 359–70; and the detailed contributions in *Treuhandanstalt. Das Unmögliche wagen*, eds. W. Fischer, H. Hax, and H. K. Schneider (Berlin: Akademie Verlag, 1993).
47. Heslop and Roberto, "Property rights," 261–2; Rodenbach, "Reprivatisierung," 314–16, and Carl-Heinz David, "Provision of Land for Development and the Status of Restitution in the New Federal States in Germany," unpublished paper, Central European University, Prague, 18–19 October 1994, 5–6.
48. Press release, Bundesamt zur Regelung offener Vermögensfragen, 7 November 1996.
49. Author's interview, Mayor Wolfgang Blasig, Kleinmachnow, 22 January 1997. Also see Dahn, *Wir bleiben hier*, 149–57; and Hugo Holzinger, "Vermögensrechtliche Ansprüche der Verfolgten des Nazi-Regimes," unpublished speech before the Berlin Fachseminare, 17–18 April 1996.
50. Adenauer's words are cited from "German Restitution for National Socialist Crimes" (German Information Center, April 1997), 1. On postwar West German policy, see Nana Sagi, *German Reparations: A History of the Negotiations* (New York: St. Martin's Press, 1986), and Jeffrey Herf, *Divided Memory: The Nazi Past in the Two Germanys* (Cambridge: Harvard University Press, 1997), 289.
51. On the regime's anti-Jewish policies, see Herf, *Divided Memory*, Chap. 5.
52. For an example of this rationale, see the BVerfGE decision of 3 March 1995 – 1 BvR 236/95.
53. Anita Kugler, "Erst arisiert, dann SEDisiert," *taz*, 18 July 1990, 13.
54. BK/0 (49) 180 der Alliierten Kommandantur Berlin vom 26. Juli. 1948. For the relevant West German judgments, see Beschluß des BVerwG vom 8.12.1994 BVerwG 7 B 180.94. For a discussion in which both documents are cited, see *Das Vermögensgesetz in der praktischen Anwendung* (Berlin: LARoV, 1996), 8–10.
55. Author's interview, Körner, Berlin, 14 January 1997. Also see Fricke and Märker, *Enteignetes Vermögen*, 170.
56. *taz*, 18 December 1996, 24 and *Wall Street Journal*: 12 November 1996, A1, A6.
57. See Norman Naimark, *The Russians in Germany* (Cambridge: Harvard University Press, 1995), 150–66, and Jonathan J. Doyle, "A Bitter Inheritance:

East German Real Property and the Supreme Constitutional Court's 'Land Reform' Decision of 23 April 1991," *Michigan Journal of International Law* 13, no. 4 (summer 1992): 844.

58. Peter Hermes, in *RM*, 7 September 1990, 4. Also see the critiques of Hans von Arnim, *FAZ*, 6 September 1990, 8; Friedrich Karl Fromme, *FAZ*, 19 September 1990, 1; and Andreas Hartisch and Harald Kreuz, *Handelsblatt*, 12 September 1990, 6. For legal commentary, see Fricke and Märker, *Enteignetes Vermögen*, 97–9.

59. See, for example, the reflections of Modrow's economics minister, Christa Luft, *Die Lust am Eigentum* (Zurich: Orell Füssli Verlag, 1996), 105–9.

60. Statement from TASS news agency, 27 March 1990. In my reading of the evidence, the Soviet stand largely reflected pressures originating in the GDR. Hans Modrow, in particular, pleaded with Moscow to oppose any attempt to reopen the land reform question. See his 7 March 1990 letter to Mikhail Gorbachev expressing the concern that "40 years of hard work devoted to the creation and expansion of people's property in the GDR might turn out to have been for naught." (*StZ*, 8 March 1990, 2.) Also see his earlier letter of 2 March 1990 to Helmut Kohl regarding escalating popular tensions "about property relationships in the GDR." *BPA/DDR Informationen*, 3 March 1990, 5.

61. Quint, *The Imperfect Union*, 128, 374, fn. 28.

62. Naimark, *The Russians in Germany*, 145–50.

63. See ibid., 136–7; Heslop and Roberto, 264–5, esp. fn. 123; and Doyle, "A Bitter Inheritance," 851–2.

64. BVerfGE, 84, 90 judgment of 23 April 1991 – 1 BvR 1170, 1174, 1175/90.

65. BVerfGE, judgment of 23 April 1991, 109–11, 128–9. In 1996, the court agreed to reconsider these issues, in response to purportedly new evidence that the Soviet Union had not made the land reform issue a precondition for unification. After considering the evidence, the court concluded that German officials had correctly diagnosed the situation: the Unification treaty would not have been realized without the exclusion of the contested properties from restitution. BVerfGE, 84, 12 judgment of 18 April 1996 – 1 BvR 1452, 1459/90 und 2031/94. For a critical analysis arguing that the "last word" on the dispute has yet to be written, see Johannes Wasmuth, "Der Bodenreform II – Beschluß des Bundesverfassungsgerichts," *VIZ* 6, no. 7 (1996): 361–5.

66. BVerfGE, 23 April 1991, 122.

67. Ibid., 122–3.

68. See Doyle, "A Bitter Inheritance": 856–62; Heslop and Roberto, "Property Rights": 265–70; and Walter Leisner, "Das Bodenreform – Urteil des Bundesverfassungsgerichts," *NJW* 4 (1991): 1569–75.

69. Doyle, 861.

70. BVerfGE, 23 April 1991, 124.

71. See the discussion of §129 of the GDR criminal code, in *Waren Sie unlauter?*, 30–1.

72. See footnote 7 and the related decision, of 24 March 1994 (*ZOV*, 3/1994, 203) as cited in Rodenbach, "Die Reprivatisierung," 295.
73. In "Bewältigung der rechtlichen Probleme," 294.
74. This interpretation was confirmed by successive administrative court decisions in the early 1990s. See the analysis by BARoV Vice-President Horst-Dieter Kittke, "Das Mauergrundstücksgesetz," *NJ* 9 (1996), 464–6.
75. VermG, §4(2) [2].
76. Dirk Brouër, "Einleitung oder von Ängste und Ansprüchen," *Offene Vermögensfragen*, 31.
77. On this theme, see Franz-Josef Peine, "Zur Verfassungswidrigkeit der 'Stichtagsregelung,'" unpublished brief, 4 February 1994, as part of a 28 July 1994 complaint by the state of Brandenburg to the Federal Constitutional Court on the constitutionality of the threshold date. Also see Brouër, "Einleitung," 31–4, and Alexander von Falkenhausen, "Das Vermögengesetz oder Wer bekommt was?" in Brouër, Cornelia Ebert, Alexander von Falkenhausen, Michael Freier, Holger Matthiessen, Rüdiger Postier, Klaus Rellermeyer, and Trimbach, *Offene Vermögensfragen*, 70–1.
78. See McAdams, *Germany Divided*, 205–6; Elizabeth Pond, *Beyond the Wall* (Washington, DC: Brookings Institution, 1993), 170–2.
79. Peine, 45–6.
80. GemErk §13(d).
81. The separation of title to a house and the underlying land was a feature peculiar to socialist law. On the extraordinarily complex issues the Property Adjustment law sought to address, see Michael Freier and Herbert Trimbach, "Das Sachenrechtsbereinigungsgesetz oder Eigentum auf fremden Grund," in Brouër, Cornelia Ebert, Alexander von Falkenhausen, Michael Freier, Holger Matthiessen, Rüdiger Postier, Klaus Rellermeyer, and Trimbach, *Offene Vermögensfragen*, 116–72.
82. For this reasoning, see Friedrich Karl Fromme, "Kein Dienst am Rechtsfrieden," *FAZ*, 27 December 1996, 1.
83. For this and related disputes, see the analysis by Quint, *The Imperfect Union*, 141–4.
84. Gesetz über die Entschädigung nach dem Gesetz zur Regelung offener Vermögensfragen und über die staatliche Ausgleichsleistungen für Enteignungen auf besatzungsrechtlicher oder besatzungshoheitlicher Grundlage (EALG) vom 27.7.1994, BGBl, I, 1994, 2624. See Richard Motsch, "Verfassungsmäßigkeit des Entschädigungs- und Ausgleichsgesetzes," *NJW* 48, no. 35 (30 August 1995), 2250–2255. Also, Bernd Zimmermann, "Wiedergutmachung zwischen materieller Gerechtigkeit und politischem Kompromiß," *DtZ* 11 (1994): 359–62.
85. FAZ, 2 December 1996, 2. Also, see the article by Saxony's justice minister, Steffan Heitmann, "Keine alten Wunden aufreißen," *FAZ*, 12 June 1996, 11; and Quint, *The Imperfect Union*, 143 and 381–2, fn. 118.

86. Gesetz über den Verkauf von Mauer- und Grenzgründstücken an die früheren Eigentümer vom 15.7.1996, BGBl. I, 980. Also see Kittke, "Das Mauergrundstücksgesetz," 464–6.
87. *Deutschland Nachrichten*, 16 February 1996, 7.
88. Ibid.
89. Author's interviews, G. Körner, 14 January 1997, and G. Rohde, Humboldt University Berlin, 21 January 1997.

Chapter 6

1. *BM Online* (www.berliner-morgenpost.de) 9 November 1999. See BGH judgment of 8 November 1999 – 5 Str 632/98. For background, Roman Grafe, "'Die Politbüro-Beschlüsse waren Bedingungen der tödlichen Schüsse,' Der Prozess gegen sechs Mitglieder des SED-Politbüros (1996–1999)," *DA* 1 (January–February 2000): 19–25.
2. *BZ Online* (www.berlinonline.de), 10 November 1999.
3. *Spg Online* (www.spiegel.de) 3 November 1999; *Spg Online*, 4 November 1999; and *Spg Online*, 5 November 1999.
4. On this sometimes contradictory path, see Gisela Helwig, "Gebremste Zuversicht," *DA* 1 (January–February 1999): 1–3, and Gisela Helwig, "Abgestraft," *DA* 5 (September–October 1999): 721–3.
5. *BZ Online*, 15 November 1999.
6. *BM Online*, 1 October 1999.
7. *Tsp Online* (www.tagesspiegel.de) 13 July 1999.
8. *Vierter Tätigkeitsbericht* (Berlin: BStU, 1999), 32.
9. *BZ Online*, 2 May 1999.
10. *Statistische Übersichten*, 4/99 (Berlin: BARoV, 31 December 1999), 2.
11. *BM Online*, 24 November 1999. See BVerfGE, judgment of 23 November 1999 – 1 BvF 1/94, 1 (www.bundesverfassungsgericht.de).
12. For example, this sentiment was in evidence at the second annual meeting of the Frankfurter Forum in late October 1997. An array of commentators (ex-GDR Interior Minister Peter-Michael Diestel, Brandenburg's Justice Minister Hans Otto Bräutigam, publicist and former West German representative to the GDR Günter Gaus, CDU politician Heinrich Lummer, and PDS leader Gregor Gysi) criticized the FRG for supposedly undermining eastern Germans' faith in the rule of law. From "Kohlhaas, Kleist und die Gerechtigkeit der Deutschen," Frankfurter Forum, 26 October 1997, unpublished document.
13. For example, Wolfgang Dümcke and Fritz Vilmar, eds. *Kolonialisierung der DDR* (Münster: Agenda Verlag, 1995).
14. See his lecture at the University of Notre Dame, "The Tragic Element in Modern International Conflict," *Review of Politics* 12, no. 2 (April 1950): 148.
15. Annette Weinke, "Die DDR-Justiz im Jahre der 'Wende,'" *DA*, 1 (January–February 1997): 45–7.

16. As cited in Silke Schumann, *Vernichten oder Offenlegen? Zur Entstehung des Stasi-Unterlagen-Gesetzes* (Berlin: BStU, 1995), 17.

17. *taz*, 6 September 1990, cited in ibid., 111–2.

18. Schumann, *Vernichten*, 16.

19. Wolfgang Schäuble, *Der Vertrag* (Stuttgart: Deutsche-Verlags Anstalt, 1991), 268.

20. LG Berlin ([523] 27/2 Js 568/92 Ks), judgment of 19 November 1997, 1–23. Original document, courtesy of Staatsanwaltschaft II bei dem Landgericht Berlin.

21. See Peter Jochen Winters, "Zwiespältiges Urteil im letzten Politbüro-Prozess," *DA*, 4 (2000): 525-8; and *SdZ*, 8–9 July 2000, 55. Because of Häber's special role, his case received significant press attention in spring 2000. For example, see Peter Jochen Winters, "Als Moskau Druck ausübte, ließ Honecker seinen deutschlandpolitischen Berater fallen," *FAZ*, 9 May 2000, 5. For background, see his interview with *Spg* 22 (26 May 1997), 34–8, and Detlef Nakath and Gerd-Rüdiger Stephan, eds., *Die Häber Protokolle* (Berlin: Karl Dietz Verlag, 1999). Also, see my interviews with Häber, in *GDR Oral History Project*, Hoover Institution, Stanford University, 19 March 1990 and 8 March 1991.

22. *Spg Online*, 10 January 2000. Also, *Spg Online*, 8 January 2000, and the commentary by Knut Teske, "Wieso Baumgarten?" *DW Online* (www.welt.de), 11 January 2000.

23. *Viertertätigkeitsbericht*, 10–11.

24. *BM Online*, 24 November 1999. For a more guarded interpretation of the consequences of the Federal Constitutional Court decision, see the press release by BARoV President Hansjürgen Schäfer, "Wem nutzt oder schadet das Urteil des Bundesverfassungsgerichts zur Stichtagsregelung?" BARoV, Berlin, 10 January 2000.

25. *The Human Condition* (Chicago: University of Chicago Press, 1958), 241. For a recent statement, see Carlos Niño, *Radical Evil on Trial* (New Haven: Yale University Press, 1996). On Germany, see especially Charles S. Maier, *The Unmasterable Past: History, Holocaust, and German National Identity* (Cambridge: Harvard University Press, 1988), 161. I owe Maier a debt for provoking my thinking in several parts of this chapter.

26. On this theme, see the arguments of Jürgen Kocka and Rainer Lepsius before the Bundestag's Enquete commission on 3 and 4 May 1994, respectively, in Deutscher Bundestag, *Protokoll der 75. Sitzung der Enquete-Kommission*, 3 May 1994, 20–33, and Deutscher Bundestag, *Protokoll der 76. Sitzung der Enquete-Kommission*, 4 May 1994, 40–5.

27. For legal and moral perspectives on this issue, see Juan E. Méndez, "In Defense of Transitional Justice," in *Transitional Justice and the Rule of Law in New Democracies*, ed. A. James McAdams (Notre Dame: University of Notre Dame Press, 1997), 4–7.

28. See Jürgen Habermas, "Die Last der doppelten Vergangenheit," *Zt*, 20 May 1994, 16, and "Dankes Rede des Friedenspreisträgers Fritz Stern," *DW Online*, 18 October 1999.
29. *FAZ*, 22 December 1999, 2.
30. *BZ Online*, 8 February 2000.
31. *DW Online*, 25 March 2000. Also see Johannes Leithäuser, "Ost–westdeutsche Gewichtsverlagerung," *FAZ*, 23 March 2000, 1.
32. The first report appeared in *Tsp Online*, 28 March 2000.
33. On the decision to destroy the telephone records, see *FAZ*, 29 March 1990, 4.
34. *BZ Online*, 5 April 2000.
35. Ibid.
36. Indeed, a poll conducted by *Die Welt* found that 61.9 percent of *all* Germans it surveyed supported the use of the Stasi records in the Bundestag commission on the CDU's finances. See *DW*, 10 April 2000, 3.
37. *Tsp Online*, 28 March 2000.
38. *Spg Online*, 10 April 2000.
39. *Spg Online*, 3 April 2000.
40. Robert Leicht, "Die Stasi-Versuchung," *DZ Online*, 6 April 2000. One possible opening for those wanting to use the Stasi transcripts to scrutinize Kohl's and other CDU leaders' behavior was availed by the Stasi Records law (Part III, Chap. 3, §32, *StUG*), which provided for the disclosure of information about "contemporary historical personages, political officeholders or public law officials while in office." This provision applied unless, in the statute's terms, "publication would impair the overriding legitimate interests of the persons involved."
41. In interviews in Bonn and Berlin in the mid-1990s, I was surprised to learn that German politicians did not show much interest in learning from other countries' experiences. For example, the organizers of the Enquete commission on the GDR apparently did not investigate the approaches of other truth commissions. Author's interview, M. Jansen, 6 June 1995.
42. For representative cases, see Jorge Correa Sutil, "'No Victorious Army has ever been Prosecuted . . . ': The Unsettled Story of Transitional Justice in Chile," in *Transitional Justice*, ed. A. James McAdams 142–9, and Aryeh Neier, *War Crimes: Brutality, Genocide, Terror, and the Struggle for Justice* (New York: Random House, 1998), Chap. 6.
43. I am grateful to Venelin Ganev for information about these cases. On Hungary, see Gábor Halmai and Kim Lane Scheppele, "Living Well Is the Best Revenge: The Hungarian Approach to Judging the Past," in *Transitional Justice and the Rule of Law in New Democracies*, ed. A. James McAdams (Notre Dame: University of Notre Dame Press, 1997), 155–85.
44. This is a major theme in Neier, *War Crimes* (e.g., xiii), which has influenced my thinking on this subject.

45. Aryeh Neier, "Toward a Permanent International Criminal Court," *Open Society News* (winter 1998–1999): 19.
46. José E. Alvarez, "Seeking Legal Remedies for War Crimes: International versus National Trials," *The Journal of the International Institute* 6, no. 1 (fall 1998): 1, 22.
47. Ibid., 22.
48. Ibid.

Glossary

Frequently Used Terms

Bundestag	lower house of German parliament
CDU	Christian Democratic Union (Christlich-Demokratische Union Deutschlands)
CDU/CSU	alliance of Christian Democratic Union and Christian Social Union (Christlich Demokratische Union/Christlich-Soziale Union)
FDP	Free Democratic Party (Freie Demokratische Partei)
FRG	Federal Republic of Germany (Bundesrepublik Deutschland)
GDR	German Democratic Republic (Deutsche Demokratische Republik)
Die Grünen	Greens
HM	regular Stasi officer (Hauptamtlicher Mitarbeiter)
IM	unofficial collaborator of the Stasi (Inoffizieller Mitarbeiter)
Land (Länder)	state(s)
NSDAP	Nazi party (Nationalsozialistische Deutsche Arbeiterpartei)
NVA	National People's Army (Nationale Volksarmee)
NVR	National Defense Council (Nationale Verteidigungsrat der DDR)
PDS	Party of Democratic Socialism (Partei des Demokratischen Sozialismus)
Rechtsstaat	constitutional state

SED	Socialist Unity Party (Sozialistische Einheitspartei Deutschlands)
SMAD	Soviet Military Administration in Germany
SPD	Social Democratic Party (Sozialdemokratische Partei Deutschlands)
Stasi, MfS	Ministry for State Security (Ministerium für Staatssicherheit)
Volkskammer	GDR parliament
ZAIG	Central Analysis and Information Group (Zentrale Auswertungs- und Informationsgruppe)

Laws/Treaties/Legal Institutions

BAG	Federal Labor Court (Bundesarbeitsgericht)
BARoV	Federal Office for the Settlement of Open Property Questions (Bundesamt zur Regelung offener Vermögensfragen)
BGBl	official publication of federal laws (Bundesgesetzblatt)
BGH	Federal Court of Justice (Bundesgerichtshof)
BStU	Federal Authority for the Records of the State Security Service of the former GDR (Bundesbeauftragte für die Unterlagen des Staatssicherheitsdienstes der ehemaligen DDR)
BVerfGE	Federal Constitutional Court decisions (Entscheidungen des Bundesverfassungsgerichts)
BVerwG	Federal Administrative Court (Bundesverwaltungsgericht)
FCC	Federal Constitutional Court (Bundesverfassungsgericht)
GemErk	Joint Declaration (Gemeinsame Erklärung)
GBl DDR	official publication of GDR laws (Gesetzblatt der DDR)
GG	Basic Law (Grundgesetz)
LAG	State Labor Court (Landesarbeitsgericht)
LARoV	State Office for the Settlement of Open Property Questions (Landesamt zur Regelung offener Vermögensfragen)
LG	Regional Court (Landgericht)

LStU	State Authority for the Records of the State Security Service of the former GDR (Landesbeauftragte für die Unterlagen des Staatssicherheitsdienstes der ehemaligen DDR)
OVG	Administrative Appeals Court (Oberverwaltungsgericht)
StUG	Stasi Records law (Stasi-Unterlagen-Gesetz)
VerfGH	State Constitutional Court (Verfassungsgerichtshof)
VermG	Property statute (Vermögensgesetz)

Journals/Newspapers

AA	Arbeit und Arbeitsrecht
BM	Berliner Morgenpost
BZ	Berliner Zeitung
DA	Deutschland Archiv
DPA	Deutsche Presse Agentur
DtZ	Deutsch–deutsche Rechts–Zeitschrift
DW	Die Welt
EuGRZ	Europäische Grundrechte-Zeitschrift
FA	Foreign Affairs
FAZ	Frankfurter Allgemeine Zeitung
FR	Frankfurter Rundschau
GA	General Anzeiger
GPS	German Politics and Society
GSR	German Studies Review
HRQ	Human Rights Quarterly
JW	Junge Welt
JZ	Juristenzeitung
JR	Juristische Rundschau
KJ	Kritische Justiz
LKV	Landes- und Kommunalverwaltung
NJ	Neue Justiz
NJW	Neue Juristische Wochenschrift
NYRB	New York Review of Books
NYT	New York Times
RM	Rheinischer Merkur
RoP	Review of Politics
RuP	Recht und Politik

SächZ	Sächsische Zeitung
Spg	Der Spiegel
StB	Stenographische Berichte
SdZ	Süddeutsche Zeitung
StZ	Stuttgarter Zeitung
taz	die tageszeitung
Tsp	Der Tagesspiegel
VIZ	Zeitschrift für Vermögens- und Investitionsrecht
ZRP	Zeitschrift für Rechtspolitik
Zt	Die Zeit

Bibliography

Ackerman, Bruce. *The Future of Liberal Revolution*. New Haven, CT: Yale University Press, 1992.

Acuña, Carlos, and Catalina Smulowitz. "Guarding the Guardians in Argentina: Some Lessons about the Risks and Benefits of Empowering the Courts." In *Transitional Justice and the Rule of Law in New Democracies*, edited by A. James McAdams, 9–122. Notre Dame: University of Notre Dame Press, 1997.

Adams, Kif Agustine. "What Is Just? The Rule of Law and Natural Law in the Trials of Former East German Border Guards." *Stanford Journal of International Law* 29 (1993): 271–314.

Alivizatos, Nicos, and P. Nikiforos Diamandouros. "Politics and the Judiciary in the Greek Transition to Democracy." In *Transitional Justice and the Rule of Law in New Democracies*, edited by A. J. McAdams, 27–61. Notre Dame: University of Notre Dame Press, 1997.

Alvarez, José E. "Seeking Legal Remedies for War Crimes: International versus National Trials." *The Journal of the International Institute* 6 (fall 1998): 1, 22.

Arendt, Fritz. "Die MfS-Überprüfung im öffentlichen Dienst." In *Eine Diktatur vor Gericht*, edited by Jürgen Weber and Michael Piazolo, 159–80. Munich: Olzog Verlag, 1995.

Arendt, Hannah. *The Human Condition*. Chicago: University of Chicago Press, 1958.

———. *The Origins of Totalitarianism*. New York: Harcourt, Brace, Jovanovich, 1973.

Aretz, Jürgen, and Wolfgang Stock. *Die vergessenen Opfer der DDR*. Bergisch Gladbach: Bastei–Verlag, 1997.

Bakker, Jeanne L. "The Defense of Obedience to Superior Order: The *Mens Rea* Requirement," *The American Journal of Criminal Law* 17, no.1 (1989): 55–75.

Bartlsberger, R. "Einstellung des Strafverfahren von Verfassungswegen," *Deutsches Verwaltungsrecht* 7 (1993): 333–49.

Beckermann, J. "Ein Landesverfassungsgericht als Revisionsgericht," *Neue Zeitschrift für Verwaltungsrecht* 5 (1993): 409–19.

Besier, Gerhard. *Die SED-Staat und die Kirche.* Munich: C. Bertelsmann Verlag, 1993.

Benz, Arthur; Heinrich Maeding; and Wolfgang Seibel, eds. *Verwaltungsreform und Verwaltungspolitik im Prozeß der deutschen Einigung.* Baden-Baden: Nomos, 1993.

Berg, Wilfried; Bodo Pieroth; and Christian Starck. "Der Rechtsstaat und die Aufarbeitung der vorrechtsstaatlichen Vergangenheit." In *Veröffentlichungen der Vereinigung der deutschen Staatsrechtsleher* no. 51, 11–176. Berlin and New York: Walter de Gruyter, 1992.

Berkowsky, Wilfried. "Kündigungen wegen Stasi-Tätigkeit in der Rechtsprechung." *Arbeit und Arbeitsrecht* 4 (1996): 125–8.

Bisky, Lothar; Uwe-Jens Heuer; and Michael Schumann. *'Unrechtsstaat'?: Politische Justiz und die Aufarbeitung der DDR-Vergangenheit.* Hamburg: VSA Verlag, 1994.

Bock, Petra. "Von der Tribunal-Idee zur Enquete-Kommission." *Deutschland Archiv* 11 (1995): 1171–83.

Böhringer, W. "Zum Schicksal von 'Modrow' – Kaufverträgen." *Offene Vermögensfragen* 21/96, special issue (7 November 1996): 334–7.

Borneman, John. *Settling Accounts: Violence, Justice, and Accountability in Postsocialist Europe.* Princeton: Princeton University Press, 1997.

Bortfeldt, Heinrich. "Die Ostdeutschen und die PDS." *Deutschland Archiv* 12 (December 1994): 1283–7.

Bracher, Karl Dietrich. "Die Unterdrücker zur Rechenschaft ziehen." *Universitas* 11 (1991): 1025–34.

Brandenburger, Maren. "Stasi-Unterlagen-Gesetz und Rechtsstaat." *Kritische Justiz* 28, no. 3 (1995): 351–68.

Brocke, Rudolf, and Wilfried von Bredow. *Das deutschlandpolitische Konzept der SPD.* Erlangen: Deutsche Gesellschaft für zeitgeschichtliche Fragen, 1987.

Broer, Bärbel. *Die innere Struktur der Behörde für die Unterlagen des Staatssicherheitsdienstes der ehemaligen DDR.* Magisterarbeit, Universität Hannover, 1995.

Brouër, Dirk; Cornelia Ebert; Alexander von Falkenhausen; Michael Freier; Holger Matthiessen; Rüdiger Postier; Klaus Rellermeyer; and Herbert Trimbach. *Offene Vermögensfragen – ein Ratgeber.* Berlin: Rowohlt, 1995.

Brunner, Georg, and Gábor Halmai. "Die juristische Bewältigung des kommunistischen Unrechts in Ungarn." In *Juristische Bewältigung des kommunistischen Unrechts in Osteuropa and Deutschland,* edited by Georg Brunner, 9–40. Berlin: Berlin Verlag, 1995.

Buruma, Ian. *The Wages of Guilt: Memories of War in Germany and Japan.* New York: Penguin Group, 1995.

Butterfield, Herbert. "The Tragic Element in Modern International Conflict." *Review of Politics* 12, no. 2 (April 1950): 147–64.

Cassel, Jr., Douglas W. "International Truth Commissions and Justice." *Aspen Institute Quarterly* 3 (1993): 77–90.

Childs, David, and Richard Popplewell. *The Stasi: The East German Intelligence and Security Service.* New York: New York University Press, 1996.

Cohen, Stanley. "State Crimes of Previous Regimes: Knowledge, Accountability, and the Policing of the Past." *Law and Social Inquiry* 1 (1995): 7–50.

Comisso, Ellen. "Legacies of the Past or New Institutions?: The Struggle Over Restitution in Hungary." *Comparative Political Studies* 28, no. 2 (July 1995): 200–38.

Correa Sutil, Jorge. "'No Victorious Army Has Ever Been Prosecuted . . . ': The Unsettled Story of Transitional Justice in Chile." In *Transitional Justice and the Rule of Law in New Democracies,* edited by A. James McAdams, 123–54. Notre Dame: University of Notre Dame Press, 1997.

Currie, David. *The Constitution of the Federal Republic of Germany.* Chicago: University of Chicago Press, 1994.

Czada, Roland. "Das Prinzip 'Rückgabe': Die Tragweite des Eigentums." In *Studieneinheit,* no. 11. DIFF: Tübingen (1998): 1–40.

Dahn, Daniela. *Wir bleiben hier oder Wem gehört der Osten.* Berlin: Rowohlt, 1994.

Dalton, Russel J., and Andrei S. Markovits. "Bundestagswahl 1994: The Culmination of the Superwahljahr." *German Politics and Society* 1, special issue (1995): 1–11.

Davenport, T. R. H. *The Transfer of Power in South Africa.* Capetown: David Philip, 1998.

David, Carl-Heinz. *Provision of Land for Development and the Status of Restitution in the New Federal States in Germany.* Working Paper, Central European University, Prague, 1994. 1–11.

Diestel, Peter-Michael. "Vier Jahre Stasi-Unterlagen-Gesetz: Erfahrungen aus arbeits- und verwaltungsrechlicher Sicht." *Neue Justiz* 12 (1995): 631–4.

Dörr, Erwin, and Dietmar Schmidt. *Stasi Unterlagengesetz.* Cologne: Datakontext Verlag, 1993.

Doyle, Jonathan J. "A Bitter Inheritance: East German Real Property and the Supreme Constitutional Court's 'Land Reform' Decision of April 23, 1991." *Michigan Journal of International Law* 4 (1992): 832–64.

Dugard, John. "International Law and the South African Model." In *Transitional Justice and the Rule of Law in New Democracies,* edited by A. James McAdams, 269–90. Notre Dame: University of Notre Dame Press, 1997.

Dworkin, Ronald. *Nunca Más: The Report of the Argentine National Commission on the Disappeared.* New York: Farrar, Straus and Giroux, 1986.

Engelmann, Roger. "Zum Quellenwert der Unterlagen des Ministeriums für Staatssicherheit." In *Aktenlage: Die Bedeutung der Unterlagen des Staatssicherheitsdienstes für die Zeitgeschichtsforschung,* edited by Klaus Dietmar Henke and Roger Engelmann, 23–39. Berlin: Ch. Links, 1995.

Eppelmann, Rainer. "Anmerkungen zu Geschichte und Folgen der SED-Diktatur in Deutschland: Rückblick und Konsequenz." *German Studies Review,* ed. Wolfgang-Uwe Friedrich (fall 1994/special issue): 205–11.

Fieburg, Gerhard, and Harald Reichenbach. "Zum Problem der offenen Vermögensfragen." *Neue Juristische Wochenschrift* 6 (1991): 321–9.
———. *VermG. Gesetz zur Regelung offener Vermögensfragen: Kommentar.* Munich: C. H. Beck'sche Verlagsbuchhandlung, 1996. 1–38.
Filmer, Werner, and Heribert Schwann. *Opfer der Mauer: Die geheimen Protokolle des Todes.* Munich: C. Bertelsmann, 1991.
Finkielkraut, Alain. *Remembering in Vain: The Klaus Barbie Trial and Crimes against Humanity.* New York: Columbia University Press, 1992.
Fischer, W.; H. Hax; and H. K. Schneider (eds.). *Treuhandanstalt. Das Unmögliche wagen.* Berlin: Akademie Verlag, 1993.
Fitzpatrick, Sheila. *Everyday Stalinism: Ordinary Life in Extraordinary Times.* Oxford: Oxford University Press, 2000.
Frei, Norbert. *Vergangenheitspolitik: Die Anfänge der Bundesrepublik und die NS-Vergangenheit.* Munich: C. H. Beck, 1996.
Fricke, Karl Wilhelm. "Honecker unter Anklage." *Deutschland Archiv* 10 (1992): 1009–10.
Fricke, Weddig, and Klaus Märker. *Enteignetes Vermögen in der Ex-DDR: Ein Wegweiser mit praktischen Tips.* Bollschweil: Verlag Dr. Grüb Nachf., 1992.
Friedrich, Wolfgang-Uwe. "Utopie und Realität: zur Misere posttotalitärer Gesellschaften." *German Studies Review,* special issue (fall 1994): 219–33.
Fulbrook, Mary. *Anatomy of a Dictatorship.* Oxford: Oxford University Press, 1995.
Garstka, Hansjürgen. "Probleme des Datenschutzes beim Umgang mit Stasi Akten." In *Wann bricht schon mal ein Staat zusammen!,* edited by Klaus Dietmar Henke, 49–55. Munich: Deutscher Taschenbuch Verlag, 1993.
Garton Ash, Timothy. *In Europe's Name: Germany and the Divided Continent.* New York: Vintage Books, 1993.
———. *The File: A Personal History.* New York: Random House, 1997.
———. "The Truth about Dictatorship." *New York Review of Books* 45 (19 February 1998): 36–40.
———. *History of the Present.* London: Penguin, 1999.
Gauck, Joachim. *Die Stasi Akten: Das unheimliche Erbe der DDR.* Reinbek bei Hamburg: Rowohlt, 1991.
———. "Dealing with a Stasi Past." *Daedalus* 1 (winter 1994): 277–84.
Gaus, Günter. *Wo Deutschland liegt.* Hamburg: Hoffmann and Campe, 1983.
Geiger, Hansjörg. "Erfahrungen mit der Staatssicherheit und ihre rechtsstaatliche Aufarbeitung." In *Eine Diktatur vor Gericht,* edited by Jürgen Weber and Michael Piazolo, 147–58. Munich: Olzog Verlag, 1995.
Geiger, Hansjörg, and Heinz Klinghardt. *Stasi-Unterlagen-Gesetz: Mit Erläuterungen für die Praxis.* Cologne: Deutsche Gemeindeverlag, 1993.
Gellately, Robert. *The Gestapo and German Society.* Oxford: Clarendon Press, 1990.
———. "Rethinking the Nazi Terror System: A Historiographical Analysis." *German Studies Review* 14, no. 1 (February 1991): 23–38.
Gelpern, Anna. "The Laws and Politics of Reprivatization in East-Central

Europe: A Comparison." *University of Pennsylvania Journal of International Business Law* 14, no. 3 (1993): 315–72.

Gill, David, and Ulrich Schröter. *Das Ministerium für Staatssicherheit.* Berlin: Rowohlt, 1991.

Glaeßner, Gert-Joachim. *Die andere deutsche Republik.* Opladen: Westdeutscher Verlag, 1989.

———, ed. *Die DDR in der Ära Honecker.* Opladen: Westdeutscher Verlag, 1988: 332–53.

Goeckel, Robert F. *The Lutheran Church and the East German State.* Ithaca, NY : Cornell University Press, 1990.

Grafe, Roman. "'Niemals Zweifel gehabt': Der Prozeß gegen die Grenztruppen Führung der DDR." *Deutschland Archiv* 6 (November–December 1996): 862–71.

———. "Die Strafverfolgung von DDR-Grenzschützen und ihren Befehlgebern." *Deutschland Archiv* 3 (May–June 1997): 377–83.

———. "Generalstaatsanwalt Christoph Schaefgen: 'Wenig aufbauend ist die zahlenmäßige Bilanz unserer Arbeit.' " *Deutschland Archiv* 1 (January–February 1999): 6–8.

Halmai, Gábor, and Kim L. Scheppele. "Living Well Is the Best Revenge: The Hungarian Approach to Judging the Past" In *Transitional Justice and the Rule of Law in New Democracies*, edited by A. James McAdams, 155–85. Notre Dame: University of Notre Dame Press, 1997.

Havel, Václav. "The Power of the Powerless." In *Living in Truth*, edited by Jan Vladislav, 36–122. London: Faber and Faber, 1987.

Hayner, Priscilla B. "Fifteen Truth Commissions – 1974 to 1994: A Comparative Study." *Human Rights Quarterly* 4 (1994): 597–655.

Helwig, Gisela. "Abgestraft." *Deutschland Archiv* 1 (September–October 1999): 721–23.

———. "Gebremste Zuversicht." *Deutschland Archiv* 1 (January–February 1999): 1–3.

Hénard, Jacqueline. *Geschichte vor Gericht.* Berlin: Corso bei Siedler, 1993.

Henkys, Reinhard. "Thesen zum Wandel der gesellschaftlichen und politischen Rolle der Kirchen in der DDR in den siebziger und achtziger Jahren." In *Die DDR in der Ära Honecker*, edited by Gert-Joachim Glaeßner, 332–53. Opladen: Westdeutscher Verlag, 1988.

———. "Kirchengeschichte im Bundestag: Anmerkungen zu einem Teilergebnis der Enquete-Kommission." *Politik und Geschichte* 3 (1994): 440–53.

Herf, Jeffrey. *Divided Memory: The Nazi Past in the Two Germanys.* Cambridge: Harvard University Press, 1997.

Heslop, Jessica, and Joel Roberto. "Property Rights in the Unified Germany: A Constitutional, Comparative, and International Legal Analysis." *Boston University International Law Journal* 2 (1993): 243–98.

Hillermeier, Heinz. "Stasi Mitarbeiter im öffentlichen Dienst." *Landes- und Kommunalverwaltung* 5, no. 4 (1995): 141–3.

Hilsberg, Stephan. "Vergangenheitsaufarbeitung als Bewährungsprobe der Demokratie." *German Studies Review*, ed. Wolfgang-Uwe Friedrich (fall 1994 special issue): 213–18.

Hirsch, Gerd Dieter. *Auskünfte zur Überprüfung durch Institutionen. Analysen und Berichte aus der Veranstaltungsreihe des Bundesbeauftragen* (series B 3). Berlin: BStU, 1993. 83–91.

Hoffmann Christa. *Stunden Null? Vergangenheitsbewältigung in Deutschland 1945 und 1989*. Bonn: Bouvier, 1992.

Holmes, Stephen. "The End of Decommunization." *East European Constitutional Review* 3, nos. 3–4 (summer/fall 1994): 33–6.

Holzinger, Hugo. "Vermögensrechtliche Ansprüche der Verfolgten des Nazi Regimes." Unpublished speech at the Berlin Fachseminare. 17–18 April 1996.

Hruschke, Joachim. "Die Todesschüsse auf der Berliner Mauer vor Gericht." *Juristische Zeitung* 13, no. 2 (1992): 650–70.

Huyse, Luc. "Justice after Transition: On the Choices Successor Elites Make in Dealing with the Past." *Law and Social Inquiry* 1 (1995): 51–78.

Jarausch, Konrad. *The Rush to German Unity*. Oxford: Oxford University Press, 1994.

Jaspers, Karl. *The Question of German Guilt*. Translated by E. B. Ashton. Westport, CT: Greenwood Press, 1978.

———. *Wohin treibt die Bundesrepublik?* Munich: Piper Reprint, 1988.

Jesse, Eckhard. " 'Entnazifizierung' und 'Entstasifizierung' als politisches Problem." In *Vergangenheitsbewältigung durch Recht*, edited by Josef Isensee, 9–36. Berlin: Duncker und Humblot, 1992.

———. " 'Vergangenheitsbewältigung' nach totalitärer Herrschaft in Deutschland." *German Studies Review*, special issue (fall 1994): 157–71.

Jochum, Dietmar. *Das Politbüro auf der Anklagebank*. Berlin: Magnus Verlag, 1996.

Judt, Tony. "The Past Is Another Country: Myth and Memory in Postwar Europe." *Daedalus* 121, no. 4 (fall 1992): 83–117.

Juling, Peter. "Alle hatten damals recht und alle hatten auch Erfolg." *Das Parlament* 46–7 (November 1993): 11.

Karau, Gisela. *Stasiprotokolle: Gespräche mit ehemaligen Mitarbeitern des "Ministeriums für Staatssicherheit" der DDR*. Frankfurt: Dipa, 1992.

Kinkel, Klaus. "Wiedervereinigung und Strafrecht." *Juristenzeitung* 47, no. 10. (22 May 1992): 485–9.

Kinzer, Stephen. "East Germans Face Their Accusers." *New York Times Magazine*. 12 April 1996.

Kirchheimer, Otto. *Political Justice: The Use of Legal Procedure for Political Ends*. Princeton: Princeton University Press, 1961.

Kittke, Horst-Dieter. "Das Mauergrundstücksgesetz." *Neue Justiz* 9 (1996): 464–6.

Köhler-Apel, S., and R. Bodenstab. "Fünf Jahre Vermögensgesetz: Überblick über die Gesetzes- und Rechtssprechungsentwicklung." *OV Spezial* 19 (10 May 1995): 310–18.

Kommers, Donald. "Basic Rights and Constitutional Review." In *Politics and Government in the Federal Republic of Germany, Basic Documents*, edited by Karl Christoph Schweitzer, Donald Kommers, Detlev Karsten, R. Taylor Cole, and Anthony Nichols, 113–37. Coventry: Berg, 1984.

———. *The Constitutional Jurisprudence of the Federal Republic of Germany*. Durham, NC: Duke University Press, 1989.

Kozminski, Andrzej. "Restitution of Private Property: Re-privatization in Central and Eastern Europe." *Communist and Post-Communist Studies* 30, no. 1 (1997): 95–106.

Krisch, Henry. "The Party of Democratic Socialism: Left and East." In *Germans Divided*, edited by Russell Dalton, 109–31. Oxford, UK: Berg, 1996.

Kritz, Neil, ed. *Transitional Justice: How Emerging Democracies Reckon with Former Regimes*. 3 volumes. Washington, DC: U.S. Institute of Peace, 1995.

Kutscha, Martin. " 'Politische Säuberung' des öffentlichen Dienstes?" *Neue Justiz* 6 (1995): 284–8.

Kvistad, Gregg O. "Accommodation or 'Cleansing': Germany's State Employees from the Old Regime." *West European Politics* 17 (October 1994): 52–73.

Lang, Jochen V. *Die Gestapo*. Hamburg: Rasch und Roehring, 1990.

Lang, Jürgen; Patrick Moreau; and Viola Nev. "Auferstanden aus Ruinen . . . ? Die PDS nach dem Super-Wahljahr 1994." In *Interne Studien*, no. 111. Sankt Augustin: Konrad Adenauer Stiftung (1995): 1–219.

Lansnicker, Frank, and Thomas Schwirtzek. "Der Beweiswert von Stasi-Unterlagen im Arbeitsgerichtsprozess." *Deutsch–deutsche Rechtszeitschrift* 5 (1994): 162–5.

Leggewie, Claus, and Horst Meier. "Zum Auftakt ein Schlußstrich?" In *Wir Kollaborateure: Der Westen und die deutschen Vergangenheiten*, edited by Cora Stephan, 51–79. Reinbek bei Hamburg: Rowohlt, 1992.

Leisner, Walter. "Das Bodenreform-Urteil des Bundesverfassungsgerichts." *Neue Juristische Wochenschrift* 25 (1991): 1569–75.

Lemke, Christiane. "Trials and Tribulations: The Stasi Legacy in Contemporary German Politics." *German Politics and Society* 26 (1992): 43–53.

Leonhard, Wolfgang. "Erich Honecker und die Berliner Mauer." *Kursbuch*, no. 111 (1993): 125–31.

Leutheusser-Schnarrenberger, Sabine. "Bewältigung der rechtlichen Probleme der Wiedervereinigung." *Deutsch–deutsche Rechtszeitschrift* 9 (1994): 417–19.

Lindheim, Thomas von. "Zum Begriff der Zusammenarbeit des inoffiziellen und hauptamtlichen Mitarbeiters mit dem MfS." *Deutsch–deutsche Rechtszeitschrift* 12 (1993): 358–61.

Livingston, Robert G. "The Party's Over: Kohl's Disservice to German Democracy." *Foreign Affairs* (May–June 2000): 13–17.

Lochen, Hans-Hermann. "Der Umgang mit den Stasi-Unterlagen." In *Juristische Bewältigung des kommunistischen Unrechts in Osteuropa und Deutschland*, edited by Georg Brunner, 251–83. Berlin: Arno Spitz, 1995.

Lüderssen, Klaus. *Der Staat geht unter – das Unrecht bleibt?* Frankfurt am Main: Suhrkamp, 1992.

Luft, Christa. *Die Lust am Eigentum*. Zurich: Orell Füssli Verlag, 1996.

Maier, Charles S. *The Unmasterable Past: History, Holocaust, and German National Identity*. Cambridge: Harvard University Press, 1988.

———. *Dissolution: The Crisis of Communism and the End of East Germany*. Princeton: Princeton University Press, 1997.

Majer, Diemut. "Ein halbierter Rechtsstaat für Ostdeutschland?" *Kritische Justiz* 2 (1992): 147–67.

Markovits, Inga. *Imperfect Justice: An East–West German Diary*. Oxford: Oxford University Press, 1995.

Materialien der Enquete-Kommission "Überwindung der Folgen der SED-Diktatur im Prozeß der deutschen Einheit." 13 volumes. Baden-Baden: Nomos Verlag, 1999.

Materialien der Enquete-Kommission "Aufarbeitung von Geschichte und Folgen der SED-Diktatur in Deutschland." 18 volumes. Baden-Baden: Nomos Verlag, 1995.

Maurer, D. "Der Verfassungsgerichtshof und das Strafverfahren." *Juristische Rundschau* 3 (1993): 89–95.

Mayorga, René. "Democracy Dignified and an End to Impunity: Bolivia's Military Dictatorship on Trial. In *Transitional Justice and the Rule of Law in New Democracies*, edited by A. James McAdams, 61–93. Notre Dame: University of Notre Dame Press, 1997.

McAdams, A. James. *East Germany and Detente*. Cambridge: Cambridge University Press, 1985.

———. *Germany Divided: From the Wall to Reunification*. Princeton: Princeton University Press, 1993.

———. "The Honecker Trial: The East German Past and the German Future." *The Review of Politics* 1 (1996): 53–80.

———, ed. *Transitional Justice and the Rule of Law in New Democracies*. Notre Dame: University of Notre Dame Press, 1997.

McFalls, Laurence. "Political Culture, Partisan Strategies, and the PDS: Prospects for an East German Party." *German Politics and Society* 1 (1995): 50–61.

Méndez, Juan. "In Defense of Transitional Justice." In *Transitional Justice and the Rule of Law in New Democracies*, edited by A. James McAdams, 1–26. Notre Dame: University of Notre Dame Press, 1997.

Meuer, D. "Der Verfassungsgerichtshof und das Strafverfahren." *Juristische Rundschau* 3 (March 1993): 89–95.

Mielke, Kai. "Der vermögensrechtliche Restitutionsgrundsatz." *Kritische Justiz* 27, no. 2 (1994): 200–13.

Miller, John. "Settling Accounts with a Secret Police: The German Law on the Stasi Records." *Europe–Asia Studies* 2 (1998): 305–30.

Motsch, Richard. "Vom Sinn und Zweck der Regelung offener Vermögensfragen." *Zeitschrift für Vermögens- und Investitionsrecht* 2 (1993): 305–30.

Naimark, Norman. "'To Know Everything and to Report Everything Worth Knowing': Building the East German Police State, 1945–1949." Working Paper No. 10. *Cold War International History Project*. Washington, DC: The Woodrow Wilson Center, August 1994.

———. *The Russians in Germany*. Cambridge: Harvard University Press, 1995.

Neff, Michael. "Eastern Europe's Policy of Restitution of Property in the 1990s." *Dickenson Journal of International Law* no. 2 (winter 1992): 357–81.

Neier, Aryeh. "Toward a Permanent International Criminal Court." *Open Society News* (winter 1998/1999): 17–19.

———. *War Crimes: Brutality, Genocide, Terror, and the Struggle for Justice*. New York: Random House, 1998.

———. "What Should Be Done about the Guilty?" *New York Review of Books* v. 31 February 1, 1990: 32–5.

Niederleithinger, Ernst. "Restitution als Grundsatz." *Vermögens- und Investitionsrecht* 2 (1992): 55–6.

Niño, Carlos. *Radical Evil on Trial*. New Haven: Yale University Press, 1996.

Offe, Claus. "Disqualification, Retribution, Restitution: Dilemmas of Justice in Post-Communist Transitions." *Journal of Political Philosophy* 1 (1993): 17–44.

Orentlicher, Diane. "Settling Accounts: The Duty to Prosecute Human Rights Violations of a Prior Regime." *Yale Law Journal* 100 (1991): 2537–2615.

Osiel, Mark, J. "Why Prosecute? Critics of Punishment for Mass Atrocity." *Human Rights Quarterly* 22, no. 1 (2000): 118–47.

Peine, Franz-Josef. "Zur Verfassungswidrigkeit der 'Stichtagsregelung.'" Unpublished brief. 4 February 1994: 1–57.

Peschel-Gutzeit, Lore M. "Zur rechtlichen Auseinandersetzung mit dem SED-Regime." *Recht und Politik* 3 (1995): 130–4.

Petersen, Antje. *The First Berlin Border Guard Trial*. Occasional Paper No. 15. Bloomington, IN: Indiana Center of Global Change and World Peace, 1992.

Polakiewicz, Jörg. "Verfassungs- und völkerrechtliche Aspekte der strafrechtlichen Ahndung des Schusswaffeneinsatzes an der innerdeutschen Grenze." *Europäische Grundrechte Zeitschrift* 9–10 (1992): 177–90.

Pond, Elizabeth. *Beyond the Wall: Germany's Road to Unification*. Washington DC: Brookings Institution, 1993.

Popkin, Margaret, and Noami Roth-Arriaza. "Truth as Justice: Investigatory Commissions in Latin America." *Law & Social Inquiry* 1 (1995): 79–116.

Potthoff, Heinrich. *Die 'Koalition der Vernunft': Deutschlandpolitik in den 80er Jahren*. Munich: Deutscher Taschenbuch Verlag, 1995.

Probst, Lothar. "German Pasts, Germany's Future: Intellectual Controversies Since Reunification." *German Politics and Society* 30 (1993): 21–33.

Prützel-Thomas, Monika. "The Property Question Revisited: The Restitution Myth." *German Politics* 4, no. 3 (December 1995): 112–27.

Quint, Peter. "The Constitutional Law of German Unification." *Maryland Law Review* 3 (1991): 475–631.

———. *The Imperfect Union: Constitutional Structures of German Unification.* Princeton: Princeton University Press, 1997.

———. "Judging the Past: The Prosecution of East German Border Guards and the GDR Chain of Command." *Review of Politics* 61, no. 2 (spring 1999): 303–29.

Reich, Jens. "Á la Lanterne?" *Kursbuch*, no. 111 (February 1993): 3–12.

Reinold, Michael. "Die Enquete-Kommission des deutschen Bundestages: 'Überwindung der Folgen der SED-Diktatur im Prozess der deutschen Einheit.'" *Deutschland Archiv* 6 (June 1996): 913–19.

Rellermeyer, Klaus, and Cornelia Ebert. "Das Grundbuch oder kein Buch mit sieben Siegeln." In *Offene Vermögensfragen – ein Ratgeber*, edited by Dirk Brouër and Herbert Trimbach, 208–37. Berlin: Rowohlt, 1995.

Richter, Peter. *Kurzer Prozess.* Berlin: Elefanten Press, 1993.

Rodenbach, Hermann-Joseph. "Die Reprivatisierung in den neuen Bundesländern." In *Juristische Bewältigung des kommunistischen Unrechts in Osteuropa und Deutschland*, edited by Georg Brunner, 3–9. Berlin: Berlin Verlag, 1995.

Roggemann, Herwig. "Zur Strafbarkeit der Mauerschützen." *Deutsch–deutsche Rechtszeitschrift* 1 (1993): 10–19.

Rosenberg, Tina. *The Haunted Land: Facing Europe's Ghosts after Communism.* New York: Random House, 1995.

———. "Tipping the Scales of Justice." *World Policy Journal* (fall 1995): 55–64.

Roth, Dieter. "Wandel der politischen Einstellungen seit der Bundestagswahl 1990." *German Studies Review* 2 (1993): 265–98.

Sa'adah, Anne. *Germany's Second Chance: Trust, Justice, and Democratization.* Cambridge: Harvard University Press, 1998.

Sagi, Nana. *German Reparations: A History of the Negotiations.* New York: St. Martin's Press, 1986.

Schäuble, Wolfgang. *Der Vertrag: Wie ich über die deutsche Einheit verhandelte.* Stuttgart: Deutsche Verlags-Anstalt, 1991.

Schlink, Bernhard. "Rechtsstaat und revolutionäre Gerechtigkeit." *Öffentliche Vorlesungen, Humboldt-Universität zu Berlin.* Berlin: Juristische Fakultät, 1996.

Scholz, Uwe R. "Kündigung in der Privatwirtschaft wegen Tätigkeit für das Ministerium für Staatssicherheit/Amt für nationale Sicherheit." *Arbeit- und Sozialrecht* 34 (1992): 2424–29.

Schöneberg, Birgit. "Die Rechtsentwicklung im Bereich der Regelung offener Vermögensfragen." *Neue Justiz* 6 (1993): 253–7.

Schumann, Silke. *Vernichten oder Offenlegen? Zur Entstehung des Stasi-Unterlagen-Gesetzes.* Berlin: BStU, 1995.

Schuster, Gunnar. "The Criminal Prosecution of Former GDR Officials." In *The Unification of Germany in International and Domestic Law*, edited by R. Piotrowicz and S. Blay, 117–71. Am Herdam: Rodopi, 1997.

Schwan, Gesine. *Politik und Schuld*. Frankfurt am Main: Fischer, 1997.

Schwan, Heribert. *Erich Mielke: Der Mann, der die Stasi war*. Munich: Drömer Knaur, 1997.

Schwartz, Herman. "Lustration in Eastern Europe." In *Transitional Justice: How Emerging Democracies Reckon with Former Regimes*, vol. 1, edited by Neil Kritz, 461–83. Washington, DC: United States Institute of Peace, 1995.

Schwartz, Paul. "Constitutional Change and Constitutional Legitimation: The Example of German Unification." *Houston Law Review* 4 (1994): 1027–1104.

Seibel, Wolfgang. "Lernen unter Unsicherheit: Hypothesen zur Entwicklung der Treuhandanstalt." In *Verwaltungsreform und Verwaltungspolitik im Prozeß der deutschen Einigung*, edited by W. Seibel, A. Benz, and H. Maeding, 359–70. Baden-Baden: Nomos, 1993.

Selbmann, Erich. *Der Prozeß*. Berlin: Spotless, 1993.

Shnayerson, Robert. "Judgement at Nuremberg." *Smithsonian* 7 (1996): 124–41.

Simitis, Spiros. "Das Stasi-Unterlagen-Gesetz – Einübung in die Zensur?" *Neue Juristische Wochenschrift* 10 (1995): 637–40.

Sinn, Gerlinde, and Hans-Werner Sinn. *Jumpstart: The Economic Unification of Germany*. Cambridge, MA: The MIT Press, 1992.

Southern, David. "Restitution or Compensation: The Open Property Question." *German Politics* 3 (1993): 436–49.

Staff, Ilse. "Wiedervereinigung unter Rechtsgesetzen." *Zeitschrift für Rechtspolitik* 12 (1992): 462–69.

Stapelfeld, Ait. "Zum aktuellen Stand der Rechtsprechung und zur Praxis des Sonderkündigungsrechts im Einigungsvertrag wegen Tätigkeit für MfS/AfNS." *Deutsch–deutsche Rechtszeitschrift* 6 (1995): 186–92.

Stephan, Cora. *Wir Kollaborateure: Der Westen und die deutschen Vergangenheiten*. Reinbek bei Hamburg: Rowohlt, 1992.

Stern, Fritz. "Democracy and Its Discontents." *Foreign Affairs* 72, no. 4 (September–October 1993): 108–25.

Stoltenberg, Klaus. *Stasi-Unterlagen-Gesetz: Kommentar*. Baden-Baden: Nomos Verlagsgesellschaft, 1992.

Suckut, Siegfried. "Die Bedeutung der Akten des Staatssicherheitsdienstes für die Erforschung der DDR-Geschichte." In *Aktenlage: Die Bedeutung der Unterlagen des Staatssicherheitsdienstes für die Zeitgeschichtsforschung*, edited by Klaus Dietmar Henke and Roger Engelmann, 195–206. Berlin: Ch. Links, 1995.

Taylor, Telford. *The Anatomy of the Nuremberg Trials: A Personal Memoir*. New York: Alfred A. Knopf, 1992.

Teitel, Ruti. "Transitional Jurisprudence: The Role of Law in Political Transformation." *The Yale Journal of Law* 106 (1997): 2009–80.

Thaysen, Uwe. *Der runde Tisch: Oder Wo blieb das Volk?* Opladen: Westdeutscher Verlag, 1990.

Tismaneanu, Vladimir. *Fantasies of Salvation*. Princeton: Princeton University Press, 1998.

Torpey, John. "The Abortive Revolution Continues: East German Civil-rights Activists Since Unification." *Theory and Society* 24 (1995): 105–34.

———. *Intellectuals, Socialism, and Dissent: The East German Opposition and Its Legacy*. Minneapolis: University of Minnesota Press, 1995.

Veen, Hans-Joachim, and Carsten Zelle. "Zusammenwachsen oder Auseinanderdriften?" *Interne Studien* 78 (1994): 6–48.

Walicki, Andrzej. "From Stalinism to Post-Communist Pluralism: The Case of Poland." *The New Left Review* 185 (January–February 1991): 93–121.

———. "Transitional Justice and the Political Struggles of Post-Communist Poland. In *Transitional Justice and the Rule of Law in New Democracies*, edited by A. James McAdams, 185–239. Notre Dame: University of Notre Dame Press, 1997.

Wasmuth, Johannes. "Der Bodenreform II–Beschluss des Bundesverfassungsgerichts." *Zeitschrift für Vermögens- und Investitionsrecht* 7 (1992): 361–5.

Wassermann, Rudolf. "Zur Aufbereitung des SED Unrechts." *Aus Politik und Zeitgeschichte* 4 (1993): 3–12.

Weichert, Thilo. "Überprüfung der öffentlichen Bediensten in Ostdeutschland." *Kritische Justiz* 24 (1991): 457–75.

Weinke, Annette. "Die DDR-Justiz im Jahre der 'Wende.'" *Deutschland Archiv* 1 (January–February 1997): 45–7.

Weisskirchen, Gert. "Ambivalenzen der Entspannungspolitik." *Deutschland Archiv* 5 (May 1992): 526–30.

Weschler, Lawrence. *A Miracle, a Universe: Settling Accounts with Torturers*. New York: Random House, 1990.

Wesel, Uwe. *Ein Staat vor Gericht: Der Honecker Prozess*. Frankfurt am Main: Eichborn, 1994.

Welsh, Helga. "Dealing with the Communist Past: Central and Eastern European Experiences after 1990." *Europe–Asia Studies* 48, no. 3 (1996): 413–28.

Winters, Peter Jochen. "Das Urteil gegen Krenz und andere." *Deutschland Archiv* 5 (September–October 1997): 693–6.

———. "Ein Sieg der Gerechtigkeit." *Deutschland Archiv* 10 (October 1993): 1121–2.

———. "Zwiespältiges Urteil im letzten Politbüro-Prozess." *Deutschland Archiv* 4 (2000): 525–8.

Wollenberger, Vera. "Eine zweite Vergewaltigung." In *Aktenkundig*, edited by Hans Joachim Schädlich, 154–65. Reinbek bei Hamburg: Rowohlt, 1993.

Zalaquett, José. "Balancing Ethical Imperatives and Political Constraints: The Dilemma of New Democracies Confronting Past Human Rights Violations." *Hastings Law Journal* 6 (1992): 1426–32.

Zimmermann, Bernd. "Wiedergutmachung zwischen materieller Gerechtigkeit und politischen Kompromiss." *Deutsch–deutsche Rechtszeitschrift* 11 (1994): 359–62.

Zimmermann, Hartmut. "The GDR in the 1970s." *Problems of Communism* 27, no. 2 (March–April 1978): 1–40.

Index

A

Adenauer, Konrad, 4–5, 138, 165
Albania, 185
Albrecht, Hans, 35, 39–41, 45, 50, 53
Alliance' 90, 89, 112
"Alliance for Germany" coalition, 55
apartheid, 7, 173
Arendt, Hannah, 11, 176
Argentina, 1, 3, 12, 46, 122–3
Ascherson, Neal, 43

B

Bahr, Egon, 86
Barbe, Angelika, 89
BARoV. *See* Federal Office for the
  Settlement of Open Property Questions
Basic Law, 4, 29, 33, 37, 41, 51, 55, 59, 77,
  127, 130, 139, 142, 144–5, 149, 166
Basic treaty, between the Germanys, 29,
  102
Baumgarten, Klaus-Dieter, 47, 171
Bavaria, 85
Benda, Ernst, 45
Berlin: 5, 24, 35, 45, 48, 52, 115, 128,
  133–4, 138, 140, 148, 157, 159, 162,
  170, 176, 178; Constitutional court of,
  38; regional (or state) court of, 47, 50,
  52, 168, 170, 189–90; screening for Stasi
  informants in, 58, 64, 67, 73, 75–77, 79
Berlin Wall: 13, 112, 179; construction of,
  13, 18–19, 36, 94; expropriations for,
  128, 146–9, 155–8, 175; opening of, 23,
  28, 30–1, 33, 70, 151; shootings at, 2–3,
  15, 23–5, 38–9, 41, 43, 47–8, 52–3,
  168–71, 177
Biermann, Wolf, 14
Böhme, Hans-Joachim, 169–70
Böhme, Ibrahim, 55, 60, 164

Bohl, Friedrich, 155
Bohley, Bärbel, 7
border code, of the GDR: 23, 33, 197 n.
  30
border guards, of the GDR: 23–5, 27, 30,
  32–5, 43–8, 168, 171
border trials: 26, 30–1, 33, 35, 38–9, 41–3,
  45, 51, 53, 55, 57, 71, 113, 126, 147,
  160, 162, 167, 169, 173, 190. *See also*
  border guards
Boß, Hans, 39–40, 44, 50
Bräutigam, Hansgeorg, 38–39, 52, 198 n.
  44
Bräutigam, Hans-Otto, 76, 219 n. 12
Brandenburg, 45, 73, 75–6, 80, 93, 100,
  115, 159, 175, 182
Brandt, Willy, 105, 107, 120
BStU. *See* "Gauck agency"
Bulgaria, 129, 184–5
Bundestag: 157; elections to, 89, 115;
  legislation, 60, 83, 139, 152–5, 163;
  response to finance scandal, 159–60,
  166, 180–2. *See also* Enquete
  commission
Bush, George, 158
Butterfield, Herbert, 161

C

CDU. *See* Christian Democratic Union
Chile, 3, 7, 12, 36, 91, 122–3, 175, 184,
  186, 188
China, 187
Christian Democratic Union (CDU), 6,
  17, 28, 55, 75, 97, 99, 100, 105–9, 118,
  120, 158, 179–81, 183, 221 n. 40
civil service, of the GDR, 7–8, 73
Claus, Roland, 182
collaborator, of the Stasi. *See* IM